Too Migrant, Too Muslim, Too Loud is a memoir and manifesto from outspoken trouble-maker and multicultural icon Mehreen Faruqi. As the first Muslim woman in any Australian parliament, Mehreen has a unique and crucial perspective on our politics and democracy. It is a tale of a political outsider fighting for her right and the rights of others like her to be let inside on their terms.

From her beginnings in Pakistan and remaking in Australia, Mehreen recounts her struggle to navigate two vastly different, changing worlds without losing herself. This moving and inspiring memoir shares shattering insights learned as a migrant, an engineer, an activist, a feminist and a politician.

Praise for *Too Migrant, Too Muslim, Too Loud*

'An inspiring and powerful memoir by one of the most fiercely principled, courageous and compassionate leaders in this country. Mehreen paves the way for a new generation, offering them an example of the moral courage it takes to shift power in favour of the marginalised from the centre of the most powerful institutions in this country.' **Randa Abdel-Fattah, author of *Does My Head Look Big in This?***

'Mehreen writes just as she speaks in parliament: with an unwavering passion and conviction. Her memoir is a refreshing insight into her life, sharing with us the experiences that made her the inspiring leader she is today.' **L-Fresh the Lion, hip-hop artist and musician**

'Faruqi's story is one of defiance, tenacity, and hope. She lays bare the hypocrisy of parliament house, and counters its banal toxicity with a commitment to integrity and care. Above all, her story of coming to Australia and making her home here is a wonderful and compelling read. If only all political memoirs were this honest.' **Bri Lee, author of** *Eggshell Skull* **and** *Who Gets to be Smart*

'To write of your life with honesty requires integrity. To do it in the face of overwhelming bigotry is courageous beyond measure. Faruqi is a shining light I'm not sure Australia deserves, but is infinitely lucky to have.' **Omar Sakr, author of** *The Lost Arabs*

'An intelligent and electrifying book. This is not a typical political memoir, but a mirror held up to Australia which asks difficult and essential questions. *Too Migrant, Too Muslim, Too Loud* confronts the gigantic issues of our time: racism, climate change, feminism, as well as our family lives. An extraordinary book, from an extraordinary woman.' **Bridie Jabour, journalist and author of** *The Way Things Should Be*

'An inspiring, intimate insight into the life of Australia's groundbreaking first Muslim woman senator. From her journey as a migrant from Pakistan to Australia, breaking barriers as an engineer in a male dominated profession, and standing up to racist abuse as a high-profile woman of colour, it is a passionate outline of Faruqi's core political beliefs and what drives her passion for environmental and social justice. This unapologetically "feminist as fuck" memoir is a must-read manifesto of a game-changing outsider shaking up the pale, stale males in the corridors of power.' **Sarah Malik, journalist**

'*Too Migrant, Too Muslim, Too Loud* takes a heavy hammer to the overworn notion of Australia's "good migrant" and from the fragments builds something far more powerful.

In her spirited political memoir, Senator Mehreen Faruqi takes us on a tour of her diverse life experiences—from touching and formative memories of her migration from Pakistan to Australia, her work as an engineer, standing up for women's rights in parliament, and her passion for racial, animal and environmental justice, while having to withstand plenty of abuse and detractors along the way.

She is, in fact, the "best" kind of migrant, showing us what love of country truly means: a life dedicated to public service, speaking truth to power and fighting for a better future.'
Monica Tan, journalist and author of *Stranger Country*

'In her passionate autobiography, Mehreen Faruqi lays bare the truth of navigating politics in Australia while being a woman of colour. This is an unapologetic account of one woman's mission to make this country a fairer place to live.'
Saman Shad, journalist and writer

'The idea of Mehreen Faruqi frightens the establishment. The actual Mehreen Faruqi is a gift, a woman of great integrity and purpose, who follows through on the egalitarian ideals of this country like few others. This country needs her. She also swears like a sailor.' **Tim Levinson/Urthboy, hip-hop artist and producer**

TOO MIGRANT TOO MUSLIM TOO LOUD

A Memoir

MEHREEN FARUQI

First published in 2021

Copyright © Mehreen Faruqi 2021

All rights reserved. No part of this book may be reproduced or transmitted in any form or by any means, electronic or mechanical, including photocopying, recording or by any information storage and retrieval system, without prior permission in writing from the publisher. The Australian *Copyright Act 1968* (the Act) allows a maximum of one chapter or 10 per cent of this book, whichever is the greater, to be photocopied by any educational institution for its educational purposes provided that the educational institution (or body that administers it) has given a remuneration notice to the Copyright Agency (Australia) under the Act.

Allen & Unwin
83 Alexander Street
Crows Nest NSW 2065
Australia
Phone: (61 2) 8425 0100
Email: info@allenandunwin.com
Web: www.allenandunwin.com

 A catalogue record for this book is available from the National Library of Australia

ISBN 978 1 76087 818 4

Except where otherwise stated, photos are from the author's collection.

Set in 12.5/18 pt Fairfield Light by Midland Typesetters, Australia
Printed in Australia by McPherson's Printing Group

10 9 8 7 6 5 4 3 2 1

 The paper in this book is FSC® certified. FSC® promotes environmentally responsible, socially beneficial and economically viable management of the world's forests.

For Omar, Osman, Aisha and Cosmo

CONTENTS

A note from the author	xi
1 Becoming a migrant	1
2 The best and worst of politics	43
3 Feminist as fuck	99
4 Muslim, Brown and proud	139
5 Three decades an environmentalist	177
Epilogue: Is it all worth it?	219
Acknowledgement and gratitude	253
Notes	257
Index	277

A NOTE FROM THE AUTHOR

This book is part memoir and part manifesto. It is about a life lived challenging dominant mindsets, bucking the trend and pushing boundaries—both in Pakistan where I grew up, and in Australia where I migrated to three decades ago with my husband, my one-year-old son and two suitcases, to make a new life.

This is the story of a Brown, migrant Muslim woman breaking into a white man's world and striving to change it without being changed. It is an honest, no-holds-barred account of what happens when reality meets perception and when you shatter long-held stereotypes and confront a system steeped in privileged hierarchies, racism and sexism. It is my story—the tale of a political outsider fighting for her rights and for the rights of others like me to be let inside on our terms.

TOO MIGRANT, TOO MUSLIM, TOO LOUD

I explore my making in Pakistan and my remaking in Australia, as I try to navigate two contrasting worlds which are changing, sharing insights hard-won through the wildly different cultural experiences of my life as an engineer, a migrant, a feminist and a politician.

Finally, and most importantly, I share my hopes for the future regarding the climate crisis and gender, racial and social equity. And I contemplate the price I have paid for feeling the fear and doing it anyway and ask, was it all worth it?

Mehreen

1
BECOMING A MIGRANT

—

'You are not really Australian, Mehreen. Why don't you fuck off to the cesspit you came from?'

'Piss off back to your shithole of Pakistan, ya maggot.'

This is not something I expected to hear—ever, let alone in Australia. Yet from day one of my public life, I have felt pummelled and beaten almost every day by this unrelenting demand to go back to where I came from. I feel the heavy weight of this hate physically bearing down on me, crushing me, squeezing the air out of my lungs until I feel suffocated. This has only got worse with time. For the first time, I have started to question my belonging in this place I call home. For the first time since arriving in Sydney in 1992, I've started to doubt my decision to migrate from Lahore.

TOO MIGRANT, TOO MUSLIM, TOO LOUD

No matter what I say, my motives are constantly questioned. Whether I'm advocating for stronger animal welfare laws, for abolishing fees for university and TAFE education or for more funding for public schools or women's rights, or speaking out against racism, the disgusting abuse thrown at me by my detractors is always the same. It's echoed on my social media accounts, in emails and in phone calls to my office. I can provoke this reaction by simply opening my mouth.

Why are you even here? they ask.
You weren't born here. What right do you have to tell us what to do?
Your country is shit. Why are you bringing that filth here to our country?
You don't belong here. You should be deported.
Go back.
Go back.
Go back.

Being born a person of colour outside Australia is a permanent mark that is used to render me, and people like me, irrelevant and voiceless in white-colonised countries. This rule doesn't apply to white politicians who were born overseas and migrated here, like Julia Gillard or Tony Abbott.

Perhaps I should feel powerful in my ability to poke the proverbial bear without even trying. I don't.

Plenty of people have extended a hand of support, and

BECOMING A MIGRANT

I am grateful for this. The reality, though, is that however well-meaning they are, they cannot understand the personal toll that such abuse takes—on me, on my family and on my staff.

My daughter, Aisha, was sixteen when I came into the public eye. Just a couple of years after that, on a Saturday night, we were walking along the bridge on the beautiful Brisbane River, enjoying the view and an increasingly rare moment of catching up. I casually tweeted some photos of this lovely scene with my daughter. A short time later an anonymous Twitter user responded:

> @MehreenFaruqi @GreensNSW Before your husband blows it up?
> —alahs-snackbar (@wesi12) July 25, 2015

Up until then, I had chosen to ignore the xenophobic messages sent my way, but this one really ate away at me. It felt so malicious and full of hate. I decided to expose it on my Facebook page. What followed was a seemingly endless stream of racist and offensive communications.

I was told that white Australia was the real victim, not a 'whingeing' Muslim. People called my office to harass my staff. An image of my face was photo-shopped onto a flag-waving Islamic State militant and then spread online. One person even created an online petition calling for evidence that I had renounced my Pakistani citizenship.

My daughter was so burned by the experience that for years afterwards she did not want to discuss politics or my work at all.

Vicious insults and abuse hurt. So does the advice to stay silent in the face of such vitriol. 'Helpful' advice like 'They're just trolls' or 'Just ignore them' rings hollow when it comes from people who haven't had to worry about their own safety or that of their family. 'Trolls' are real people sending hate-filled messages to other real people, who then have to live with the consequences. I've had days when I've wanted to crawl under the doona and never get out. Ever.

It took me a while to understand that the horrid, hateful backlash pitched at me is about who I am, and not necessarily what I stand for. The loathing always boils down to my identity as a migrant Muslim woman.

One of the first questions I fielded from the media after being elected to the New South Wales Parliament in 2013 was how I would reconcile my faith with the Greens Party support for LGBTQI+ rights. It is a question rarely—if ever—asked of other MPs of faith, no matter where they sit on the political spectrum.

Why do I support equal rights for LGBTQI+ people? I hold strong values of justice and compassion. Like every other person, these values are a product of my upbringing and the influence of my family, my friends, the people I've met and the places I've been. I held these views when I lived in Pakistan. They have only strengthened while I've been in Australia. I understand the trials and tribulations of being a member of a marginalised minority community. I know what it feels like to face prejudice. It matters to me that people have the same rights and dignity regardless of their race, religion, ability, sex, sexuality or gender identity.

I'm often berated online by people who accuse me of taking my parliamentary oath on the Qur'an. This is incorrect—I did not. But even if it were true, so what? Countless MPs have sworn on the Bible yet are free from the criticism I am subjected to.

I chose not to make my parliamentary pledge of allegiance on the Qur'an because I firmly believe in the separation of state and religion. I'm committed to a secular system of governance. My integrity and worth come from my character and my track record, not from swearing on my holy book.

There is nothing suspicious about my beliefs. There's no ulterior motive here. This is just me. Shouldn't I be able to express my values and opinions on social justice, democracy, civil rights and other issues like any other Australian, without abusive messages on social media, threatening phone calls and vile emails becoming a regular part of my life? Why am I silenced? Why are my life experiences, my professional qualifications, my career, my intellect and my agency rejected?

Because I'm a migrant, a Muslim and a Brown woman.

I did not expect this of Australia.

What *did* I expect from Australia?

***

TOO MIGRANT, TOO MUSLIM, TOO LOUD

The Australia I came to was one my Abbu (my dad) had raved about. He had travelled to Canada, the United States, Europe and Australia. For him, Sydney was always the most beautiful city in the world. Abbu's first trip to Australia was in the 1950s to do his Master of Engineering on a Colombo Plan* scholarship. This was followed by visits to conferences during his academic career. My dad carried his cameras everywhere. My three siblings and I grew up watching his movies and looking at slides and photos of the Sydney Harbour Bridge and the Opera House nestled in the glimmering harbour, the beaches of New South Wales and the bush. We heard stories about koalas and kangaroos, and Australia's unique wildlife. Even now, I still get goosebumps driving over the Harbour Bridge. It is entwined with my sweet childhood memories and Abbu's love for Sydney—and, of course, the nerd in me that marvels at the steel arch structural engineering feat that it is.

As a student in Sydney, Abbu lived with a couple he called 'Mum and Dad'. After he went back to Pakistan, got married and started a family, his Australian dad and a few of his colleagues and professors visited us in Lahore at different times. To make them feel at home, my Ammi (my mum) would make banana pavlovas. At the dinner table we would swap cricket stories. After dinner we all played bridge. (Yes, we lived in a weird household where all the kids became civil engineers and we all learned to play bridge at a young age.

---

*The Colombo Plan was an intergovernmental program to strengthen relations between Asia and the Pacific and included scholarships offered by the Australian government to students from other member countries.

Go figure!) Abbu brought home a Blinky Bill book from one of his trips, along with a cuddly koala soft toy that adorned our mantelpiece for years. Our house was the only one in the entire neighbourhood with a very tall gum tree in our garden—so our home was literally among the gum tree(s)! It seems inevitable that if I was to ever leave Pakistan, it would be to go to Australia. This path had been carved out for me years before I was born.

In Pakistan, I imagined that 'developed' countries like Australia were free from bias and discrimination, and that equality prevailed in all aspects of society. The narrative that had filtered down to me while growing up in a land that was once a British colony was that of Western supremacy in intellect, power and prowess. The developed countries could always do things better, I thought, and we in the developing countries always had something to learn from them so we could be better too. I was looking forward to experiencing a life free from sexism, discrimination and the class divide—the things that most irked me in Pakistan.

Pakistan is a country of wild contradictions. Gender disparities in Pakistan are large and stark. Discrimination against women is the leading cause of female poverty, poor education and health, domestic violence and abuse. A vast majority of women have little economic freedom or access to financial assets. Yet despite the huge gender gap, the first female prime minister of Pakistan was elected years before the first female prime minister of Australia. It is a conservative country seen as strict and religious, but it has another side in which song and dance are ingrained and even alcohol flows freely in many homes.

Although it has a tiny Christian population, Pakistan has a large number of convent schools. Along with many children in my neighbourhood, I did my schooling from kindergarten to Year 11 at the Convent of Jesus and Mary. It was there I developed a love of netball, drama, maths and Urdu literature. It was also where I developed a fear of nuns. Some of them weren't shy of using the ruler on your open palms or whacking a notebook on your head as punishment for not producing your homework. I dreaded going to school as much as I looked forward to being there.

Pakistani society was visibly divided. The rich and the poor. The professionals and the working class. The educated and the illiterate. Occasionally the lines were crossed, but the social structure was mirrored in the physical infrastructure of divided neighbourhoods for the rich, the poor and the middle class—an ever-present reminder of inequality. Without serious intervention, closing these chasm-like divides was an impossibility, even over many generations.

At first sight, Australia fulfilled many of the promises I had envisioned. Yet I was blithely unaware of the conundrums waiting for me on the day I stepped out of the plane into the sun of a Sydney autumn to brave a new world.

***

I still vividly remember my excitement as our plane landed on the tarmac of Kingsford-Smith Airport on a March

BECOMING A MIGRANT

morning in 1992. Hopes, dreams and excitement all rolled into one big ball of anticipation pulsating in my stomach as I held my nineteen-month-old son, Osman, close to my chest and squeezed the hand of my husband, Omar, tightly.

My friends often tell me what a courageous move it was to pack up our bags and leave a settled, comfortable life in Lahore for a totally new and unknown one in Sydney. I never really thought about it that way. We told our parents we would try living here for a year. If the move didn't work out, we would come back. This was our security blanket and their reassurance.

It was only later I realised that once you've made this epic journey, there is no going back. As I packed our two suitcases, it hadn't felt like I was extricating myself from my past so profoundly. But I was. Those two suitcases became the only physical remnants of our past life.

My first impression of Australia was a place where you could do whatever you wanted if you worked for it. I saw an Australia that was egalitarian, that had worked hard for all ordinary people to be treated with dignity and respect regardless of their origin, their family history, their gender or their bank balance. Tradies lived next door to engineers, everyone could read and write, and there wasn't the poverty that forced people to beg for food or money.

I thought women in general had broken through the glass ceiling. I thought the colour of people's skin or where they came from was not held against them.

I realise now my first sight of Australia was through rose-coloured glasses.

While some things were definitely better in Australia than in Pakistan, equality was far from the reality. I was used to being one of a handful of female engineers in Pakistan, but was quite shocked to see that there was only one female academic in the entire School of Civil and Environmental Engineering at the University of New South Wales (UNSW) when I started my postgraduate degree there in 1992. Since then, change has been very slow. Engineering is still a male-dominated profession. Patriarchy is still the system. Violence against women results in one woman's death every week. Our first female prime minister was hounded by sexism and misogyny during her short stint as leader. We still have a long way to go.

The more I learned about Australia, the more troubled I became by the treatment of Aboriginal people. While the violence of dispossession and colonisation was touched on in history books, I did not expect the depth and breadth of prejudice against First Nations people that was still rooted in law enforcement, societal attitudes and institutional systems. The same year I arrived in Australia, the landmark *Mabo v. The State of Queensland (No 2)* (1992) case was decided, overturning the concept of *terra nullius*. There was much hope, perhaps misplaced, that this would spark Australia's reckoning with its past. Yet decades later, systemic racism is still killing First Nations people.

BECOMING A MIGRANT

The ignorance and insensitivity about the past and present injustices perpetrated against First Nations people runs deep. The current prime minister of our country, Scott Morrison, displayed just how out of touch with history he is when, just before 26 January 2021, he compared the experiences of those on board the First Fleet to those of First Nations people subjected to the violent colonisation of this continent. Saying he acknowledges history when announcing the changes to the Australian national anthem—from 'for we are young and free' to 'for we are one and free'—is one thing, but doing something about it is another thing entirely. First Nations disadvantage results in their shorter life expectancy and poorer health. They are disproportionately overrepresented in prisons. There have been more than 450 Aboriginal deaths in custody since the Royal Commission into these deaths handed down recommendations in 1991. Many of the 339 recommendations have still not been fully implemented. Symbolic changes are only helpful if they are accompanied by concrete actions. Otherwise they are just empty words.

For years after migrating here, I was determined not to find any fault with my adopted country. After all, I had left Pakistan to make a better life in a better place. Even when I saw something that troubled me, I would turn a blind eye. I wanted to fit in. I wanted to be an Aussie. I didn't want to be a troublemaker. This now familiar migrant story of keeping your head down and working hard to prove your worth was unknown to me when I arrived here.

But the longer I lived here, the more I discovered the weaknesses of my assumptions.

I had not expected an Australia where politicians and media figures denigrate minorities to gain popularity. In the last twenty years, the country that proudly dismantled the White Australia Policy to welcome people from all nations has changed to one that now indefinitely locks up asylum seekers, demonises Muslims and whips up anti-immigrant hysteria.

I've seen the inequality gap widen with time. As the ethos of public investment in essential services like housing, transport, education, health and aged care shifted to a culture of privatisation and profit making, I saw egalitarianism crumbling. The public sector was gutted. Job insecurity rose. Homelessness soared. Clear geographic divides emerged between suburbs based on property prices.

I've now lived in Australia for as many years as I have in Pakistan. Pakistan has changed in that time. Australia has changed too. So have I. I have learned that, as a first-generation migrant, I will always straddle two countries, two cultures, three languages. But that doesn't mean I'm at odds with any of them. Humans are complex creatures, and we are pretty good at adapting, given the chance. I can speak Urdu, Punjabi and English fluently. I wear shalwar kameez with as much ease as I wear jeans and a T-shirt. I'm now quite at home in a pub with friends or at an impromptu political meeting without drinking alcohol. I admire and criticise both Pakistan and Australia when

BECOMING A MIGRANT

needed. I'm quite comfortable with an identity that spans two belongings.

I've also learned that, for some, I will never be enough. For Pakistan, I've become too Aussie. For Australia, I'm still too Pakistani.

***

It's strange how a plane trip can take you from a secure, predictable life and land you into the turbulence of a completely unpredictable future.

My middle-class family had lived in Pakistani Punjab for generations. My dad was a civil engineer and academic at the University of Engineering and Technology in Lahore, where I studied later on. My mum was the matriarch of the family. We lived in campus housing surrounded by other university staff doing the same, and students residing in hostels.

As far as the predictability of my life in Pakistan goes, unless something went awry, there was a path marked out for me. I would finish school and university. I would work professionally if I chose to. Then would come the expectations of marriage and children. Within this big picture there were, of course, many smaller frames that made up the colourful collage of my life.

Early-morning walks with my grandmother have a special place in my memory. We used to walk through Jinnah Gardens (then called Lawrence Gardens) in the middle of Lahore city. I would collect leaves, write down the botanical names of the trees they'd fallen from and go home to press them. I had reams and reams of books with beautifully pressed leaves. Walking in leafy Centennial Park in Sydney takes me back to those days. I attribute my love of trees to those walks of my childhood and happily embrace the label of a 'greenie tree hugger', even though it's used as a derogatory tag to describe someone from my political party.

Just thinking of the long, hot summer afternoons spent eating mangoes, freshly salted fruits like falsas and jamuns makes my mouth water. When the monsoon rains broke the dry hot season with their thunderous roar, all the neighbourhood kids would get together and float paper boats in front yards full of murky brown water up to our knees.

I still remember the little fights and the big battles. Quarrels with my mum over getting permission to do what my older brothers didn't even have to ask approval for: flying kites from the roof of our home, playing cricket with the boys in the neighbourhood and going out late at night. Many were won, but some were lost. There were loud, passionate clashes between parents, uncles and aunties at the dinner table about religion, politics and women's rights. The one voice from these debates stuck in my memory is my favourite aunt's—intelligent, articulate, fervent and courageous. She understood the true meaning of what my scuffles with my parents were about: equality and fairness. She was a feminist. She was left of centre. From her, I learned to speak out. From her, I learned to hold onto my convictions even when in the minority.

In Lahore, I grew up in a large extended family within a close-knit society. Our family connections went back generations. Quite often I'd meet a stranger at a large wedding or at the shops but very soon find a common connection.

These cultural expectations were by and large a happy place for me. That doesn't mean I didn't think about what life would be like without always having to share physical space, emotions and everything in between. I had an unfulfilled need for independence. Being free from family obligations—first parents, then in-laws—was a tantalising prospect. Migrating to Australia gave me that opportunity.

In Sydney, I knew no one, and no one knew me.

Like a butterfly emerging from its cocoon, I felt free. I had flown out into the world without the strings of family attached. Omar and I could set up our first home as an independent family unit without someone looking over our shoulders most of the time. We could make our own decisions without always having to consider someone else's feelings or opinions first.

But freedom came at a price.

We landed in Australia right in the middle of what Paul Keating famously described as the 'recession we had to have'. The information we'd been given in Pakistan by the Australian High Commission was that engineers were much-needed professionals and there would be plenty of jobs available. When we arrived, we found that was far from the reality.

Finding jobs was impossible. Rejection letters to our job applications for engineering positions came thick and fast. Even though we were fully qualified and experienced engineers, we were told we were no good because we had no local experience. How do you get local experience when no one is willing to give you a chance? Migrants like us are told to 'go get a job', but we are not given the opportunity to get that job.

I'm sure the recession was partly to blame for doors not opening for us, but résumé racism deliberately kept those doors shut. Other migrants we met told us they had faced the same barriers even before the recession. Even today, I hear very similar stories from newly arrived engineers from South Asia. Many fully qualified and experienced migrant engineers never work in their area of expertise. This is pretty ironic, since engineering is the qualification that allowed them entry to Australia in the first place.

For us, not having Anglo names meant our CVs often went straight into the bin. We would joke about changing our names and other details to 'whiten' our résumés, just to see if there would be a different response. We now know this is far from funny. The grim truth is that there is pervasive bias in the labour market against people who have Asian or Middle Eastern names. I don't for a moment fall for the argument that this isn't racism but a desire for employers to find the right 'cultural fit' for their organisations. These employers might still want to live in the 'white Australia' that was forced upon First Nations people, but that Australia no longer exists, except in their imagination and longing.

There are plenty of examples of our accents and our names being made fun of. My name gets mispronounced and misspelled as Maureen, Mireen and even Maria. During one community forum in the Australian parliament, Liberal MP Craig Kelly couldn't get my name right. He mispronounced my name and then told a room full of people from the subcontinent 'we should have simple names'.

When Liberal senator Ian Macdonald kept mispronouncing my surname during a Senate Estimates hearing in 2019—even after being corrected a few times—it really struck a chord with many people familiar with the agony of dealing with this every single day of their lives. Many, but not all, were sympathetic to our struggle. Some people thought that those of us with non-Anglo names were being unreasonable in requesting our names be pronounced correctly. Someone tweeted at me: 'This is why Asians are better migrants than Pakistanis Muslims [sic]. The Asians actually try to assimilate and change their first names to Western names. They don't just land here and demand everyone learn their bizarre names.'

Bizarre or foreign they may be to some, but names are an integral part of identity, no matter what your background is. They connect us to our culture, our ancestors, and the countries and regions of our heritage. Getting someone's name right is a sign of respect. It's an indication you see them as an equal. We shouldn't have to compromise on this with our colleagues, employers, friends or acquaintances. Yet so many have. Many people with non-Anglo names like mine have just given up and offer other names, or even change their names to save themselves the torment of repeatedly correcting others.

Many migrant engineers I know, dejected by rejections from prospective employers, started driving taxis and never worked as engineers again. Some say Australian taxi drivers are some of the most qualified in the world. I can't help but feel extremely frustrated that even while we lament engineering skill shortages, migrant engineers face such an uphill battle to find jobs. Expertise, experience and skills are lost because of discrimination. This hurts migrants and it hurts our country.

Omar and I decided we would not be the ones to give up engineering. I started my Master of Engineering Science, focusing on water and waste management. My husband kept looking for that elusive job, then began training to be a taxi driver at the same time. So began our lives as migrants.

We had to live. We went on the dole.

We would line up every fortnight at our local Department of Social Security office to hand in the filled-out form with a list of our job applications to the nice person behind the counter. In response, money was deposited in our bank account every other Thursday. This welfare safety net allowed us to have a roof over our heads and food on the table in those early months. It gave us a start to make a new life in Australia.

Depending on state welfare for survival was still hard. It wasn't just having to live hand-to-mouth, or letting go of a more comfortable life we were used to in Pakistan. It was the loss of dignity that came from the shame, stigma and negative attitudes targetting those receiving what was considered a 'handout' as 'bludgers'.

The stigma continues, but this support has slowly but surely eroded over time. People on income support at the start of 2020 suffered shocking levels of deprivation. They were expected to live on $40 a day because payments have not increased in real terms since 1994. Young people on youth allowance are being forced to live in poverty. They skip meals, couch-surf and live in all sorts of unstable accommodation, teetering on the edge of homelessness.

It took the COVID-19 pandemic for the government to increase these payments for a few months before snapping them back to below the poverty line. The social security system is now corporatised and impersonal. The pleasant person behind the counter that I encountered has been replaced by an answering machine. The obligations on welfare recipients have become tougher and inflexible. Recipients were put through the robodebt debacle, designed to extort money: in 2016, hundreds of thousands of people were sent letters from Centrelink through an automated system demanding they pay back outstanding 'debts' dating back from 2010. For some, this debt was for thousands of dollars, and they were given only days to pay it back. This has caused enormous harm and trauma to people and was proved to be illegal, but the damage was done. It later emerged that many of these so called 'debts' didn't really exist and were unlawful and incorrect.[1]

A system designed to provide those in need with a basic standard of living has morphed into one that maligns them. Prime Minister Scott Morrison wants us to 'have a go to get a go'. He had the gall to label calls to raise the social security safety net 'unfunded empathy'—perhaps because he has no empathy. Others continue the stigmatising of 'dole bludgers' and 'dole cruisers' who are told to get a job and to stop milking taxpayers. My husband and I lined up in the dole queue not because we didn't want jobs or out of any desire to sponge off hardworking taxpayers. We were there because we were new migrants and, despite trying our hardest, no one would give us a go. The lines of people needing to access welfare payments in 1992 may not have been as long as those outside Centrelink at the start of the COVID-19 pandemic, when hundreds of thousands of people lost their jobs, but the feelings of anxiety, stress and helplessness were the same.

No one should be stripped of their dignity because they need support to survive. It is the responsibility of a government to look after the welfare of its citizens. No one should be made to feel ashamed of being a welfare recipient in times of need. It's those blatantly shaming our most vulnerable who should be ashamed.

***

People ask me why we left Pakistan. It's not an easy question to answer three decades after the decision was made. My husband and I don't fully see eye to eye on all the reasons we left, but some are still crystal clear.

BECOMING A MIGRANT

We never really had any grand plans for making a new life in a foreign country. We were happy in Pakistan. We had loving families, great friends, good jobs.

Yet I yearned for more. I had a real hunger for seeing the world outside Pakistan. I wanted to travel. I wanted to see the alluring world my parents had described after their overseas travels.

I wanted to study more, like my older brothers.

By the time I reached my twenties, corruption was taking hold in Pakistan. It was deep-seated and widespread. It was entrenched in politics, bureaucracy and institutions. Straightforward things like getting a passport, a driver's licence or a telephone connection required paying someone a bribe or knowing someone in the right place. Large sums of money regularly exchanged hands to win big consulting or construction projects. This went against the strong ethical values I had grown up with. For my father, integrity was the measure of your worth. There were no two ways about it. Either you had integrity in everything you did, or you didn't.

Once, a Palestinian student of my father's came to say goodbye after completing his civil engineering degree. He brought a box of mangoes as a farewell gift for my father. With true Lahori hospitality, he was invited in for tea. When it was time to say farewell, I saw Abbu hand him back the box of mangoes. He told his student in no uncertain terms that accepting a gift, no matter how small, could be perceived as a reward for doing him a favour. He explained it could be seen as a 'thank you' for helping the student pass his exam, even though the papers had been marked and the results long declared. I saw the embarrassment on the student's face at being returned a gift he had brought with love and respect. At the time, I felt this was a rather rude and heartless gesture on my dad's part. Now it is a reminder of the standard of integrity he set for me to follow.

Omar and I were both uneasy working in a system that had become corrupted from top to bottom in just one generation. We had a baby boy to think of as well. Osman's survival in a society whose values now clashed with ours worried me no end.

Eventually the catalyst that actually pushed us into applying for permanent residency in Australia was completely unexpected. But before I can tell you that story, you need to know how I met the man of my dreams.

I met Omar at work. We were both civil engineers working in NESPAK, the largest engineering firm in Pakistan. I started work there in 1988, a freshly minted civil engineer and the proud recipient of a gold medal in geotechnical studies. Omar had just returned to work after finishing his Master of Civil Engineering at Oregon State University in the United States. We knew of each other because of family connections. Our eyes met across the entrance lobby of the iconic WAPDA House building where our office was located. When we met, it was love at first sight.

I come from a family of civil engineering tragics. My dad, my two older brothers, me and then my younger sister all followed in my Abbu's footsteps and graduated as civil engineers. It was only fitting that I fell for a civil engineer.

In a few months our families arranged our marriage. We were married a year later.

I was the only woman engineer in the structural engineering division of NESPAK. After college, all my close friends who wanted to study further went off to medical schools or to study humanities at university. I was tempted to do the same, but the desire to go against the grain took over. Engineering was seen as a man's domain. It bothered me that women were discouraged from pursuing it. I wanted to push back. A little nudge from my dad was all I needed. I didn't have to fight to do what my two older brothers were allowed to do. I was being encouraged to do it!

As Omar and I started a blissfully married life, we were unaware of making our older, more conservative colleagues irate by falling in love at our workplace. I was conscious of a level of discomfort some of the more senior colleagues felt with me being the only female engineer in the office. Falling in love right in front of their eyes definitely didn't make things easier. It had disrupted the order of their conservative male domain. There were, however, enough younger, more progressive people around to take the edge off the situation. Many of my colleagues had been my father's students. Their respect for him as their teacher probably held them back from targeting me in any way. But they didn't hold back where my husband was concerned.

While I was on maternity leave, his harassment started. One of his bosses claimed Omar was an Ahmadi, a member of a persecuted minority who had been declared non-Muslims in Pakistan. They wanted him to prove he wasn't.

Omar's boss called him into his office one day and asked him to denounce Ahmadis. Of course, he refused to do so. Omar is not an Ahmadi. Neither is anyone in his family. But for him, that was no one's business but his. His ethics did not allow him to decry anyone else's religion either.

Omar's defiance of his boss's request, no matter how unreasonable that request was, made it untenable for him to stay on in that office. He transferred from structural engineering to the water and agricultural division. His appalling treatment was the final prompt for us to seek a life elsewhere.

This was also a shuddering reminder of the ongoing discrimination against Ahmadis in Pakistan. The Ahmadiyya religion originated in British India in the late nineteenth century, and Ahmadis set up their headquarters in Pakistani Punjab after the partition of British India in 1947. The founder of this faith reinterpreted some branches of Islamic thought and claimed to be a prophet.[2] Since one of the tenets of mainstream Islam declares the Prophet Muhammad (PBUH) to be the last prophet of Allah, this has remained a contentious issue. The animosity in Pakistan towards the religion and its followers reached a peak during the reign of Prime Minister Zulfikar Ali Bhutto, who, bowing to pressure from religious political parties, declared this religious minority 'non-Muslims' in 1974, and a constitutional amendment was made to set this in stone.

In Lahore, my family's neighbours across the street were Ahmadi. I only found this out during the riot after Bhutto's declaration. I was ten years old. A large, rowdy mob of angry university students came marching down our street at night, chanting and screaming their hate. I remember looking through our lounge room window as some of them jumped our neighbours' boundary wall, got their car out of the porch, doused it in petrol and set it alight.

I can still feel the fear gripping me as some of the students jumped the wall into our garden. The street was too narrow to hold them all. The chaos and violence in front of me brought to life the stories I had repeatedly heard from my parents, grandparents, aunts and uncles about the partition of British India into the nations of Pakistan and Hindustan (India). I had seen similar scenes of trauma and devastation of the people of the subcontinent in movies and documentaries when friend turned against friend, neighbour against neighbour. I had thought those days were behind us.

I remember the visceral emotional reaction I felt at the unfairness of it all. One of my good friends was the youngest daughter in our neighbour's family, and I adored her three older sisters. They were a softly spoken family, highly respected in the neighbourhood. Now their home was being invaded, and their car set alight. They did not deserve this violation of their lives. Even as a young person, it confused and angered me. Hadn't Pakistan been created to provide refuge for people who, as a minority, were persecuted during the British Raj because of their religion? Why were my friends now being vilified for the same reason by those who knew the terrible consequences of such discrimination? I could not reconcile such injustice. I still can't. Having now been the target of racism and discrimination, I do, however, understand better where it comes from—fear, dogma, superiority, power and politics.

This was the beginning of my political awakening. The fire that was sparked within my ten-year-old self that night still burns in my belly to this day. It burns brighter than the flames that consumed my innocent neighbours' car. It burns to rid society of discrimination, hate and bigotry. It burns to rekindle hope in a world struggling under the weight of inequality and despair. I know I'm not alone in my quest. Flames like mine flicker across the world. I hope one day all these flickering flames of hope will join together in a roaring blaze whose intensity will light up the world and make it a brighter place for all.

Australia seemed like a place where my flame could take hold.

Approval for our permanent residency in Australia came exactly at the same time as the offer of an AusAID scholarship, accompanied with the acceptance of my application for a master's degree at UNSW. But there was a catch. If I accepted the AusAID scholarship, we'd no longer be eligible for permanent residency (PR); if we accepted PR, I'd no longer be eligible for the scholarship. An officer at the Australian High Commission recommended accepting PR, which would allow me to study for free and give us the flexibility of living permanently in Australia if we wanted to.

While this made sense, I was reluctant. I had worked hard to get the highly competitive scholarship. I had earned it. I took pride in that, and felt a sense of satisfaction. I felt like I was in control. The offer of PR was not the same. It was being handed to us just because we had met some arbitrary criteria set by the Australian government. At the time we were deemed worthy because we are both engineers. It felt like a favour, even when it was obviously Australia that needed *us*.

In the end we took the offer of PR. I swallowed my pride, as I have done many times since moving here. I swallowed my pride when a customs officer at Sydney Airport started speaking very, very slowly to me: 'Do . . . you . . . understand . . . what . . . I . . . am . . . saying?' I swallowed my pride after every rejected job application. I swallowed my pride when I had to accept an entry-level engineering position in a large consulting firm in Sydney, despite my master's degree and PhD, after the head of the division interviewed me to check my 'cultural fit' with the company. I swallowed my pride every time I was presumed to be a staffer of an MP, rather than an MP.

***

In my new country, the family strings I was so desperate to cut were gone but so was the protective shield. The huge leap from knowing 'everyone' in Lahore to hardly anyone in Sydney was unexpectedly tough.

Loneliness set in pretty quickly.

I'm writing this in the middle of the global coronavirus pandemic in 2020. The isolation so many are experiencing right now reminds me of how alone I felt in the first few months in my newly adopted country. As COVID-19 was declared a pandemic, my mother was in Pakistan, my daughter was in the United States and my son was in Melbourne. The feeling of not knowing when I will meet them again is similar to how I felt after moving to Australia. Then, I wasn't sure when I'd have the money to board a flight back home. Now, there are no flights to board.

I'm anxious because I have no inkling of, or control over, when I'll see my children and mother. I go to bed clutching this fear as if it was them, then wake up in tears realising it's not. It's a lonely anxiety and panic. I fear if I share my own troubles during this very difficult time, I will somehow be minimising the distress so many who are worse off than me are feeling. I keep telling myself I'm so much better off than most. I fear that if I say anything, I will appear ungrateful. After all, so many have lost lives and livelihoods. I have a steady income. I should be grateful.

I keep crying myself to sleep. I wake up exhausted. I put on a brave face (along with make-up to hide the ravages of the night) and head out to do my job. No one will know I am carrying a broken heart inside me. I keep pretending nothing had changed. The body has a knack of catching up with the turmoil in the mind. In 2020, I gained weight. Pasta and chips temporarily alleviated the mental pain I was feeling. I fell and fractured my ribs during a sitting week in Canberra. I broke one of my toes while filming a video. The bones mended. The heartache continued.

But the loneliness that hit me after migrating to Australia was nothing like I've felt before. It was the early 1990s. There was no internet, no FaceTime, no Zoom, no mobile phones, no WhatsApp—all the things that have kept us connected during the pandemic. In the early 1990s, I called my Ammi on a landline once a week on strictly limited time. It was expensive and we did not have money to spare. Letter writing was the only way to communicate in any detail.

It seems like yesterday that we booked into a motel on Anzac Parade in the Sydney suburb of Kensington straight from the airport after our arrival. I remember writing a letter to my mum the next morning about how much I had enjoyed eating fresh strawberries (then a rarity in Pakistan) with my cereal and then having to wait two weeks until I got her reaction. In Lahore, my parents' place was just a three-kilometre drive away from ours. We saw each other every other day. In Sydney, they were a 10,500-kilometre flight away. I did not know when I'd see them again.

When we arrived in Australia, however, Omar and I made a decision to take full advantage of what our new country offered—especially the rich diversity of people who lived here. While it was tempting to just reach out to the Pakistani community, we didn't. In Pakistan, almost everyone was, well, from Pakistan. In Australia there were people from hundreds of different countries. What a wonderful way to fulfil my dreams of seeing the world through meeting the culturally diverse people living here!

As fate would have it, the first friends we made from another country were our neighbours. They were from India, and they lived in the unit below ours. A couple of them were international students at UNSW. The others were migrants. We became each other's family-away-from-family.

Anyone looking at us all enjoying a barbecue in Centennial Park could have been forgiven for thinking we had known each other all our lives. We looked like we came from the same place and we spoke the same language. In reality, we came from warring nations, from two countries that had violently split apart after two centuries of British colonisation and oppression. The hostility that was set in stone on the night of 14 August 1947 led to further wars in 1948, 1965 and 1971. I experienced two of these as a young child. I remember blackouts, sirens, hiding in trenches, the sound of bombs dropping and of war planes being shot down. One of my first memories is sitting in a trench on my mother's lap in pitch darkness, cottonwool in my ears and a pencil between my teeth, with war planes flying over our heads and bombs blasting in the distance. With these wars came the rise in nationalism, the further entrenchment of hatred between people who are essentially culturally the same, who had lived in peace for hundreds of years, but who are now always on the brink of war. My parents and grandparents held the scars of partition all their lives.

My generation grew up loving Bollywood. The songs of Lata Mangeshkar, Mohammed Rafi and Kishore Kumar boomed all day from our cassette player. Yet the tinge of animosity was always under the surface, ready to burst out at the first hint of a skirmish between the two nations. As recently as 2019, airstrikes over Kashmir, a flashpoint for nuclear-armed India and Pakistan, triggered public calls for war. This happened during one of my visits to see Ammi in Lahore. As the airspace and airports closed down, strong sentiments were stirred up. As the young and the old on both sides of the border started calling for war, my childhood wartime memories returned to haunt me. Only this time it was scarier. As an adult, I know the devastation of armed conflict.

My neighbours in Sydney were the first Indians I had ever met. Given our countries' fraught history, I expected some awkwardness, some hesitation in extending a hand of friendship. It never came. We bonded from the very first moment we met. Our home became an extension of theirs. They often looked after Osman when I was at uni and Omar was working as a cabbie. I was their adopted sister who lovingly tied a rakhi around their wrist and who would cook endless meals for them. We would all sit around our living room, chatting for hours over chai and samosas. The rather uncomfortable mismatched furniture we had mainly picked up on council kerbside collection days didn't bother any of us. We joined in to celebrate each other's religious festivals—Eid, Ramadan, Raksha Bandhan, Holi. The loneliness eased as our friendship blossomed. The nights I would cry myself to sleep soon became a memory.

To me, this was the best of Australia. Here was a multicultural country where people came from all around the globe and easily shed their long-held enmities, no longer subject to the arbitrary physical borders that divide people of common heritage via narratives of toxic nationalism. It was also a sad realisation of the strength and depth of the very deliberate legacy of colonisation, which to this day can start the beating of chests and the sound of war drums in both India and Pakistan at the merest whiff of conflict.

UNSW soon became my second home, where I found my people, my first job and my political feet. As my study load increased, it became clear that I would need permanent childcare options for my baby boy, and I could not afford the available childcare in my local area. That's why I got involved in a campaign to establish affordable, student-centred childcare at the university. That's how the first cooperative childcare centre at UNSW, the Honey Pot, was established. I would not have been able to complete my master's and PhD, nor embark on my career in engineering and academia—and then, eventually, state and federal politics—without the availability of childcare at the university.

In our patriarchal society, many women have to give up work, study and career opportunities because childcare is too expensive or not accessible at all. Caring work has long been seen as 'women's work'. It is undervalued, underpaid and unpaid, even when our whole economy relies on it. It is not by accident that this feminisation of labour has created the heavily casualised and underpaid conditions for many workers in childcare and early learning. In my mind there is no question about the importance of publicly provided universal early childhood education and care that is accessible to anyone who needs it. Making childcare free and well funded, and supporting carers and educators with higher wages, is essential to dismantling the retrograde ideas that don't value early education or caring work.

Women have always known this, but it took a pandemic to bring the government around to recognising childcare as an essential service. Early childhood education and care was made free for all families for a few months. It is time for this view to stick.

Those early years as new migrants were difficult and liberating at the same time. The hardships of isolation, the constraints of living from week to week and the complexities of finding our feet in a new culture were accompanied by the sheer delight of discovering new things I had never experienced before. The azure blue of the coastline, public transport, avocados and ATMs were all novelties. So were McDonald's and Pizza Hut—and they were also the only places we could afford to eat out in. We had many Wednesday-night dinners at the Pizza Hut on Barker Street across from UNSW, thanks to the all-you-can-eat meal deal.

TOO MIGRANT, TOO MUSLIM, TOO LOUD

We were impatient to explore Sydney and its surrounds. Having no money to buy a decent car, we decided to use our engineering ingenuity and skills. Omar found two Datsuns (the classic 120Ys, of course!) for $400 advertised in the *Trading Post*. One had a decent body, the other a working engine. Now it was only a matter of putting the two together and voila—we would have a whole car. Omar has always been a car buff. It rubbed off on me too. Our first car in Pakistan was a 1969 Volkswagen Beetle. We fixed it up and painted it bright orange (even the saucepan-shaped air cleaner).

The shared backyard of our apartment building became a mechanics' garage for a couple of weeks. There, in the narrow space between the Hills hoists, we cranked up a crane to lift the engine from one car and lower it into the other. I sanded the rust off the bonnet and the body. We broke up the set cement in the footwells and wiped the interior clean. We were ready to see the sights of New South Wales. Our loyal white-and-rust(ed) 120Y took us to Wollongong, the Blue Mountains, the Central Coast, Palm Beach and all around Sydney. Among the rubble of the cement we found $12 in coins—enough for the three of us to celebrate with a family meal deal at Maccas!

It's true: the simple pleasures in life are the best.

A few of my cousins had been to Australia at various times. They were forthcoming in giving advice as we were leaving. We should stay at the Kings Cross Medina, one said: 'That's where all the action and nightlife is!' Another was adamant that attending the Mardi Gras was a must. 'It's in

BECOMING A MIGRANT

March. Make sure you go!' he chimed in. Yet another told us that Australia was a great place with wonderfully generous and welcoming people. Some years ago he was in Sydney for a conference and ended up sick at St Vincent's Hospital in Darlinghurst. The hospital did not charge him a single cent because he was a guest in Australia. 'You must try your best to make it your home' was his sage counsel.

Did we do as we were told? You bet we did! And more.

Bondi Beach was a must-do once a week. Sitting on the sand, looking out on the Pacific Ocean while hearing the waves break on the rocks was a new pleasure for Lahoris from a river city.

Walking up and down Darlinghurst Road in Kings Cross late at night with our baby boy in a stroller also became a weekly ritual. It was the only place that came close to the bright lights, sound and movement we were used to in Lahore. This didn't exist elsewhere in Sydney in the early 1990s, as everything except pubs shut down at 5 p.m. Being teetotallers with a young child, we didn't think a pub was an appropriate place. It was only later we discovered that the Cross was perhaps an inappropriate place for a two-year-old! We also went to watch the Mardi Gras Parade and loved every minute of the pride and expression of the LGBTQI+ community. Who knew then that two decades later I'd be on a Greens float, dancing and singing along, with others watching on?

***

TOO MIGRANT, TOO MUSLIM, TOO LOUD

My two children grew up in Australia without any extended family. They listen to my stories about weekends and holidays spent with grandparents, uncles, aunts and cousins playing cricket, cards and carom board with longing. With dozens of cousins around, there was always someone to talk to, to play with, to confide in. When we visited Pakistan, usually over summer holidays, they were always fascinated by the sheer number of people my family knew. The phone in my mum's home would ring all day. There would be people knocking on the door at all hours without prior notice. They were always invited in for a cup of tea, or to sit down at the table and share food for lunch or dinner. In a city of more than ten million people, you would still often meet someone you knew when you were shopping or running errands. This prompted the innocent and wondrous question from my then five-year-old daughter: 'Mama, do you know everyone in Pakistan?'—which is exactly how I felt growing up.

This big-city girl found those community links again in a small town in coastal New South Wales when, at the turn of the 21st century, the direction of my life changed once more.

After making the life-changing move from Lahore to Sydney, I never anticipated ever moving again. Nor did I want to. We had finally found our feet. We had jobs. We had bought a small apartment. Both children were happy at school. Like many working parents, though, we were struggling to balance life and work. Our children attended before- and after-school care. Omar worked very long hours.

BECOMING A MIGRANT

There was little time for all of us to be together. We started to re-evaluate our lives.

Then a few traumatic events jolted us into action.

My mother-in-law passed away in early 2001, soon after she was diagnosed with motor neurone disease. She was only 64 years old, fit and well, and had been working full-time before the diagnosis. This was a big shock for us. We all loved Omar's Amma. She was an incredible woman who had been widowed quite young when the youngest of her four children was only eight years old. With her children grown up, it had been her time to take it easy and enjoy life. Fate, sadly, had other plans.

Then, a month after her death, Omar was at a training exercise with the Army Reserve when he nearly drowned in the ocean off the coast of Sussex Inlet. Omar had joined the Corps of Engineers in the Australian Army Reserves in 1996 as a way of using his engineering skills to serve the community. The training included a weekend away every month and two weeks away every year. Every time Omar got back from his time away with the Reserves I could tell how rewarding he found the work by the way he would tell me about projects they had worked on: constructing an airstrip for the Royal Flying Doctors near Maralinga to provide medical access for remote communities, or building public housing in Cape York.

Both of these were moments of realisation. While Omar was still recovering in hospital, we made the decision to pack our bags once more. Life was too precious, and too short. We wanted to move to a smaller town with a slower pace, a place where we could spend more time with each other, get to know our neighbours, smell the roses. A few days after we made that decision, two jobs advertised in the paper caught my eye. Hastings Council in Port Macquarie, four-and-a-half hours drive north of Sydney, was looking for two engineers. We applied, got the jobs and were living there a few months later.

I'd grown up in the large metropolis of Lahore, then moved to Sydney, the most populous and multicultural city in Australia. I wasn't sure what to expect in a town of 36,000 mainly white people. Some of our friends did warn us against the move, given the sheer lack of cultural diversity. We were apprehensive too, but also confident that we could cope with it. It turned out to be the best move we ever made.

On the first day of the job in Port, my boss told me family was priority. The culture of smaller towns makes it easy to do that. Many move there to get away from the mundanity of city life. People have time to stop and talk to each other. Rather than rushing through a supermarket you have time to explore and chat to the person at the checkout without feeling you are delaying them or the person behind you. In fact, the person behind you is very willing to engage in the conversation as well. I started to meet friends, and people who knew my friends, in the street, at functions and while out and about. Within a couple of years we were pretty much a part of the community. We made friends all across the region from Johns River to Wauchope, Lake Cathie, Bonny Hills and Coffs Harbour. It was some of these friends who

BECOMING A MIGRANT

led me to join the Greens in this regional town, the conservative National Party heartland.

This is what I had missed most since leaving Pakistan. *This* was the home I'd been looking for. I never thought I would find it in a small coastal town in the mid-north coast of New South Wales.

In Pakistan, having a huge circle of family, friends and neighbours came with countless benefits. There's always help available when you need it—for weddings, at funerals, in sickness. There's always a doctor close by when needed, or a driver to give you a lift, or a friend when you need a shoulder to cry on or someone to celebrate and laugh with. You are never lonely or alone.

There are downsides too. There is never any privacy. There is always someone there. My husband tells me as a teenager he slept in the lounge room, not his bedroom, for years because there was always a guest to accommodate. The situation in my home wasn't as drastic but there was always an aunt, an uncle, a grandma, or a first, second or third cousin staying over. You had to give up your room, your bed, your space for them. When my sister and I whinged about always being kicked out of the room we shared, my Ammi told me to have a big heart. She said, 'To welcome guests you only need space in your heart—then there will always be enough in the home.' That's what I told my children when they too were asked to give up their bedrooms for friends who came to visit us in Port Macquarie, or those who came from Pakistan to visit Australia or make it home.

We've always had plenty of visitors since moving to Australia. My mother and mother-in-law would tell anyone they knew coming this way, 'Go and stay with Mehreen and Omar!' Lahoris are famous for their hospitality. My Ammi ingrained this generosity in me. I hope I've done the same in my children.

***

As it happened, our one-year trial of Australia turned into a lifetime of making a home here. Despite the trials and tribulations of being first-generation migrants, I did feel welcome in Australia on arrival. People coming to our shores today would not be able to say the same. While support for new migrants has eroded, bigotry and xenophobia has been allowed to flourish. Things sure have changed.

There was what is called 'everyday racism' and 'casual racism', but there definitely wasn't the searing heat of hate that I feel now. Migrants of colour were not used so blatantly as fodder for the inherent biases and white supremacy that this nation seems to be steeped in. There weren't the calls for changing the 'composition of our migration program' or for a migration program that reflects 'the historic European-Christian composition of Australian society'. The visceral hostility towards migrants, Muslims and refugees expressed by the politics of hate from One Nation and adopted by mainstream politicians has been normalised in our society. It makes us feel unwanted unless we toe the line drawn by jingoistic notions of patriotism. The major parties fan

BECOMING A MIGRANT

the flames of racism and xenophobia. The Coalition have been touting the rhetoric of 'us' and 'them', targeting the Sudanese community, Lebanese Muslim migrants, asylum seekers and refugees.

The relentless demands for me to prove my Australianness, while ridiculous, do hurt. I've dedicated the last eight years of my life to serving the people of New South Wales and Australia. I've given up my birthright to do this. I'm no longer a citizen of the country where generations of my family have lived, a country for whose independence they had fought. This was not easy. After filling out the forms to renounce my Pakistani citizenship to be able to run for the Senate, the papers sat in my desk drawer for many days. I could not bring myself to sign on the dotted line. I know it was only a piece of paper. But signing it had symbolic as well as actual implications.

I can see why so many would not do it. Why should we have to? Why should we be forced to extinguish ties with our roots, to deny who we are just to satisfy a misplaced sense of loyalty? This makes no sense in a country where almost one-third of us were born overseas and almost half of us have a parent born overseas. This only alienates people from engaging with democracy. How does forcing someone to renounce their citizenship of their country of birth guarantee their loyalty to their adopted country anyway? Surely it's their track record, their integrity, their work that should be up for scrutiny and judgement. I know people who would make great representatives but don't want to give up their ancestry. For me, sadly, even giving up my birthright isn't enough. I'm still harassed constantly to prove my Australianness.

To those who question my Australianness, when you abuse me, that reflects on me, my family, my community, my heritage and migrants as a whole. We are not here to be insulted or marginalised if we don't fall into the narrow conception of what you think it means to be 'Australian', or tolerated if you deem us to be Australian enough. You can't whitewash a country with Black foundations.

I am made in Pakistan. I am proud of my roots. I'm even prouder of my heritage. Now Australia is my home. Yes, Australia did give me the opportunity to be changed and now to fight for change. That's great, but don't expect me to be eternally grateful and stay in the corner you've created for migrants, where you pat us on the head if we fit your notion of what an Australian is, but vilify us, silence us and try to hound us out of our homes if we don't. My husband and I have worked hard to be where we are now. We are proud and upstanding citizens of this country and we make Australia a better place.

You can call me names. You can call me a maggot, a whore, a cockroach, a cow. You can demand I fuck off back to where I came from. Sorry, not sorry. This is my home. I'm not going anywhere. You will not grind me down. You will not shut me up. I'm not a maggot, a cockroach, a whore or a cow. I am a migrant. I am a Muslim. I am a woman. I am an engineer. I am here to stay.

2

THE BEST AND WORST OF POLITICS

—

I was sworn into the New South Wales Parliament on 19 June 2013. After the adrenaline rush of pure elation dissipated, along with my supporters and family who had stood around me, I found myself alone in my new office.

I'd just come out victorious from perhaps the largest member-driven preselection in Australia. A majority of grassroots Greens members across New South Wales had voted for me as their new MP. In the spirit of affirmative action, they had decided on a women-only preselection. There was a real atmosphere of camaraderie, not competition, among the eight women running. I was buoyed by the love I received as we travelled across the state for candidate forums. I had a clear-cut goal: to win the preselection and get into parliament.

Now, here in Macquarie Street, that clarity went out the window. There were only negative thoughts going through my head: 'What the fuck do I do now? What the hell am I even doing here? Why, oh why, did I quit my dream job as an academic?'

Winning my party's preselection, and the respect of members who hold similar values to mine, was one thing. Coming into a place infamously known as 'the Bear Pit' to fight for those values was quite another.

New South Wales' Parliament House is rumoured to be haunted by ghosts, said to be there from its days as the 'Rum' hospital with a morgue. Now, I never saw ethereal soldiers or old ladies in rocking chairs, but there is no doubt, it has its share of skeletons in its closets. Some secrets may never see the light of day, but plenty are out there, from corruption scandals and dirty deals to clandestine relationships and sexual harassment.

Macquarie Street has been complicit in so much suffering. After all, the man who the very street is named after, Governor Macquarie, famously issued the orders for the Appin massacre of the Gundungurra and Dharawal people, where soldiers drove men, women and children down the cliffs of a gorge of the Cataract River. The laws and regulations that have come from this place have aided and abetted so much to be ashamed of—child removals, theft of Indigenous land, targeting of First Nations people by police, gross injustices towards LGBTQI+ people, and denial of women's rights.

THE BEST AND WORST OF POLITICS

New South Wales' history of corruption is well known, from the countless colonial abuses to the rampant corruption of the Bob Askin era, to the more recent misconduct of Eddie Obeid and co.

Alleged improprieties continued through my time in New South Wales Parliament, with Premier Barry O'Farrell and that infamous $3000 bottle of Grange. The scandal surrounding Premier Gladys Berejiklian and Daryl Maguire and their years-long secret relationship is just another chapter in this dreary saga of deception. A culture of patriarchy, power and corruption is embedded within the politics of my state.

When I entered the New South Wales Parliament, the Liberals were midway through their first term, which they had won in a landslide after sixteen years of Labor governments. They were eagerly putting together plans to privatise public assets, gut environmental regulations, cut public-service jobs and restrict workers' rights. The conservative cross bench in the Legislative Council looked eager to assist them.

The Greens were preparing to resist this agenda, and push for opposite measures. We were a small minority party in parliament, with five out of 42 members in the upper house and only one member in the lower house. How could I help unravel the government's regressive attacks and implement the Greens' progressive vision? Why did I ever think I could?

I wish I had had a crystal ball. Gazing through it, I would have seen how different I would feel five years later, on my last day in the New South Wales Parliament, as I headed to the Australian Senate. The challenges that had seemed unsurmountable on that first day, I recognised, had given me the strength to keep doing my job. Through all the unseen pitfalls, the pleasant and unpleasant surprises, the good, the bad and the ugly of politics, I was determined to be myself.

I am idealistic. I believe the world can be a better place.

I'm not a politician. I'm an engineer.

I follow my convictions. I don't compromise on my values.

I'm not a wheeler and dealer. I convince people with evidence.

I was confident of learning the mechanics of parliament. It was the dynamics that worried me.

The city I was born in, Lahore, was a world away. I had never, not even in my wildest dreams, imagined myself in Australia, let alone as a member of the oldest parliament in Australia. I was an outsider.

I had not come through the political ranks, as a student unionist, a party apparatchik or a political staffer. My experience comprised my years of work as an engineer in Australia and in Pakistan, as a consultant, an academic and a local government officer. I'd lived in the real world, not the political realm most politicians inhabit.

When you're an outsider like me, you don't have access to the many informal established networks of politics. While in the smallish New South Wales upper house it was relatively easy to break down barriers, it was much harder in the

Senate. The physical vastness of the building means senators don't run into each other in the corridors. Not having existing political or historical connections made it harder to break through and establish connections. And if you're not part of the after-dark scene in Canberra's bars, where booze and gossip flow freely, you miss out on another opportunity for networking.

The drawbacks of not being a product of this entrenched political system signify its brokenness. When young people interested in politics ask me what they should do to become a politician, I have no hesitation in telling them to go work in the real world before they decide to run for parliament. They should live the life of the people they want to represent, I tell them, whether that means working as a barista or a barrister (although we do have too many lawyers in politics!). But they should also talk to people who they wouldn't usually engage with, taking the time to understand their lives and their points of view.

Getting involved in politics doesn't necessarily mean striving to become an MP, either. That might seem strange coming from me, but I do believe the spark for political change can come as easily from outside parliament. In fact, history tells us that society is almost always running ahead of politicians, who are usually dragged into supporting change once they see the writing on the wall.

It gives me boundless hope to see people agitating for social and climate justice. The few voices for First Nations justice have now become roaring crowds that speak louder than ever before on Invasion Day each year, demanding truth and treaties. The school strikers for climate action are the new heroes for climate justice. When these voices are amplified in parliaments, the momentum will become unstoppable.

I was alien to the 'game' of politics when I started in the New South Wales Parliament, but politics has never been far from my mind. For nineteen of my 28 years in Pakistan, my country was under military rule, and the rest was mainly under corrupt political regimes. My family did have a connection with politics. My paternal grandfather was the first speaker of the Punjab assembly after partition. He died long before I was born. But by the time I grew up, 'politician' was a rather dirty word. We were all very proud of my grandfather's legacy, but no one in my family considered it a respected profession anymore.

While heated political debates were devoured around the dinner table along with my mum's hot curries, politicians were pilloried for being self-interested, egotistical and crooked. My elders reminisced about the good old days of statesman-like politicians like my grandfather who dedicated their lives to the good of people and country. The system is so broken now, they would say, that the idea of respectable, ordinary folk joining politics to fix it was as ridiculous as it was unrealistic. How could one good person even hope to change an entrenched system of corruption? Even if they were brave enough to try, how could they even hope to get elected without the right connections and money? They'd end up disillusioned, burnt out and marginalised, without having made a dent in the system. So what was the point?

Hearing these conversations, first as a child and then as a young adult, I had so many questions. Surely, if the state of politics was so bad, someone had to do something? How would things change if we gave up? Were we really willing to give the crooked politicians or the military dictators free rein? Shouldn't we be the change? I was never satisfied by the answers I got, but the strength of the opinion and the emotion that flew around the dinner table seeped into me. So, I did not even consider following my grandfather's path into parliament.

You'd be right to ask why I changed my mind. There was no real light-bulb moment, but rather a series of insights and observations that spanned quite a period. Some were just accidental twists and turns of life, others deliberate and well-thought-through choices. The first one goes back to those childhood conversations. While Pakistani politicians were seen as villains embroiled in corruption, nepotism and cronyism, politicians in Western countries were viewed very differently. They were public servants with honesty and integrity, something apparently long lost in our politicians. That's why, I was told, those nations were doing so well. That's why they were wealthy. That's why they treated everyone the same. That's why, when someone worked hard they were rewarded, no matter who they were or where they came from.

So the virtues of Western democracies that trickled down to me were endless, and I had high hopes of Australian politicians, and of the political system itself.

Soon after I joined politics in Australia, my belief in corruption-free, selfless politicians came crashing down.

In my first year in the New South Wales Parliament, a staggering ten state Liberal MPs resigned from the party or from their positions under the shadow of corruption, along with Premier Barry O'Farrell. This happened at the same time the NSW Independent Commission Against Corruption was investigating previous Labor ministers Eddie Obeid and Joe Tripodi for misconduct in public office. I was shattered by these revelations, especially since one of the reasons my husband and I had left Pakistan was the political corruption that had set in over there. I was hoping for things to be different in Australia.

The more I see of politics, the more I see the omnipresence of corruption. It may not be as confronting or as openly acknowledged as in Pakistan, but in my view that makes it worse. It is worse because it is denied, covered up and even defended. It is worse because some of the outright corruption is largely legal.

The very concept of political donations is about buying influence, which ultimately results in the abuse of taxpayer money. There is simply no other explanation. In the two decades to 2019 inclusive, the resource industry's political donations amount to $136.8 million.[1] For corporations, it is simply an investment. Give a hundred thousand dollars today, unlock tens of millions of dollars through a policy change tomorrow. Fossil-fuel companies that donate millions of dollars to political parties end up getting $12 billion worth of taxpayer-funded subsidies every year. They go on to make huge profits while paying zero or little tax. Labor, Liberal, Nationals, One Nation—they are all the same when it comes to accepting corporate bribery. Unlike these parties, the Greens refuse to take corporate donations intended to buy influence.

Public money is freely used by governments to advance their odds of winning an election without any recriminations. In 2020, both the federal government and the New South Wales government were caught rorting grants funding by funnelling it into Coalition-held and marginal seats in an obvious bid to influence the 2019 election outcomes.

The 'sports rorts' were federal grants directed at marginal and targeted electorates, approved by the then sports minister, Bridget McKenzie. After a frenzy of media attention, public and political backlash, the minister resigned from Cabinet and gave up her position as the deputy leader of the National Party. But it was not her department's failure to follow proper process, nor the immorality of 'pork-barrelling', that took her down in the end. It was her failure to declare membership of a club to which one of the grants was directed. Of course, this conflict of interest was a problem, but it was clearly also a deflection from the bigger issue of underlying corruption. Even under intense public pressure, Prime Minister Scott Morrison got away without setting up a federal ICAC that might have powers to investigate cases of misuse of public funds by politicians seeking election advantage.

In New South Wales, Premier Gladys Berejiklian and her government approved $252 million in grants to councils, 95 per cent of which were directed to councils in Coalition-held seats or marginal electorates.[2] After the denials and cover-ups were exposed following the release of copies of shredded documents which the premier's office had been ordered to produce, Berejiklian quickly went into self-defence mode.[3] Favouring 'certain areas', she said, was 'not something the community likes . . . but it's an accusation I will wear'.[4]

How did it become so easy to brush off accusations of wrongdoing and pork-barrelling? There is something very wrong with a political process that lets politicians shore up their seats using public money. This is routine in our country. Again and again, politicians get away with behaviour which does not meet the community's expectations of honesty, integrity and transparency.

When ministers leave parliament, they often swing straight into lucrative positions in companies they once regulated. Or they swing right back into politics as 'lobbyists', and are paid obscene amounts of money by corporations to influence decisions and outcomes using their well-established political networks. How many pieces of legislation have been passed in Australian parliaments, I wonder, under both Labor and Coalition governments, purely at the behest of corporate lobbying or as a favour to 'one of the boys' in the club?

I've sat in parliament and watched career politicians pass bills written by lobbyists. I've sat in committees and watched MPs ignore expert advice and evidence because it doesn't match up with what their donors are telling them. I've sat in inquiries where witnesses have begged the major parties to listen to common sense and act in the interests of the people, but the interests of developers win out. If we are to have a parliament of integrity, then we must have a parliament that can't be bought.

I remain astounded by the depth and breadth of this corruption. It is so normalised that it goes on right under our noses. If it ever gets brought to light, there have occasionally been repercussions, resignations and even jail for some. But so much of it is sanctioned by our lax laws and the well-established web of privileged connections that no one is held accountable.

I often talk about this with my brothers and sister, who are scattered all over the world. We recall how, as young people, we were so trusting in Western countries. Now I know it is the Western supremacist narrative that is to blame for our naivety. We were surrounded by it while we were growing up. As people with a colonial history, we were conditioned to think of ourselves as the problem, one the colonialists fixed when they occupied and ruled us. We were taught to believe in a world where developed rich nations were morally and intellectually superior to developing poor nations. In fact, their ruthless pursuit of power and self-interest shows just how devoid of morality they were.

These conversations with my siblings leave me with a tinge of sadness. As if someone has robbed me of this better, more moral world we all thought was there outside Pakistan. That world never existed. Sadly, everyone is corruptible. Looking at it another way, this puts us on an equal footing, however lowly it is. The moral high ground often taken by white folk is revealed as being without foundation. In any case, talking about this has helped me decolonise my mind. It has shown me how deep and wide the manifestations of structural oppression run.

We can't lull ourselves into thinking that decolonising our world and ourselves is an easy task. It's hard. It must be purposeful. It's a task that has to be taken on by the colonised. Colonisers can't, and won't, decolonise.

***

I've always taken pride in my work. As an engineer, I've worked at consulting firms in Pakistan and Australia, and at local councils in Sydney and Port Macquarie. As an academic, I've taught for a few different university faculties. I've walked into completely new workplaces without any qualms about how I would fit in, or how my presence might shape the organisation or indeed influence my colleagues. I've often managed to initiate change in unlikely places. The head of a local council I once worked at gave me a leather whip as a gift. He wanted me to symbolically whip the organisation into becoming more environmentally sustainable, not because he had a particular interest in it, but because he had seen my passion for it.

But as I sat alone in my new office in the New South Wales Parliament on that first day, any confidence I had in my experience and ability flew out the window. I had more than a few moments of panic as I contemplated how I would make the transition from a migrant engineer to a politician.

I did not know anyone in my new workplace place other than the Greens MPs. Frankly, even among my Greens colleagues, the only person I really knew was the late Dr John Kaye—or Dr K, as I called him. It was my comeback to his 'Dr F'. He was a friend, a mentor, a fellow engineer, a fellow University of New South Wales academic, a fellow campaigner and an animal lover just like me. Dr K took me under his wing and passed on his knowledge in the very forensic way that he was known for. He introduced me to other members of parliament and parliamentary staff. He became my go-to person for advice. I was never disappointed. The New South Wales Parliament was never the same for me after his death in 2016.

I've always found it easy to get along with people at the many places I've worked, whether they have similar or vastly different worldviews to mine. I was beyond touched to see friends and colleagues from every one of these workplaces at my inaugural speech to the New South Wales Parliament.

In politics, the world is often a binary black or white. It's 'my way or the highway'—'I'm right, therefore you're wrong'.

People are squashed into two boxes—left-wing or right-wing, progressive or conservative, believer or denier, Labor or Liberal, friend or foe, capitalist or socialist. I've always believed people are more complex than the labels affixed to them suggest.

While there are some who fit neatly into one or the other box, the vast majority of us are an endless permutation of these schisms and the influences on our lives. These nuances are conveniently ignored within the adversarial argy-bargy of politics. We become two-dimensional cut-outs of our real selves, debating just two sides of an argument. One's right and the other's wrong. How can we ever hope to resolve multifaceted problems like the climate crisis and racial injustice within such narrowly defined frames, which bear no resemblance to the real world?

In politics, the barriers come up quickly as newcomers are viewed through the lens of their political party. As a result, I was really nervous about how I would bridge the divide in my new workplace. I hoped people wouldn't view me simply as a Greens MP. I came into politics with an open mind and heart, bringing with me all my professional and my lived experience. I thought my life, which straddled two continents and cultures, would allow me to offer some useful, even unique insights into the political issues our state faced.

I could only remember being this nervous once: right before I delivered my first lecture at the Institute of Environmental Studies to my master's students. My heart was beating fast, and my hands were sweaty with apprehension. Dr Ronnie Harding, the founder and director of the institute, had hired me in 2004 for this job, my first as an academic. She has since become my mentor and a very dear friend. Teaching was all I'd desired as a career. It was a lifelong goal which had finally come true.

I wanted to be a good teacher—but what if I didn't have an answer to the students' questions? What if I didn't meet their expectations? What if they hated me? Ronnie came to my office to wish me luck. Seeing my anxiety, she stopped to have a chat, and gave me some advice that I've carried with me since. Advice on being true to myself. On being honest and not pretending that I knew everything. On not being afraid to be challenged, and above all on valuing the knowledge others have. 'They just want to have a yarn, Mehreen,' she said.

When the thoughts swirling around my head that first day in the New South Wales Parliament made me feel hopeless and hopeful in quick succession, I remembered Ronnie's wisdom. I took a deep breath and walked into the Legislative Council chamber. I was going to be myself. I was determined to listen to views that were different to mine. I wanted to be heard, too. I was ready for a debate. Bring it on.

***

Believe it or not, politics does have its good side. It has bad and ugly sides too. I've seen them all. A politician's life is full of highs and lows, and mine has been no different. One of the things that frustrates me most is how easily vested interests trump both evidence and community input in political decision-making.

I'm not naive. I am acutely aware of the complexities of political decisions. I know they are bounded by political ideologies. I know they are dominated by political donors, lobbyists and connections. But where do expertise, evidence and the community's needs fit in the dimensions of decision-making? In my experience, unless they are aligned with the wants of the government of the day, they rarely do. As someone who has relied on hard scientific data to substantiate decisions, I am astounded by how conveniently facts are discarded to fulfil narrow political agendas.

'Community consultation' is for ticking a box. It's an orchestrated public relations exercise with a predetermined outcome. People's submissions and contributions do little to sway it. The voices of corporate donors and powerbrokers in the corridors of parliament drown out community voices.

Political debate is a misnomer. Governments come into the parliamentary debate with their minds already made up. By the time they introduce a piece of legislation into parliament, it's often just for a rubber stamp. If the government has the majority or the numbers, then it's an easy ride and the bill is rammed through. No logic, reason or compassion need be employed. How often have I read out a constituent's personal story or an expert's report to a row of empty chairs? Politicians march in and march out with their orders on how to vote.

My most brutal experience of this in New South Wales was the passing of the Biodiversity Conservation Bill 2016 and the cognate Local Land Services Amendment Bill

2016, also known as the 'Land Clearing Laws'. These pieces of legislation are nothing short of ecocide. It was very clear from the start that weakening environmental protections for native vegetation would be disastrous for the environment, climate and wildlife. When the Queensland government of Campbell Newman passed similar laws that severely undermined native vegetation rules, it resulted in doubling of land clearing, the removal of almost 300,000 hectares of bushland, and the release of 35 million tonnes of carbon dioxide annually in its first two years.[5] The example was there for New South Wales to heed; all it required was a gaze. But the government looked away.

The panel set up to provide an 'Independent Biodiversity Legislation Review' was a farce, a tokenistic exercise to tick the 'public consultation' box. Even though 80 per cent of the thousands of submissions to this review asked for the environmental protections to be retained or strengthened, the final recommendations called for the exact opposite: the wholesale repeal of the *Native Vegetation Act 2003*, which had been instrumental in stopping broadscale clearing.

Things got so bad that a few days before the bill was brought to parliament, Professor Hugh Possingham, a member of the Review Panel, quit because his advice was being ignored. He warned of the massive increase in land clearing under the proposed laws, and the ramification this would have for extinctions. This should have been the end of this terrible legislation, but we can never underestimate the power of vested interests—Big Agriculture, Big Mining, Big Development, and of course the anti-environment National Party.

The bills were introduced. We started debate in the Legislative Council at 3 p.m. on the afternoon of 15 November 2016 and finished at 2 a.m. the next morning. I moved dozens of amendments to try to improve the bill. Not a single one passed. The bill itself, however, did pass. And what the experts warned would happen was exactly what happened. Three years on from these weakened laws, there was a 60 per cent increase in land clearing in New South Wales. This destruction and fragmentation of habitat have put koalas on track for extinction by 2050. At a time when climate change is biting, unprecedented bushfires are consuming lives and livelihoods, deliberately clearing habitat is not just murder, it's self-sabotage as well.

In the case of land-clearing laws, the Liberal/National government's interests aligned with those of the Shooters and Fishers Party. They easily had the numbers for this act of environmental vandalism. From where I sat, the upper house of the New South Wales Parliament had failed its role as an effective legislature.

When the government can't easily get the numbers for a piece of legislation to pass, they do secret deals with those crossbenchers who are willing to exchange their vote for something in return. Voters may never find out what has been bought and sold in these transactions. What the public see is the final performance of a well-rehearsed play. Voters have no access to the rehearsals or backstage, where the wheeling and dealing takes place. Not even all the actors in the final production are privy to what goes on behind the scenes. We just speculate, then rebuke those who've sold out.

At no time was this more evident than in 2020, by which time I was a senator for New South Wales. The year that changed the world forever didn't change much about the way political decisions are made in Australian parliaments. There was the same deal-making. The same triumph of ideology over evidence, with critical thinking replaced by autocratic conformity and a neoliberal agenda. No alternatives are entertained. There is only contempt for those with a different opinion. The end result is dangerous policies with terrible consequences. The 'Job-Ready Graduates Bill' of 2020 is a prime example of this defective decision-making.

Under the cover of a global pandemic, governments wielded even more authority than in normal times. They were under less media and public scrutiny. And they struck while the iron was hot.

The weight of evidence against this bill was heavy. It was widely criticised by higher education experts, economists, the business lobby, academics, unions and students alike. I wasn't shy to call it a 'shit bill' on the floor of the Senate. Why? Because it was. It doubled the fees of humanities degrees, while also hiking fees for law and economics, condemning students to decades more of debt. It slashed close to a billion dollars a year of core learning and teaching funding from universities. It punished struggling students by taking away their student loan if they failed half their subjects. While it lowered the fees for STEM courses like engineering, the government funding to deliver them was also reduced.

If this bill became law, I knew it would move us even further away from the vision of fully funded public universities, fee-free for students and with security of work for staff so they can deliver high-quality research, learning and teaching. Moreover, as the bill's title suggests, it was shifting the very purpose of a university from a place of acquiring and creating knowledge to one that simply churns out a workforce.

My father always wanted his two sons and two daughters to go to uni. In Pakistan, you are more likely to get a better, well-paying job with a higher degree, but that was not his primary motivation. For Abbu, it was first and foremost about learning, about opening up our minds so that we could think critically and make decisions after considering the relevant evidence. 'Engineers can do anything and everything,' he would tell us. 'After all, we are trained to solve problems.' It's probably no surprise that all four of us became civil engineers.

My engineering expertise has been handy in my parliamentary work. In making a case against Sydney's proposed WestConnex motorway, I build a mathematical model to show the financial unviability of the toll road. I've examined the trajectory of the privatisation of public transport in New South Wales to prove it's neither less expensive nor more efficient than if it were in public hands. I've pored over thousands of pages of secret documents released through my call for papers in the Legislative Council to extract vital information quickly. So I understand very well the value of an engineering degree. I also know the value of humanities and social sciences to better understand the complex world around us and to question and find our place within it. This social engineering experiment to funnel more students into STEM degrees and fewer into the humanities is misguided.

Young people should be able to choose degrees that match their dreams and aspirations without the hurdle of high fees and the consequent debt. If we want to encourage more people to study science and engineering, and I believe we should, then let's cultivate interest in these professions. Let's raise their profile. My daughter graduated as a civil engineer 30 years after me. The glacial progress being made towards gender equality meant she still encountered many of the same barriers I did. We know what's stopping women from studying and working in these fields: gender stereotypes, a lack of visible role models, a blokey workplace culture, and inflexible work arrangements, to name just a few issues. That's what needs to change.

My engineering skills were again put to good use as our office dissected the many impacts of the bill. We wanted to make sure that we left no stone unturned as we set about revealing its flaws. After 70 days of deliberation, the Labor Party had finally expressed their unequivocal opposition.

That meant my mission was to convince my three crossbench colleagues—independent senators Jacqui Lambie and Rex Patrick and Senator Stirling Griff of the Centre Alliance—to reject the bill.

We unravelled the government's logic that fee hikes and funding cuts were justified because they allowed the creation of more Commonwealth Supported Places. According to our assessment, the 'Job-Ready Graduates Package' would fall drastically short of places as applications to study soared during the COVID-induced recession. Tens of thousands of people would be denied the chance to study and retrain. Our analysis showed that women would feel the greatest impact, as they represented two-thirds of the students in the courses with the largest fee increases. They would be saddled with much higher student debt: it would take some of them twenty years to pay off their university debts.

Education minister Dan Tehan was quick to dismiss this modelling, telling the *Sydney Morning Herald*, 'Maybe Senator Faruqi should study a mathematics unit.'

LOL. That was pretty amusing, given I'm the only engineering PhD in the national parliament.

The bill inspired not only outrage but also total bafflement. The entire sector was bewildered by the messy policy disaster this was. Even former Liberal foreign minister Julie Bishop conceded it appeared to be contrary to the government's policy intentions. It was unlikely to have the professed effect of encouraging more students to enrol in the priority science and engineering courses identified by the government. First, universities would be incentivised to enrol substantially more students in courses with the highest student contributions. Second, there's little evidence that students respond in any meaningful way to price signals when the costs of their degrees are deferred under the Higher Education Loan Program.

Labor and the three key crossbenchers joined forces to vote for my motion to refer the bill to a Senate inquiry. While that didn't give us the numbers on the day, grudgingly the government was forced to agree a little later. They weren't going to make it easy for us. The inquiry process was highly problematic. It allowed only 22 days, with just two days of hearings, to consider a complex and controversial bill. During consideration of the draft committee report, I was allowed no time to discuss my amendments to the report. The final report leans heavily on evidence that supports the bill, while omitting to convey the level of dissent heard by the committee.

Despite the government's attempts to scupper the inquiry and then to produce a biased report, independent senator Rex Patrick made clear his intention to vote against the bill. A few days later, Senator Lambie revealed her view: she would oppose the bill. Hope was rekindled. We were getting closer.

The Liberals have never pretended to be friends of universities or public education. Their benches are full of arts graduates, yet most feel a juvenile loathing for the humanities. Many Liberal politicians who benefited from free university education tried hard to deregulate university fees when Tony Abbott was prime minister, without success. In 2020, they got the opportunity to kick the sector while it was down.

Universities were shedding thousands of jobs due to the loss of international student revenue that was anticipated because of the COVID-related shutdown. Instead of coming to their rescue, the government did the opposite. They changed the JobKeeper subsidy rules three times, specifically to make public universities ineligible for the income-support payment. Among my lowest parliamentary moments of that year were seeing the exclusion of international students from government support, witnessing the passage of the university funding cuts and fee hikes, and watching the Liberals block my amendment to include universities in JobKeeper.

I never trusted the Liberals to do right by higher education. But I did expect university leaders to put up a fight for their communities, and for the value of higher education.

A vast majority of university vice-chancellors caved under the government's pressure. Fearful of government hostility, they quietly acquiesced to its demands. Back in 2019, just before the federal election, I'd met with university representatives and urged them to be more public with their demands to undo the funding freeze that had been imposed in 2017. If they didn't fight back, the government would see them as easy targets for further budget cuts. And in 2020 the government did just that. Vice-chancellors offered no resistance as their staff and students were trampled on. They acted like cowards. They don't deserve their power, their positions or their fat pay cheques.

The vice-chancellors of Australia's universities have presided over a period of increasing casualisation of their workforce, and even the systematic underpayment of wages to those casual staff—and yet they remain the highest-paid vice-chancellors in the world. This makes me angry. It makes me more determined to build democratic universities. Staff and students should control boards and senates, not government-appointed, self-promoting hacks who have corporatised universities to the extent that education is now bought and sold in a marketplace, leaving staff as 'service providers'. Education is simply not a commodity. It is a public good.

What disgusted me most was the moral bankruptcy of Pauline Hanson's One Nation (PHON) party and the Centre Alliance. In all honesty, I didn't have much hope for PHON. The government didn't have to make much effort to bring them on board. I did expect more from the Centre Alliance, though.

When the changes were announced, Rebekha Sharkie, the Centre Alliance's education spokesperson, had expressed serious concerns about the bill, believing it to be 'grossly unfair' to high school students. She was quick to come out on Twitter in praise of her arts degree, thanking Flinders University and acknowledging she would not have had a career, nor become a politician, if it were not for her degree. I thought this was a signal of the Centre Alliance's opposition to a bill that more than doubled the cost of arts degrees, robbing future students of the opportunities Sharkie had enjoyed. But in a few short months, the Centre Alliance had cut a deal with the government. The bill then passed the Senate by one vote. Theirs.

No matter how I try, I simply cannot fathom such politics. I cannot reconcile how easily facts become the casualty of politics. It happens every day.

Soon after the passage of the university fee hikes and funding cuts, legislation to expand and make permanent the cashless debit card was brought on. The cashless debit card scheme trial started in Australia in 2016 under a Coalition government. It is a mandatory income management tool which quarantines 80 per cent of social security payments on the card which can be spent only on clothes, food, health and hygiene products, and prevents spending on alcohol, illegal drugs and gambling products. This policy has been opposed and rejected by people from across the community for years because it causes harm, disproportionately effects First Nations people and doesn't even work.[6,7]

During the debate on the controversial government bill to make the scheme permanent, senator after senator from the side opposite the government's spoke against the bill. We backed our arguments with the first-hand experience of card users. We presented research that cast doubt on whether the cashless debit card was achieving its intended aims. We provided data to show how it disproportionately targeted First Nations communities. On the other hand, the evidence for continuing compulsory income management was just not there.

In the House of Representatives, the Centre Alliance voted against the bill. During the Senate debate, we found out that Senator Lambie and Senator Patrick had made up their minds to vote against it. There was palpable relief that, combining their opposition with that of the Centre Alliance, this punitive, racist, discriminatory policy would finally end.

But this reprieve only lasted a few minutes. It soon became apparent the Centre Alliance were now doing another deal with the government. In the end, the bill passed the Senate with the votes of One Nation and with an abstention from the Centre Alliance's Senator Griff, with the party changing its mind after securing an amendment from the government to extend the trial for two more years, not making it permanent. This is cold comfort for the people whose shame, frustration and stigma will continue for at least two more years. No one knows what the Centre Alliance got in return for cheerleading the government in this way.

***

Politics can break your heart. It can shatter your confidence in people. But it can uplift you too, and all in the space of a few short months. It can fundamentally change the way you see the world.

Back in the New South Wales Parliament—in direct contrast to the land-clearing laws, which flouted all evidence—came then premier Mike Baird's decision to end greyhound racing in New South Wales in 2016. This ban came on the back of overwhelming evidence of animal cruelty from the Special Commission of Inquiry into Greyhound Racing. But the episode ultimately offered a painful lesson in political opportunism, and in how money trumps facts.

I must confess, my understanding of the gambling and greyhound racing industries was limited when I came into the New South Wales Parliament. The only greyhounds I was familiar with were Santa's Little Helper in *The Simpsons* and the racing greys loved by Darryl Kerrigan in the iconic movie *The Castle*.

I had seen the track at Taree while travelling around the Mid North Coast in my previous role at Port Macquarie-Hastings Council, but I hadn't given it too much thought. It wasn't until an explosive ABC *Four Corners* investigation, 'Making a Killing', broadcast in 2015, that I was exposed to the full horrors of animal cruelty in this so-called sport. Following this exposé, and the speedy resignation of the CEO and members of the board of Greyhound Racing NSW, the New South Wales government hastily put together a special commission to inquire into the industry.

Although I held the animal welfare portfolio for the Greens at the time, the charge against greyhound racing was being led by our racing and gambling spokesperson, Dr John Kaye. Initially, John had believed that the industry could be reformed, but the more he saw of the evidence brought to him by activists and whistle-blowers, the more strongly he felt that the industry was rotten to the core. Sadly, Dr Kaye passed away before the commission handed down its final report. It was left to me to run our campaign to shut down greyhound racing.

By now I was a fierce advocate for the greys. I knew enough about the use and abuse of greyhounds for gambling profits. I had also met dozens of these gentle, adorable dogs, and had fallen in love with them. I could not comprehend how anyone could inflict pain and death on them so callously. I found out the hard way. Money does make the world go round for some.

The Special Commission of Inquiry into Greyhound Racing had its term extended a few times. I wasn't holding out much hope, expecting a lukewarm report with inadequate recommendations that would barely touch the edges of the deep pool of animal cruelty that was greyhound racing. So you can imagine the eruption of joy in our office, accompanied by rivulets of tears down our faces, when Premier Baird announced on 7 July 2016 he would ban greyhound racing in New South Wales. On the eve of my birthday, this was the best present I could have hoped for.

The truly heinous nature of this industry was laid bare by the report of the Special Commission of Inquiry, authored by Justice Michael McHugh. It was based on thirteen months of investigation, 151,000 pages of evidence, 115 hours of video evidence, 804 new submissions and 69 individual testimonies. There was vast and irrefutable evidence of animal cruelty, live baiting, drugging and mass killings of dogs. Justice McHugh's report estimated that over the past twelve years, 97,783 greyhounds had been bred, and at least 50 per cent to 70 per cent were killed simply because they were not, or no longer were, capable of being competitive. That is up to 68,448 dogs killed—more than fifteen a day, on average. How can we purport to be a civilised society and allow this barbarism to go on? Ultimately, the report found that this 'sport' could not survive without the deaths of thousands of dogs.

The full extent of the brutality of this industry with no oversight was revealed. The death of dogs was a core part of the business model, as was covering up the drugging, the death pits and the catastrophic injuries. And it was clear that the industry went to great lengths not only to make no changes whatsoever—even when it knew it was being investigated by the Special Commission of Inquiry—but actively tried to cover up its failings. The industry continued to deliberately misreport greyhound deaths on track so as to avoid 'stirring up the greenies'.

Premier Baird admitted that, after these revelations, the government genuinely had no other option but to shut the greyhound racing industry down.

While we celebrated, there was uncharacteristic silence from the Labor Party. I wasn't too concerned. After all, during the 2015 election, the Leader of the Opposition at the time, Luke Foley, and New South Wales Labor had released an animal welfare plan. In its foreword, Foley had stated: 'A civilised society cares for its people and looks after those who are vulnerable. A civilised society also ensures that its animals are treated humanely.' On this basis—and with the pretty incontrovertible proof of inhumane treatment of animals in the greyhound racing industry—I was quietly confident that Labor would support the ban.

How wrong I was. I had miscalculated how cravenly opportunistic the Labor Party would be. These are times when my having come to politics in Australia from the 'outside' remains a handicap. I just cannot comprehend such base unscrupulousness. The game of politics will remain an enigma to me. People and animals are not pawns: their lives depend on what we politicians do. This manoeuvre by the Labor Party sacrificed greyhounds at the altar of political expediency.

Four days after Baird's announcement, Foley vowed to fight the ban. It was the first time I'd seen Labor actually campaign for something, and I was disgusted that they chose to fight for gambling and animal cruelty. It was a powerful lesson of the might of the gambling industry in Australia, and its nexus with the media.

The *Daily Telegraph*, which is reliant on huge amounts of advertising from the gambling industry, began attacking the ban with dozens of front pages. Just a few months later, it would announce it had acquired the major gambling tipping website, punters.com.au. TABcorp is one of the major players in the gambling and racing industry, and one of the country's most prolific political donors. It later emerged that Ladbrokes had made a large financial contribution to the campaign to overturn the ban.

The Coalition government moved swiftly. By mid-August the legislation to ban greyhound racing had passed both houses of the New South Wales Parliament.

The ban was overwhelmingly popular with the public. A poll from the RSPCA found that 64 per cent of people in New South Wales and the ACT supported the ban on greyhound racing. But the unholy alliance of the gambling industry, the Murdoch media and the Labor Party kept on savaging it. To counter them, we organised protests, wrote open letters and opinion pieces supporting and praising the ban. The Liberal Party went into paralysis. They did nothing. They ignored the majority who were supporting them.

I had reached out to Premier Baird the day he announced the ban, thanking him for his courageous decision. We organised greyhound rescue groups to come to parliament to meet and thank MPs—not a single Liberal MP turned up. I wrote to him expressing support for both the ban and the industry assistance package that was to accompany it. I'm aware there were conspiracy theories that held the government had the Greens in its inner circle, but in fact I never got so much as a response from Baird. The first we heard from them was the night before the bill was to be debated. A senior government MP later confided in me that they had expected the bill to pass with Labor's support, which may explain just how unprepared the Liberals were for the backlash. They allowed the narrative to be controlled by the opposition, and by radio shock jocks Alan Jones and Ray Hadley.

THE BEST AND WORST OF POLITICS

Pressure was clearly building on the government to back down. A by-election in Orange was looming. The deputy premier and leader of the New South Wales Nationals, Troy Grant, received death threats from people involved in greyhound breeding and training. There were rumours of a leadership spill in the Nationals party room. By the time I stood with thousands of animal advocates rallying in Martin Place, it had become clear that they were going to reverse the ban.

Then came the moment that broke my heart. On 11 October, less than two months after the greyhound ban bill had passed parliament, Mike Baird announced the backflip. I had cried tears of joy when the ban was announced. Now there were tears of sheer anger and disappointment rolling down my face. It had seemed too good to be true, and it was.

Not only was the ban reversed, but now the government was promising to pour tens of millions of taxpayer dollars into the industry. Before the ban, greyhound racing was shrinking, with industry plans to reduce the number of tracks by up to 24—a massive 70 per cent reduction. But now the Liberals were actually resuscitating the industry that they had recently said needed to be shut down because of its animal cruelty. So much for conviction politics. I sometimes wish Mike Baird had done nothing at all. Greyhound racing would probably have fizzled out on its own. Now it was having a revival, and being propped up by torrents of public money. That made it even more obscene.

When the Coalition and Labor members filed in to vote to undo the ban, I didn't hold back. I let them have it. 'Today one can almost smell the shame in this chamber,' I said. 'There are members of parliament from the Labor Party, the Liberal Party and the Nationals who supported the ban, but I suppose thousands of dogs will have to be sacrificed on the altar of political expediency. Labor's hypocrisy on animal welfare has been well canvassed in this place. I guess Luke Foley can add a notch to his belt that he managed to overturn what would have been the most significant animal welfare reform in New South Wales—one that could have reverberated across the nation. Labor is not about stopping coal seam gas mining, phasing out coal or transitioning from coal to 100 per cent renewable energy, but Labor will go into bat for gambling and racing interests with gusto. That was what woke up the sleeping Labor leader.'

The sordid greyhound saga took a few political scalps. In November 2016, the Nationals lost the Orange by-election to the Shooters and Fishers, who were buoyed by Labor Party preferences. A few days later, Troy Grant resigned as leader of the New South Wales National Party. In January 2017, Mike Baird announced his resignation as New South Wales premier, and his retirement from politics. The big winners were the gambling industry and their animal cruelty.

The power the gambling and racing industry wields on politicians and the media in this country never ceases to astonish me. Their influence, greed and audacity were reinforced during the peak of the COVID-19 crisis. While the whole country was in lockdown, greyhound racing was still going on. In Victoria, at the height of the second wave,

THE BEST AND WORST OF POLITICS

greyhound racing and horse racing continued while everything else except essential services was shut down. Since when is gambling an essential service? I guess since those who profit from it started donating to the Labor and Liberal parties.

To save face, the Coalition made a big song and dance about how they were introducing a better system to regulate animal welfare. The stark reality, though, is that, across Australia, hundreds of greyhounds continue to die at racing tracks. They are put down when they no longer turn a profit. They are drugged, and their treatable injuries turned into death sentences when their owners decide it's not worth paying the vet bills. These dogs deserve much better. They should run for fun, not for their lives.

Soon after the ban backflip, I emailed a greyhound rescue charity to put my name down to foster a greyhound. If the New South Wales government wasn't going to rescue these majestic animals, then I sure as hell was going to do my part. Cosmo joined my family not much later. It was only then that I came to know first-hand the mental and physical scars an ex-racing greyhound carries. They come out of racing scared, nervous and anxious. Cosmo had little patches of hair missing from one of his hind legs. His vet told us it was where a trainer had probably used a soldering iron–like device as a home remedy to treat his arthritis. Cosmo is a constant reminder to me of the plight of hundreds of dogs still enduring the cruelty of racing. Once you know this industry's dirty secrets, you can't un-know them.

It's taken many months, with healthy doses of love and patience, for Cosmo's personality to fully bloom. He returns that love to us many times over. We saved him from the racing industry, and he was our saviour during the loneliness of COVID-19. He was our companion when my son was locked down in Melbourne, and my daughter was locked out in the United States.

At the crushing moment of the greyhound racing ban backflip, I felt like throwing my hands up in the air and just giving up. After all, the industry probably became stronger, not weaker, as a result of the failed attempt to ban it. And now, given the poisonous political atmosphere, it was unlikely any government would attempt a major animal welfare reform for some time. But the movement for animal rights grew stronger. As I looked into the eyes of other advocates as we commiserated our loss, I could see their determination. I knew this was never about a single bill—it is about fighting a system that relies on animal death and cruelty. Our task now was to find other avenues.

One obvious target was to stop the export of Australian greyhounds to the infamous Yat Yuen greyhound racing track in Macau, known as the Canidrome. This track had been described by international animal welfare organisation GREY2K as a 'death camp for dogs', where tens of thousands of greyhounds, including animals from Australia, have been killed or raced to death over the last 50 years.

We soon identified airlines as the pathway for greyhound exports. This had to be cut off. On the day the ban was meant to go ahead, we launched our 'Don't Fly With Me' campaign to lobby airlines to commit to not carry racing greyhounds. The campaign was an incredible success, with some of the world's biggest airlines—including Air China, Thai Airways and Delta Airlines—pledging to ban the transport of racing greyhounds. Politics can still lead to good things when people decide to fight back.

In 2018 the Canidrome was shut down, and hundreds of Australian greyhounds have been rescued since then. A leaked document I obtained showed that between the start of 2013 and the end of 2015, more than 900 greyhounds were approved for export from our country, likely to end up at this death camp. Although the industry eventually banned the export of dogs after intense media scrutiny, this industry rule was virtually unenforceable given that dogs could enter Macau through third countries. And when industry participants were eventually investigated for breaking this rule, they were given slaps on the wrists.

We haven't shut down this toxic and cruel industry yet. We have exposed what happens at racetracks and behind the scenes. Greyhound racing has definitely lost its social licence. More and more people are adopting greyhounds. In my neighbourhood, there are so many that an American tourist I once ran into while walking Cosmo asked me if they were native to Australia, like coyotes in the United States. Yet I do struggle with the perverse incentives of greyhound adoption. Every dog saved just makes space for a trainer to breed another, and another. If the dog isn't a winner, they throw them onto the street and it's left to volunteers to put their blood, sweat, tears and money into rehabilitating them. But when I look into Cosmo's trusting eyes, and I know what the greyhound trainers had planned for him once he stopped turning a profit, I know we have no choice.

***

At times like these, I have questioned why I'm in parliament. What's the point of being in politics when you don't have the numbers to make change on your own terms? When decisions are so often made by ignoring facts? Even on the rare occasion that a decision is based on evidence, too often it's overturned by debased politics.

These same moments, however, also remind me of exactly why I am here: to represent those who would otherwise not be represented. The voiceless animals, the thousands in the community who are counting on you to bring their issues to the table, or even the one or two people out there who want you to say what they think and feel, or to express what they have faced and what they want to spare others. Removing pregnancy discrimination from the workplace, getting driver's licence disqualification reform, highlighting the rights of disabled people on public transport, and knocking back compulsory IDs for cyclists are just a few examples. Nothing is ever too small or too big to take on or take up.

Some laws are formulated in good faith but can have severe consequences for marginalised communities. The habitual traffic offenders scheme introduced in New South

Wales under a Labor government was one such law. It made licence disqualification periods mandatory for driving offences, irrespective of the circumstances of the case, with courts having no discretion to shorten the period. The cumulative nature of these offences meant you could end up with very lengthy disqualifications, sometimes for much longer periods than you'd get for drink-driving or even negligent driving occasioning death.

It has had disastrous consequences for marginalised communities. It's led to many people being disqualified from driving for minor offences such as not paying a fine. A vastly disproportionate number of Aboriginal people were charged with driving without a licence or driving while disqualified.

I had the chance to hear one very human and extremely sad story. A gentleman contacted my office to tell us about the devastating consequences of these laws on his brother, who eventually died of suicide as a result. He had lost his licence for failing to pay fines when he was seventeen years old. He'd never had a dangerous driving charge in his life, but ended up with a licence disqualification for 50 years. As he was an apprentice, this had a devastating impact on his ability to work. Going to court several times to have the term reduced was to no avail. I heard this story a year after this young man's tragic death. I started lobbying for change. A few years before, in 2013, a parliamentary committee on law and safety had recommended changing these laws. Eventually, in 2017, a legislative pathway was created for offenders to get their licences back.

Large parts of rural and regional New South Wales are not serviced by public transport, so not having a licence could destroy lives. It's even worse for Aboriginal communities who already face disadvantages in obtaining and maintaining a driver's licence because of difficulties obtaining birth certificates, limited access to licensed drivers to supervise learners and costs associated with getting a licence.

The people dealing with these issues are not well represented in parliaments, so their problems often go unheard. The sameness of legislators, often from a political class, means that the variety of perspectives needed to address complex problems just aren't there. The 'unintended' consequences of laws aren't considered because they don't harm the people making them. Every day I am in parliament, I am more determined to look at issues from the point of view of someone who is not (yet) at the decision-making table. Or better still, pull up a seat for them.

The mere act of asking for help or questioning a situation can be the heroic moment that we can miss. How we react to the challenges people are dealing with can be a turning point in their lives. Sometimes one person's story is representative of the experience of many in society. What might be a difficult phone call for us can be the result of a huge amount of courage on the caller's part. It might be a woman asking for help with an Apprehended Domestic Violence Order (ADVO) to escape an abusive situation she's lived with for years. Or it might be someone who has been unfairly dismissed from work.

THE BEST AND WORST OF POLITICS

In August 2016, a woman rang my office and reported that she had been fired after telling her boss she was pregnant. She had not hidden her pregnancy at the time of the interview, but had not told them she was pregnant. When she lodged a complaint, she was told it was perfectly legal to dismiss her. How could this be possible in the 21st century? My office double-checked the law—and there it was, hiding in plain sight. Two subsections in New South Wales' *Anti-Discrimination Act 1977* allowed employers to dismiss, or not hire, an employee who knew they were pregnant at the time of the job interview or at the time of hiring. I was outraged at the thought of a woman being forced to confess her pregnancy status at a job interview—to tell a complete stranger something that she may not even have told her partner. I wondered how many more women like our caller had been fired or not hired because of a pregnancy.

I went to work drafting, then introducing, a private member's bill to repeal the exemptions that allowed pregnancy discrimination to continue. I also picked up the phone to Attorney-General Mark Speakman. I wanted to convince him of the need to remove this gendered discrimination. I was apprehensive about how he would respond. My only interaction with him had been a run-in over an amendment he had put forward to the infamous Foetal Personhood Bill, also known as 'Zoe's Law'. I had led the charge in opposing this bill, and disagreed with the amendment proposed by Speakman, arguing that it only made a bad bill look slightly more palatable.

Soon enough, my chief of staff and I were sitting with the attorney-general and his team, explaining the situation. We walked out of that meeting having made a strong case but not knowing if they would take it any further. In the meantime, we launched a public campaign to raise awareness and put pressure on the government.

Six months later, as I sat in a community hall in Newcastle with Greens members for our State Delegates Council, a reporter contacted me to give the news: the government had issued a press release saying they would remove the exemption. They even went so far as to acknowledge my advocacy on the matter, which was virtually unheard of. Minister Speakman said in a television interview: '[O]ften you get loopy ideas from the Greens. But from time to time you get a good one. This is a good one.'[8]

I wasn't sure whether to take this as a compliment, but I was over the moon. While the fight for gender equality was far from over, at least one layer of discrimination against women had been peeled off. It was a moment of real pride for our campaign. It was a moment that restored some of my lost faith in politics.

Getting rid of pregnancy discrimination made me realise that, in just a few short years, I had come a long way. That first panic-stricken day in the New South Wales Parliament was a distant memory. Now I understood the art as well as the science of politics.

While some wins come within months, others, like decriminalising abortion, take years—and yet others even

THE BEST AND WORST OF POLITICS

longer. But they only happen because these issues, which have been lying dormant for years, even decades, are brought onto the political agenda. They happen because someone is brave enough to pick up the phone. They happen because someone with empathy listens. These wins happen because there's a strong movement outside parliament alongside strong voices inside parliament.

Politics is not just the domain of elected politicians. It never has been. Hopefully it never will be. Nothing motivates me more than people power. I am in awe of the incredible people I meet every single day; people whose love of natural places, passion for helping others here and elsewhere, compassion for animals, and determination to create a better shared future is an extraordinary contribution to making Australia the best we can be. I relish joining activists on the front line. I've stood with them in camping grounds in the Leard Forest and Bentley. I've been with them in torrential rain in Mullumbimby, in 50 degree heat in Menindee where my iPhone had a meltdown as I was shooting a video, and in freezing cold and strong winds. We've been together in townhalls, community centres, town squares, and in parks, pubs and the street. I work with people, not on behalf of them.

I joined the Greens because of the party's propensity to speak out on issues no one else would. I've come to appreciate the important role that we play in amplifying the difficult conversations which communities are having but politicians are ignoring. It wasn't that long ago that marriage equality or voluntary euthanasia were taboo subjects discussed on the 'political fringe'. Marriage equality was finally enshrined in law in 2017. A number of states have now passed voluntary euthanasia laws, and more are pushing for them. I look back humbly on my contribution to these debates. I was part of the cross-party groups of politicians who introduced the bills for same-sex marriage and voluntary euthanasia in the New South Wales Parliament. I'm proud of the role the Greens have played in making possible what once seemed impossible. We continue to incubate ideas that will blossom over time.

It's not easy. Some of the great injustices in this country were not accidental. They are there by design. The carefully coordinated backlash to discourage and crush you when you speak out against the powers that be is also designed. Just look at my Twitter feed to see what I'm talking about. When I 'say nup to the cup', or when I highlight racism or the rise of the fascist far right, it's soon filled with threats and abuse.

It's scary to be on the receiving end of such hate, and often I wonder if my stand is worth it. But when people tell me they shy away from public life after they see the volley of abuse sent my way, I know packing it in is not an option. I'm not going to let my detractors silence me into submission either. With that decision made, my mind focuses more sharply on telling it like it is. As a senator in our federal parliament, I have a platform shared by only 75 other people in Australia. I'm going to tell the truth. I'm going to feel the fear and do it anyway.

THE BEST AND WORST OF POLITICS

When you push boundaries on policy, you fear not being taken seriously. Bold Greens concepts are often rejected as 'pie in the sky'. We are dismissed as idealists. This must not deter us from becoming revolutionary. At its best, politics is a contest of bold ideas. We must make these ideas worth fighting for. We shouldn't just settle for incremental change.

Let's end the war machine that perpetuates militarism and nationalism. War doesn't solve the root causes of conflict: those are economic, social and environmental inequality. Wars victimise those already suffering the consequences of these injustices.

Private schools should not receive a cent of public money. Funding such a system further entrenches inequality and privilege, while providing no significant learning benefit. The real discussion we should be having is whether there should be private schools at all.

We must lead debates that question carceral logic. Locking up people in prisons doesn't help keep society safe, reform perpetrators or address the causes of offending. A disproportionate number of people in prison are those disadvantaged in society because of class and race. Discussions about the harms of putting children in prison and refugees in detention are far advanced. Let's start seriously questioning the utility of the prison industrial complex itself.

There will be backlash. The Murdoch press will hound us. But in the long term, pitching radical ideas for a more just and sustainable world is worth the risk of losing some short-term political capital. After all, leadership is about changing hearts and minds, not chasing votes.

***

While I never dreamed of being a politician, politics was never far from my mind, especially the politics of gender equality. For me, studying civil engineering was a political act. I wanted to show people that women could, and should be able to, do what they wanted to. We should not be shackled by outdated norms or patriarchal systems. I looked up to women in Pakistan who were putting themselves in the firing line, not as MPs but as agents of political change in the community.

Women like Asma Jahangir, who died in 2018. She was a Pakistani lawyer and activist who established the first all-women legal firm in Pakistan. She was one of the leading defenders of women's rights and human rights in the country. Asma defended bonded labourers in Pakistan and, as a UN envoy, the rights of the Rohingya of Myanmar, of Kashmiris, of Palestinians, and of Christians in Pakistan.

While Pakistan is far from a bastion of democracy, everybody there talks politics. The samosa-wala on the street who often catered for our iftar in Ramadan, the rickshaw-driver who I chatted to above the din of the loud engine as he drove me to college, and the women in the beauty parlour who threaded my eyebrows into perfect arches—all would enthusiastically have a yarn about the politics of the day.

My family regularly had rows over politics. A big fight between my aunt and my uncle—one a progressive, the

THE BEST AND WORST OF POLITICS

other not so much—is still etched in my memory. It was one of a few, I might add. It was a big shouting match that erupted during an extended family lunch at our place. It ended with my aunt walking out in tears, calling a rickshaw and heading home, quite distraught. This was the same aunt who unknowingly taught me to stand up for myself and be the feminist I am today. But it was a serious falling-out. My mother was later given the responsibility of patching it up. She did, and things were okay again—until the next time.

I haven't seen people in Australia thrashing out politics every day and everywhere like they did in Pakistan. Is it because politics has less relevance to our day-to-day lives here? Many of us continue to live comfortably as governments of different stripes come and go. For others, politicians seem far removed from the reality of our existence, needs and wants. I will never forget the image of Treasurer Joe Hockey and Finance Minister Mathias Cormann smoking cigars before they delivered the savage 2014 budget, which slashed thousands of public service jobs, cut income support for young people and ripped away billions from foreign aid. For many of us, they embodied the worst in politics: out of touch, arrogant and uncaring.

In the past we had prime ministers and treasurers who had been tradespeople, teachers and train drivers. Over time, though, a professional political class has crept in. Few of us can see our reflection in parliaments across the country. My friends often point out, half-jokingly, how many minority boxes I tick in parliament—migrant, Muslim, woman of colour, engineer. A study into parliamentary records also found that since 1988, government and opposition benches swelled with white men, political staffers, unionists, lawyers and bankers. While the proportion of Australians born overseas rose from 22 per cent to 33 per cent between 1988 and 2018, their representation in parliament stalled at 11 per cent.[9] That's hardly a joke.

Is it that we have tried and failed? The politically active don't feel as if their concerns are being heard. Communities are frustrated as they see their right to know being eroded. Government decisions are shrouded in secrecy. Attempts to retrieve information through regulated channels are thwarted by bureaucracy. The powerful corporate interests who profit from the exploitation of the environment and workers are putting everything they have into holding on to a system that favours them at the expense of community interest. Opposing them and the political parties beholden to them is a slow, uphill battle.

Have people turned their back on an increasingly discredited parliamentary system? Political scandals emerge and fizzle out without consequence. People feel powerless. They shrug their shoulders and move on, as if it's just a norm we have to live with. I can't really blame them. In my first week in the Australian parliament, I experienced first-hand what people had warned me about: the Canberra bubble. Politicians singularly focused on pursuing power at all cost. Politicians completely disconnected from the people they are supposed to represent.

THE BEST AND WORST OF POLITICS

I was sworn into the Australian Senate in Canberra on Monday, 18 August 2018. Malcolm Turnbull was prime minister. When I drove back home to Sydney at the end of the week, Scott Morrison was prime minister. This was the fifth time a sitting PM had been removed since 2010. Only once was it the result of a federal election; all the others were pushed out by their own parties. Twice by Labor and twice by the Liberals. Every time the reason was the same: flagging poll numbers. Opinion polling is no longer about 'taking the pulse' of the electorate—it is what drives party policy and election strategy. This is poor leadership. This is dispiriting politics.

No wonder trust in democracy, politicians and government in Australia has been plummeting. The level of democratic satisfaction has decreased steadily across each of the last four governments, from 86 per cent in 2007 (John Howard), to 72 per cent in 2010 (Kevin Rudd), 72 per cent in 2013 (Tony Abbott) and 41 per cent in July 2018 (Malcolm Turnbull).[10] In other parts of the world, this rising distrust allowed populists like Donald Trump and Boris Johnson to emerge. They took advantage of the trust divide and successfully pitched themselves as anti-establishment when they were anything but.

Is it the creep of individualism and self-interest that has now pervaded our culture? John Howard's construction of 'aspirational battlers' fragmented society. This set us on a course to become individuals focused on getting ahead. We started putting ourselves and our families ahead of the collective good. Morrison's 'quiet Australians' rhetoric has only cemented that trend.

Deep-seated xenophobia exploited for electoral gain has further divided us. Blaming immigrants for simultaneously taking 'our' jobs and draining the welfare system, while ludicrous, has successfully scapegoated migrants for the failings of the state. Bipartisan demonisation and dehumanisation of asylum seekers has maligned them as queue jumpers, boat people, illegals, criminal aliens. Mainstream Australia has swallowed the spin that paints them as a threat to national security. How else can we explain Australia's cruel asylum seeker policies, which lock innocent people in offshore prisons indefinitely?

I am concerned that this cultivated fear purposefully keeps us detached and divided so we lose faith in the power of collective action. It splits society with the intention of harvesting votes.

Democracy is at its most vulnerable when people feel helpless, or become cynical and apathetic. If this distrust, division and disengagement continues, it will keep sweeping away community cohesion. It will discourage people from political action. Politics will remain the domain of the 'big boys'.

I've been told many times, 'I don't know how you do it, Mehreen.' Others say: 'Better you than me—I couldn't do it.' While people admire me for putting my hand up, they are unwilling to do it themselves.

This does light a little spark of pride within me. I'm doing something others won't even contemplate. For the most part, though, it troubles me that ordinary citizens in a democratic society feel so helpless. It reminds me of my parents' generation in Pakistan, who had given up on making politics better because they'd come to the conclusion that the system was so rotten and rigged that ordinary people didn't even have a fighting chance of fixing it.

As challenging as it may be, our democracy is not beyond fixing. Neither is our society.

Democratic legitimacy needs public participation. Simply voting to choose our representatives every three or four years and hoping they will represent us isn't working. We can shift our representative democracy to become participatory. The public should have a genuine say on policy-making between elections. Ordinary citizens, not powerbrokers, should be at the centre of decision-making.

The lack of political discourse is intriguing in a country where voting is compulsory for citizens. I have started to question my long-held view that compulsory voting is an indisputable good. Is it too easy for politicians and political parties to garner votes when they don't have to convince people to come out to vote?

And should the boundaries of democracy be defined by your visa status? After all, governments are responsible for all those who live in a community—citizens, permanent residents and temporary visa holders. But only citizens have the right to choose who represents them. With the advent of COVID-19, it became clear that those on temporary visas—international students and migrant workers in casual and precarious employment—were being completely abandoned by our government. When push comes to shove, those without the right to vote end up the losers. In these circumstances, community-centric policy-making that genuinely engages all people, citizens or not, becomes even more essential as we try to mend the fabric of democracy.

I find it hard to understand the careerist nature of politics. When I see politicians around me who have been in parliament for decades, or who have not done much else in life but politics, it is hard to deny that winning elections is inextricably linked with holding onto power and a well-paying job. Building a political career can quickly become a focus that takes over from public service. And the longer a politician hangs on, the more their influence grows, making it harder for anyone new to break through. Imposing term limits would be one way of breaking cyclical incumbency.

In Australia, we don't have a proportional representation voting system in the House of Representatives. This may partly explain the anomaly of elected politicians and political parties being out of sync with the preferences of voters. In the 2019 federal election, the Greens banked 10.4 per cent of the popular vote but secured just one lower-house seat. In contrast, the Nationals secured only 4.5 per cent of the popular vote and won ten seats. A proportional voting system would break the stranglehold of the Labor and Coalition duopoly, and deliver a more representative parliament.

We know there is a problem with a political system that has allowed corruption to flourish unfettered right under our eyes—whether it's Aldi bags full of cash, or the influence of the

THE BEST AND WORST OF POLITICS

fossil-fuel lobby to stop action combatting the climate crisis, or the more insidious networks that allow billions of dollars of public money to be handed over to rich private schools who build orchestra pits and swimming pools while public schools go without the funds they need to meet basic standards.

We know how to fix some of these fundamental problems. For starters: a national anti-corruption body, a ban on corporate political donations, tighter restrictions on politicians working as lobbyists after leaving parliament, and transparency about whom politicians hobnob with. These changes would force politicians to be more responsible and accountable.

For a system to change, those within it must change or be replaced. The whiteness, maleness, staleness and sameness of parliaments must make way for colour, diversity and variation.

It is a pretty sad indictment of our politics that multicultural Australia lives and breathes on our streets but disappears when it comes to our parliaments. It's the same story in boardrooms and in the media. This lack of diversity is not just unrepresentative of our contemporary society, it's also a clear indicator of inequality. It means that decisions and decision-making will often be shackled by the conformity of opinions. Without the creativity that comes through the clash of a variety of perspectives and lived experiences, we end up with policies bereft of depth or complexity. They are developed within the narrow mandates of political parties, by people who have similarly narrow worldviews. That's how we end up with opinions like 'education is a privilege—people should have to pay for it', 'if you are worried about homelessness, buy a house', and the denial of the existence of racism. These views are so far away from the reality for those who are burdened by their student debt years after graduating, those who rough sleep every night, and those who face the sear of racism every day.

The best of politics will always have community at its centre. Whether it's a phone call to a politician or a mass protest in the streets. Small acts of individual courage and full-blown direct actions are necessary to start and shift debates.

When migrant communities see 'people like them' in parliament, they are more motivated to actively engage in democracy. The reception I received from ethnic migrant communities, and especially women, while campaigning to win the New South Wales Senate seat in 2019 was nothing like I'd experienced before. They organised dozens of 'Meet Mehreen' events in homes across Sydney, they connected with communities on WhatsApp, they spoke in my support at events, they were phone-banking and handing out how-to-vote cards at polling booths on election day. The eight seats where our Senate vote from the previous election grew by more than 40 per cent were all in Western Sydney, including Chifley and Werriwa, where our vote grew by more than 75 per cent. My election was no accident.

Political change comes through working with people, not on behalf of them. It has to be a relationship based on

THE BEST AND WORST OF POLITICS

partnership, on talking and listening to each other, not on telling others what to do. The conversations we have on doorsteps, at market stalls, at rallies, at public forums and at train stations can be messy and confronting. They are slow. But they are lasting.

In 2020, I came across someone whose door I had knocked on during the 2011 New South Wales election. I was a first-time Greens candidate running against the Labor premier, Kristina Keneally (who is now my colleague in the Senate). This voter told me I was the only politician to have knocked on his door in 40 years. After we met, he started voting Greens—and he's stayed with the party ever since.

This is one example of many. It's these conversations—not the clinical purity of data analysis, ad targeting, corporate fundraising or obsessive opinion polling—that can create a movement for change.

I didn't know what to expect of politics. I didn't know how I'd cope. I did know that I was there to make a difference.

I will follow my convictions. I will take the risk of shaking up the status quo. I'm here to change the face, body and soul of politics.

History will be my judge.

3

FEMINIST AS FUCK

---

25 September 2019. It's my first visit back to New South Wales parliament since taking up my role in the Australian Senate. Sitting in the public gallery of the lower house, I look down at the debate below. This is the moment we have been waiting for. The Speaker announces, 'The ayes have it.' My heart bursts with emotion, like a dam wall breaking. After 70 hours of debate, politicians have finally voted to decriminalise abortion in New South Wales. It is done.

I had imagined this moment would be bittersweet for me. Instead, I was walking on air. It had been more than a thousand days since I introduced the first bill to decriminalise abortion in the parliament's history. Although my bill was voted down, I believe it paved the way for the victory I had just witnessed. By having the courage to break the long silence, we had lifted the taboo around abortion. We had made this win inevitable.

Introducing that bill and the years-long campaign that followed were simultaneously the hardest, most challenging, most frustrating and most rewarding struggle of my political life.

I was attacked incessantly from the right. I was called a 'baby killer'. Filthy rumours were spread about this being some kind of Islamic plot to abort Western babies. I can't say these personal attacks didn't hurt, but the relentless pile-on from the anti-abortion, conservative and religious players was expected. I was more hurt by the rebukes I received from the progressives outside the Greens. That surprised me. I was warned to leave abortion alone. I was told, 'If it ain't broke, don't fix it.' But it was broke. The privilege of some MPs simply stopped them from seeing that. The politics of others stopped them from acting on it. Meanwhile, women continued to live every day with the consequences of the parliament's inaction.

The existence of abortion in the New South Wales *Crimes Act 1900* was the most visible stain of an overwhelming patriarchy that will always seek to silence women. For me, liberation from abortion laws that restricted our choices and policed our bodies was a big victory in our fight against a system that at best ignores women, and at worst seeks to control us.

I have been repeatedly asked why the New South Wales Parliament had never debated the decriminalisation of abortion before my bill. This question intrigued me no end. Why had this debate remained politically moribund for so long? Surely, the fundamental right of bodily autonomy should be demanded without fear. Ironically, it was fear itself that had stopped us.

The truth is that, for decades, campaigners for abortion rights had been told to stay quiet for fear of toppling the finely balanced applecart of abortion regulations in New South Wales. They were told not to push for change in case hard-won legal loopholes that created limited access to abortion were closed. They were told to wait for the right time and a sympathetic government. If they tried without succeeding, they would hinder rather than help the cause. They were made afraid of failure.

I was told exactly that. Bizarrely, it was the Labor-aligned pro-choice lobby that initially tried to dissuade me from introducing a bill. Labor MPs expressed their anger at me. A union leader visited me. Women from what I call the professional women's activist spaces came calling. As if reading from a well-practised script, they all told me it was not the right time. They told me that under a Liberal government, things could get worse. If that happened, I would be squarely to blame, they said in no uncertain terms.

As they spoke, I couldn't help wondering if they were telling me this firstly to justify Labor's inaction on abortion rights, and secondly to avoid spotlighting their inertia if I, not them, was the one taking action. Their reaction to my plans distressed me terribly. This was precisely the sort of political play that eats at me. By now I understood these games much better, but in the quest for women's rights I was expecting solidarity, not silencing, from progressive women. How naive was I.

In trying to prevent me from pursuing abortion law reform, there may have been an element of genuine apprehension. But there was more to it than that. The Labor Party in New South Wales has some very strong opponents of abortion rights within its ranks. Most likely, this is why they never made a move to decriminalise abortion, even when they were in government for sixteen years straight. I'm sure pro-choice Labor women were deeply frustrated by being constrained from within their own party, unable to even bring a bill forward for discussion. But this was not a good enough reason to stop me from making an attempt. The parliamentary debate had to start somewhere.

In Victoria and Queensland, these conversations had been jump-started by bills introduced by MPs outside the Labor and Liberal parties. The Greens bill could provide the cover for others to pursue reform in their own parties, I reasoned. But they feared losing control of the narrative more than they feared the consequences of the continued criminalisation of abortion.

The efforts to stop me did make me hesitate. I wouldn't have been human if they didn't. The continuous probing started to play on my mind. It put the fear of 'what if' in my heart. What if things did get worse? What if our attempt was unsuccessful? What if it put us back rather than moving us forward? Perhaps we should wait for a change of government? I started doubting myself.

This was only the start of the personal anguish I would feel. I've sustained many attacks for taking an unapologetically feminist view of abortion: that women and all people needing reproductive health care should have full and unambiguous bodily autonomy. I have been sworn at in the street. Someone yelled 'Dr Death' at me as I was walking into parliament for the debate. People rang my office repeatedly and harassed my staff. People sent horrific, graphic images and abusive messages.

It's never easy to brush off these attacks. It becomes even harder when you are being squeezed both by supporters and by opponents of abortion rights.

These questions, misgivings and accusations would haunt me for the next three years. I would have many sleepless nights, tossing and turning as I wondered if I was doing the right thing. I would question my motives for doing it. Was I doing this for personal recognition? Was my ego getting in the way? After all, others did have more political experience than me.

But every time I came to the same conclusion: the 'it's not the right time' argument is, and always has been, complete bullshit.

Women have always been told to go to the back of the queue. Our priorities have never been a top political priority. They've always been dispensable. We've always been dispensable.

We had already waited a hundred years for the right time. In that time, we'd lived with the fear of dangerous backyard abortions. The fear of persecution and prosecution hung over our heads. Shame and stigma clung to us. These fears are much more damaging than the fear of failure. I did not want to wait another century. I was sick of women being told that their issues had to wait behind other, 'more important' matters. I took strength from the Women's Abortion Action Campaign (WAAC) who enthusiastically supported my call to decriminalise abortion. After all, they had been fighting for the repeal of all abortion laws since the early 1970s.

There would never be a perfect time, I realised. There never is. We have to make the time right. Looking back, I'm glad I chose to ignore the elites who wanted to play the game of politics. I went with my heart and mind, and with the overwhelming number of people in the community who wanted change.

The arguments put to me highlighted the different faces of feminism. The mainly white, middle-class, middle-aged women politicians wanted me to wait for the right time. But it's not up to them alone to set out a feminist agenda. Feminism isn't the purview of the privileged and the white. They don't necessarily know what is best. Others have a stake too, and a say in when and how women's rights should be advanced.

Perhaps, for the middle classes living in Sydney, abortion was not a pressing issue. They had the financial means to pay for abortions, as well as the physical proximity to clinics. But this was not the case for women living in rural and remote New South Wales, in low socio-economic circumstances, or Aboriginal and Torres Strait Islander women and immigrant women. Women and girls who already face restrictive cultural and social attitudes to abortion are doubly hurt by a lack of access and culturally inappropriate health services.[1]

We all experience the world differently. If our experiences don't match those of others, that doesn't invalidate them or make them less important. If the essence of feminism is unity, then surely it must embrace the intersections of race, class, culture and gender.

My feminism is inclusive, not exclusive. It was this feminism that drove me to make a push to end forced divorces for trans people. In 2014, I and Alex Greenwich, independent member for Sydney, introduced a bill to allow married persons who have undergone sex affirmation to update their records on the Births, Deaths and Marriages register to correctly reflect their gender without having to get a divorce. At that time, New South Wales law required married transgender people to divorce their partners if they wished to alter a record of their sex on their birth certificate or live with an incorrect sex on one of the most important personal identity documents if they wanted the marriage to continue. It forced loving couples to break up, and stopped those who might wish to transition in future from even thinking about marriage.

I wanted to do whatever I could to lessen the burden on trans and gender diverse people, who face disproportionately high levels of homelessness, poverty, unemployment and sickness. It finally happened in 2018. After same-sex marriage was legalised in Australia, the New South Wales government's bill to end forced divorces passed parliament.

Every time a toxic dispute between feminism and trans rights flares up, my distress is palpable. I can only imagine how hurt transgender people feel when this happens. In Lahore, I had the privilege of getting to know someone who, despite the social stigma, was a proudly transgender person. Tufail worked for my mother-in-law. They were the life of the neighbourhood.

In Pakistan, unlike Australia, transgender people have always been very visible. Before the British colonised the subcontinent, they were also culturally accepted and respected. An intolerance for gender diverse people and social structures such as a strict gender binary were brought into my part of the world by the British through a penal code that recognised only males and females. The legacy of this cultural and gender supremacy lives on, over there and here.

Tufail passed away some years ago, but their courage to openly be who they were in a society that vilified and stigmatised sexual variance lives on as an example to me. Now, in my role as a parliamentarian, I will take up any opportunity to do something about such discrimination.

It was this belief in intersectional feminism that led me to launch an International Women's Day Breakfast event in 2014 to create a space for anyone who identified as a woman to hear exclusively from women of colour. This series has become quite well known for its honest and radical discussions on gender and race. It also gave us a platform to advance abortion rights with the inclusivity they demanded.

Feminists who resist inclusivity or intersectionality do our movement a disservice. The issues that some feminists choose to prioritise (or not prioritise) illustrates their privilege. The lack of awareness of the failings of the feminist movement to bring everyone along was evident at a forum on feminism in the New South Wales Parliament. On the panel was a very prominent white feminist. In responding to an audience question about the lack of diversity in the feminism movement, she asserted that the feminist movement had always been inclusive of all women, and that anyone suggesting otherwise was just playing into the hands of men to divide the movement.

My skin bristled. As often happens, I couldn't help myself. I had to say something. I pointed out that Aboriginal and Torres Strait Islander women have talked extensively about how they have felt isolated from the middle-class pursuits of second-wave feminism, and the movement should reflect on the different needs of different women. As I left the forum, I was pulled aside and told in no uncertain terms that I was being divisive by bringing up the issue of intersectionality.

What I was pointing out was that the spotlight on the 'gender gap' often focuses on inequality between men and women. This conceals the reality of the layered oppression diverse groups of women and individuals face—for instance, Aboriginal women, trans women, disabled women, migrant women, women of colour.

The question of diversity has been a difficult frontier for feminism, as the focus has often been on the overarching bigger causes of equality between genders. Similar challenges have faced other civil rights movements, where women did not receive the recognition they deserved. They were expected to just accept the existing sexism from within for the greater good. We understand more than most the repercussions of oppression. Solidarity means the needs of all women, and people who identify as women shouldn't just fade away in the quest for some 'greater good'. Their stories must be part of the whole story. Inclusion is not a threat to feminism. It is a strength.

The push to decriminalise abortion was for the women most affected by the criminalisation of abortion—women who weren't wealthy and didn't live in big cities. Women in small towns who found themselves pregnant and knew going to their local GP simply wasn't an option. Nor could they afford to spend days travelling to Sydney or Adelaide, then perhaps further days recovering. I remember standing on the banks of the Murray River in Albury, looking across to Victoria and realising that women there could access abortion services legally and with medical privacy, while women in New South Wales were treated like criminals. It couldn't stay like this.

When I began pushing for the decriminalisation of abortion in New South Wales, I was acutely aware of the forces of darkness that were gathering to knock off the tenuous legal loophole through which women could access a termination. If we didn't fight for more rights, I knew, we would be stripped of the fragile ones we had.

A few weeks after I'd joined the New South Wales Parliament in 2013, an attack on women's reproductive rights began. This came in the form of a bill that would legally recognise foetuses as living persons, entirely separate from their mothers. The Crimes Amendment (Zoe's Law) Bill 2013 (No 2), introduced by conservative Liberal MP Chris Spence, was a repackaged version of an earlier bill from the Reverend Fred Nile of the Christian Democratic Party to enact legal foetal personhood.

Legal personhood has been a battleground for 'pro-life' and 'pro-choice' activists in the United States for many years. The so-called personhood movement has been growing in the United States since the Supreme Court's *Roe v. Wade* decision that made abortion legal in all 50 states. It has severely undermined women's rights and their dignity. There are hundreds of documented cases of punitive actions against women.[2] In one incident, a pregnant woman was taken in shackles before a family court commissioner. She was refused a lawyer. Her foetus had already been assigned a legal guardian to represent it in court. Her crime? Telling her doctor during a prenatal visit about a pill addiction she had successfully beaten the year before. She was ordered by the court to report to and stay at an inpatient facility for drug rehabilitation because she refused to take an anti-addiction drug she didn't need.

In another case in Texas, a pregnant woman collapsed in her home. She was declared legally dead after her paramedic husband found her unconscious. Because she was fourteen weeks pregnant, doctors refused to take her off life support under a 'pro-life' state law. After winning a lengthy court battle, her life support was switched off. Both she and the 23-week-old foetus died in a hospital in Fort Worth.

In the United States, these anti-women laws have been pushed and applauded by religious and far-right groups. Here, they have been driven by the same interests through the religious right, the Christian Democratic Party and conservative MPs. Their aim is clear. They want to police women's bodies.

At the time in New South Wales, abortion was on shaky legal ground, only accessible through a lower-court ruling in 1971. Granting foetal personhood would make it more ambiguous. It could result in the prosecution of women where they may be deemed to have acted contrary to the interests of the 'living person' they are carrying. It would place doctors and lawyers in decision-making dilemmas.

This was dangerous legislation. It had to be blocked and I got to work.

I called a meeting of doctors, lawyers, women's groups and others who opposed the bill. We started organising. Coalitions were built to lobby MPs. People took to the streets, demonstrating their displeasure at the bill. Petitions were signed. Letters were sent and opinion pieces written.

Proponents of the bill insisted it had nothing to do with abortion. Lawyers and doctors had a contrary view. They knew the precarious legality of abortion was at stake. They remained unconvinced that the exclusions provided in the bill would override the risks posed by the fundamental definitional legal recognition of a foetus as a living person. When all attempts by women's groups to negotiate a compromised bill to recognise a foetus without legislating personhood failed, it became clear that this bill was about more than the recognition of harm to an 'unborn child'. It was a stalking horse for the anti-choice agenda.

In addition to the risk of weakening reproductive rights, the 'foetal personhood' law was unnecessary. The *Crimes Act* was amended in 2005 to address the harm caused to the foetus of a pregnant woman against her wishes. Such an act is considered a crime against the mother, regardless of any other harm inflicted, and is punishable with a maximum 25-year sentence.

What the proponents of this law didn't realise was that in trying to further restrict abortion access, they planted the seeds of a campaign that would ultimately do the opposite.

As the Greens' spokesperson for women, I led the charge against the bill. We unequivocally opposed it. Every Labor and Coalition MP was granted a conscience vote. This made women captive to a parliament composed mostly of men, each of whom would decide our fate. That is completely cooked. It is unconscionable that women's rights are seen as a matter of conscience. As it happened, politicians did exactly what patriarchy ordered. The bill passed the Legislative Assembly with 63 votes 'for' and 26 'against'.

It is scary that a bill so completely incompatible with a woman's right to choose passed the lower house with an overwhelming majority. Conservative ideology had won over rational debate in the LNP-dominated chamber, but in the more diverse upper house a strong public campaign had convinced a majority of MPs to reject the bill. It was shelved. The danger had been averted—for now.

During the long days, weeks and months spent opposing Zoe's Law, a few things became abundantly clear to me.

Women can never take their rights for granted. At least not while men have a majority in our parliaments.

We must be proactive, organised and bold about advancing our rights. Otherwise, all our effort and energy will be used up defending what we've already fought and won.

We had come uncomfortably close to toppling the fragile lawfulness of abortion. It would not be long before the anti-choice brigade attacked us again. We had to go on the offensive.

It was time to decriminalise abortion in New South Wales.

***

As a woman, and as the mother of a young woman, I could not—I would not—accept the reality that abortion was a criminal offence in our home state. And many of those with whom I had worked on the campaign to stop the foetal personhood laws agreed. Our realisation of how close we had come to losing the small gains made on reproductive rights spurred the formation of a small group of activists and legal and medical professionals, intent on working together to repeal laws that made abortion an offence.

FEMINIST AS FUCK

We knew full well that the road ahead would be bumpy and long. After all, no one had attempted this before. We knew we would face the full force of the anti-choice lobby, but we also had to contend with the progressives who crumbled when it was time for action. In this rocky landscape, a grassroots people's movement was essential to build momentum for change. We called ourselves 'End12'.*

People in Australia are infuriated at regressive moves in the United States that stop women from accessing reproductive health. We are rightly enraged by the disgusting harassment of women by those who are anti-choice. Many were not aware that barriers such as these were also present right here in our own backyard.

The intimidation of patients by anti-choice protesters was not unusual before safe access zones were created. They intimidated people outside clinics, hoping to change their mind or at least make them feel guilty about terminating their pregnancy. They targeted women, their partners and their friends as they were going into and coming out of clinics. They formed picket lines holding graphic images, and handing out plastic foetus dolls and pamphlets. They filmed women with the intention of naming and shaming them. They chanted prayers, walked in front of women to slow them down and threw holy water at them.

I have stood outside clinics in Sydney and in Albury. I have seen some of this disgusting behaviour with my

---

*Division 12 of Part 3 of the *Crimes Act 1900* (NSW) was entirely devoted to abortion offences.

own eyes. I've met women who have felt panic and anxiety. They have felt unsafe and violated.

Justifying such behaviour by calling it 'protest' doesn't make it so. There's a distinct line between protesting and harassment. I can see it and so can they. Couching it as 'sidewalk counselling' is demeaning. Just the notion of being 'counselled' by this gauntlet of anti-choicers is offensive. As if women don't have agency and haven't made a considered decision. As if we need these hostile saviours to shove pamphlets in our faces and shout at us under the guise of education to make us reconsider.

No one should be subjected to such treatment, let alone a patient seeking medical care. But then why was the medical care they are seeking deemed a criminal offence?

In New South Wales, until the law was changed in 2019, abortion was a crime under sections 82, 83 and 84 of the *Crimes Act*. Access to abortion was only possible because of exceptions granted through a District Court ruling in 1971. This established that abortions would be lawful if there was 'any economic, social or medical ground or reason which in the jury's view could constitute reasonable grounds upon which an accused could honestly and reasonably believe there would result a serious danger to her physical or mental health'. Later, these considerations of 'serious danger' were extended to include the social and economic factors affecting a woman's physical and psychological health.

Some thought the debate around the decriminalisation of abortion was just a semantic one. In their view, the fact that abortion was technically still a criminal offence was just an antiquated quirk of the law that had few implications in the 21st century. After all, between one-quarter and one-third of Australian women will experience an abortion in their lifetime.[3] It is a common and safe procedure. Where's the issue? I can tell you, there are many issues.

Pregnancy terminations were permissible in our state only through the interpretation of case law. Women accessing abortions, their doctors and health practitioners were doing it through this 'legal loophole'. They were exposed to the full force of the law, including up to a decade in jail.

Many doctors would not perform abortions due to the fear of prosecution and persecution. Some worried about peer pressure from anti-choice colleagues. I knew of pretty terrible incidents where women were left untreated by doctors who feared being criminalised. One of these people was Anna Groth. While undergoing a medical abortion, she ended up in hospital, septic and in excruciating pain. She was left in this pain for five days before she was treated. She told the media: 'The doctors and nurses just kept apologising. They said if it were their decision, they would have done it earlier. They said it was a political hold up.' It was the criminal offence of abortion that had made Anna's body a political battleground.[4]

Women told me they'd had miscarriages and been turned away from hospitals because doctors suspected it was an abortion. Public hospitals don't routinely provide the procedure, forcing women to go to expensive private clinics.

How you were treated depended on which hospital you ended up in. These were the very real consequences of the law in New South Wales.

The issue of reproductive rights is writ large on the District Court ruling of 1971. Medical practitioners remained the decision-makers. As Forster and Jivan highlight, 'A pregnant woman or girl must present her circumstances in the worst possible light in order to ensure that she secures a lawful abortion, a process that is demeaning and non-therapeutic.'[5]

The shame and stigma that criminality creates follows us around. Young women told me their voices dropped to whispers when they discussed abortion. I had heard those whispers from my mother, and my grandmother. I was not willing to accept that for my daughter.

Access to abortion was a geographical, racial and class lottery. It was limited, expensive and privatised. Rural and regional women, Aboriginal and Torres Strait Islander women, immigrant women and those from low socio-economic backgrounds found it much harder to gain access. Those who were saying that decriminalising abortion was unnecessary were ignoring the stories of these women.

Health lawyer Julie Hamblin best explained the unsatisfactory nature of the situation: 'There is a clear disconnect between what the law says, what most people think it says, and what happens in practice.'[6]

Women deserve better than this terrible ambiguity. We deserve full and unquestionable autonomy.

The 'brains trust' of my staff, some Greens women and a close-knit group of doctors and lawyers started the hard work of crafting a bill to address these problems. We wanted New South Wales to have the gold standard of abortion laws, taking in the best parts of laws that had been passed in Victoria, Tasmania and the ACT. It had three main aims:

1. Repeal abortion offences under the *Crimes Act 1900*.
2. Require health practitioners to advise patients if they had a conscientious objection to abortion, and refer them to another doctor who did not have this objection, or to a women's health centre.
3. Enact safe access zones around places where abortions are provided to protect the health, safety, dignity, wellbeing and medical privacy of patients and staff.

The Abortion Law Reform (Miscellaneous Acts Amendment) Bill 2016 (NSW) was centred on reproductive rights. It made sure that those seeking abortion would be the decision-makers. Once criminality was removed, there would be no other restrictions put in place. As for any other medical procedure, a qualified practitioner would provide the best possible advice and the patient would make the final decision.

This was a bold feminist bill. It was designed to bring archaic legal provisions in line with modern medical practice, public expectations and the right to bodily autonomy. While positioning abortion law reform as a feminist campaign responding to historical and entrenched sexism against women, the bill was deliberately drafted in gender neutral terms. This was an acknowledgement that a range of people need to access reproductive health care, including non-binary persons and transgender men. This was not about making women invisible, as some have claimed. The shift in language was to make gender and sexually diverse people visible.

We also wanted to make sure the community was on board. I commissioned an independent poll of community views on abortion in New South Wales. It showed overwhelming support for decriminalising abortion across party lines, gender and generations. The poll found that 87 per cent of those surveyed believed women should be able to have an abortion, 73 per cent supported decriminalisation, 78 per cent believed medical practitioners should be required to provide unbiased and independent information on options for unplanned pregnancies, and 81 per cent agreed that there should be exclusion zones outside clinics to stop harassment.[7] On the questions of decriminalising abortion and exclusion zones, support in regional and rural communities was higher than in Sydney. This did not surprise me, as these communities were bearing the brunt of this law when it came to the lack of accessibility, the additional cost and the inconvenience of travelling to find a service—to say nothing of the harassment outside clinics.

Then came the physically gruelling, but most rewarding, work of listening to and talking with people across New South Wales.

I traversed the state, going from Albury to Bega to Wagga Wagga to Gosford to Newcastle to Byron Bay, and all around Sydney. We organised public meetings, rallies and street stalls. I spoke to the Country Women's Association in Kyogle, a packed hall in Glebe, a round table in Armidale and the crowds at the folk festival in Cobargo. The people I met became supporters and active campaigners. They restored the faith I had lost in politicians.

Thousands of petitions and postcards were signed. Phone calls were made. Meetings were held with MPs. Doctors, lawyers, students, individuals and interest groups joined in to voice their support. Hundreds of doctors, and law and criminology academics signed open letters to New South Wales MPs urging them to vote to give women the right to choose.

As our campaign progressed, momentum built. Activist organisations like GetUp and the Women's March joined the calls to decriminalise abortion and provide safe access. Media attention intensified. Opinion pieces popped up. Journalists started writing about something they had steered clear of for too long. It would be remiss of me not to recognise the role journalist Gina Rushton played in bringing abortion into the limelight. She covered all aspects of the campaigns and the debates in New South Wales and Queensland. She told stories of women's experiences of abortion and of the lack of access in rural areas. In no small way, she played a big part in moving the debate forward.

Community campaigns have the power to shift political agendas. I'm quite certain that the bill would never have been debated inside parliament without this mass movement outside. It was quite clear that individual politicians and their political parties wanted to avoid having their position on abortion exposed. My first attempt to introduce the bill into the Legislative Council in June 2016 was halted by other political parties. They used procedural tactics to knock it off the running list of bills to be debated that day, even though it had been listed first in the order of precedence.

But their efforts to stymie debate were thwarted in the end, and a year later they were forced to confront their demons. The first ever bill to decriminalise abortion and create safe access zones in New South Wales was debated in the Legislative Council in May 2017.

It didn't pass. The bill was voted down, 25–14. Disappointed cries of 'Shame! Shame!' from pro-choice advocates in the gallery clashed with the jubilant chanting and drumming of anti-choice protestors on Macquarie Street.

Supporters of the bill were shocked, angry and embarrassed. They could not believe that in the year 2017, a majority of the members of parliament refused to overturn an archaic law that criminalised women and doctors because of a medical procedure. There was palpable anger among citizens at those political representatives who had ignored their wishes and continued to deny them reproductive autonomy. It was an embarrassment that New South Wales lagged behind Victoria, Tasmania, the ACT and the Northern Territory, states which had all decriminalised abortion.

People I caught up with later were crying tears of

dismay. My 21-year-old daughter and my husband were in the chamber that day. They were shocked by the chastising I had been subjected to by MPs on the floor of parliament. So distraught were they that this was the last debate they ever attended in the New South Wales Parliament.

I received emails and phone calls from women expressing their deep disappointment and anger. A few days later, frustrated by the vote, a protest organised by the University of Sydney Womens Collective and the University's Queer Action Collective named and shamed the 25 politicians (eighteen Liberal/National MPs, three Labor, two Christian Democrat, and two Shooters, Fishers and Farmers) who had voted against the bill. Their photos were pasted on coat hangers and hung on the steel fence of Parliament House with a banner reading 'Never Again'. Some of those MPs expressed indignation at being targeted by the protestors. I'm glad they felt the heat. For too long politicians have escaped accountability on this issue by avoiding it altogether. Now they were being held responsible for their actions.

I'll be honest. I knew the bill was unlikely to pass that day. I didn't know that all Liberal and National MPs—who had been granted a conscience vote by their parties—would nevertheless vote as a bloc to oppose the bill. Not even the most vocal opponent of abortion rights—the Christian Democrats' Reverend Fred Nile—spoke on the bill that day. A deal had obviously been struck. This made a mockery of the idea that the floor of parliament is a place for debate. So often it's a stage for predetermined outcomes. I'll never know whether the Liberals did a deal to keep the Christian Democrats onside, or whether Gladys Berejiklian, only a few months into her premiership after Mike Baird's sudden resignation, did not want to open the debate up any further than she was being forced to. I do know that women's rights were once again relegated to the bottom of the pile.

Those in government who claimed to be pro-choice duplicitously voted against the bill. I was stunned at their silent cowardice. Only one bothered to speak during the debate and his contribution was brief.

The anti-choice mob led by the Catholic Church and the Australian Christian Lobby ran the same tired, old scare campaigns based on mistruths and misinformation. One of the most offensive myths they peddle concerns the sensitive matter of late-term abortions. They demonise women by suggesting that we'd suddenly start having abortions right before birth if it were decriminalised. This is an obscene accusation, and bears no resemblance to reality. Only 0.7 per cent of terminations take place after twenty weeks of gestation. These are performed in cases of severe foetal abnormalities or serious danger to the pregnant woman's health. Fearmongering about these few heartbreaking decisions is completely heartless. This fear campaign tapped into the deeply patriarchal notion that women can't be trusted, and the law must keep them in line.

Such arguments can't hide the religious moralism that lies behind them. Religious beliefs, no matter how deeply felt, should have no place in public policy or laws of a country that claims to separate church from state. Neither my religion nor anyone else's should deny anyone a basic right.

Before our campaign commenced, I found it hard to understand why no one had ever attempted to change the abortion law in New South Wales. Three years later, I knew exactly why. The personal attacks, the scare campaigns and the blocking attempts by those who should be allies would make anyone think twice.

Some of the harshest attacks came on the floor of the New South Wales upper house from self-declared 'pro-choice' men who bent over backwards to justify their decision to vote against my bill, or who voted for it under great pains. In their attempt to denigrate me, they also exposed their ignorance.

The speech by Labor's shadow health minister, Walt Secord, while vilifying me, also demonstrated how out of touch he was with the people of New South Wales.

'She and her staff have cynically manufactured and manipulated the debate on this issue,' he claimed. 'Until she raised this issue in the public arena I, as shadow Minister for Health for the last three years, had not received a single representation on abortion or the need for legal clarification. I repeat: In three years as shadow Minister for Health, I had not received a single representation about the need to legalise this area of common law until Dr Faruqi began her campaign.'[8]

Secord's admission that not a single person had raised decriminalisation with him was both enlightening and perplexing. For all their protestations of being pro-choice, had no Labor MPs had bothered to raise this issue with their health spokesperson? This reinforced my belief that, without a push, this issue would never be discussed in parliament.

It surprised me how disconnected and out of touch some MPs were from their communities. If a person had money and lived in an urban centre like Sydney, they probably would not have a lot of difficulty accessing a termination. But what about women in Broken Hill, Walgett or Moree? People who did not live in the big cities are hard-pressed to find a specialist clinic. Access to terminations in public hospitals is largely based on the luck of the draw, being dependent on a particular hospital's policy and even the opinion of the particular treating physician. Would we accept this for any other health matter? I think not.

If anyone had reason to be cynical, it was me. Developing the bill was a considered, consultative and thorough process. Attacking my staff was below the belt. The bill was the culmination of months of intense consultation with health experts, women's groups, lawyers and academics. There was a three-month exposure draft process for public consultation. The parliamentary debate started a full year after the bill had been introduced. The bill had been reviewed and endorsed by many organisations, including the Royal Australian and New Zealand College of Obstetricians and Gynaecologists, the responsible professional body; the New South Wales Council for Civil Liberties; the NSW Nurses and Midwives' Association; the Public Health Association; Women's Legal Services; the New South Wales Teachers

Federation; Australian Lawyers for Human Rights; the National Tertiary Education Union; Family Planning NSW; Marie Stopes—the list went on.

I had sent copies of the bill to the relevant ministers and shadow ministers a year before the debate in parliament. I had invited their feedback and sought meetings. Members received information and updates from me. I reached out and had one-on-one meetings with whoever was willing to reciprocate, and organised meetings with experts that MPs were welcome at. My door was always open for any concerns to be raised, or amendments to be made, as long as they did not jeopardise the intent of the bill.

In the event, the one proposed amendment the bill received was circulated very late at night before the day of the debate by Labor. After reviewing it, my staff discovered it would jeopardise medical abortion by telephone, a service provided by the Tabbot Foundation. It was maddeningly frustrating that Labor had thought so little about this legislation.

The arguments presented in opposition to the Abortion Law Reform Bill were weak and disingenuous. Some attacked me rather than the bill itself. I think politicians were taken by surprise. Either they did not want to discuss abortion law reform, or they only wanted to debate it on their own terms. When they didn't get what they wanted, their discontent was on display for all to see.

I was disappointed by the result, and taken aback by the personal denigration. My mind was numb, my body drained. At the same time, I was oddly relieved and optimistic. We had broken the 100 years of parliamentary silence. Abortion law reform was squarely on the public and political agenda. Whether MPs had deigned to speak or not, each and every parliamentarian and political party room had been forced to consider abortion and women's reproductive rights. We knew there were supporters of decriminalising abortion across the political spectrum, whether they had made that position public or not.

There would be no turning back. This defeat was not a setback, I decided: it was a milestone in the journey we had just jump-started. The genie was well and truly out of the bottle. Now it was a matter of when, not if.

A year later, a bill to enact safe access zones passed parliament. A year after that, abortion was decriminalised.

***

In New South Wales, we have rid ourselves of the 'crime' of abortion, but our work isn't finished. Access to reproductive health can't remain a lottery. All public hospitals should offer pregnancy termination services through bulk-billing, so no one is left out of pocket. In addition, establishing culturally appropriate services in regional areas and in cities will help remove some of the barriers for marginalised women.

A journalist wrote to me a few years later, reflecting on that day of the debate:

> I still remember filing my story from your office (thanks for the wi-fi!) and the collective sad exhalation of your

staff when you came back into the room after the bill was defeated. Covering that debate really taught me a lot about politics and how there are necessary losses before necessary successes. I hope you know those subsequent successes couldn't have happened without your work.

This message captures exactly our feelings and the tough political lessons we learned. Advocating for abortion reform is one of the hardest things I've done. It was years of highs and lows. It was an emotional roller-coaster of fear, anger, disappointment, surprise, love, frustration, sadness, disgust and joy. It required patience (not one of my virtues!) and the good humour to smile—or grit your teeth—and carry on. That's what I did.

You see, I am unashamedly, unapologetically feminist. I am feminist as fuck.

Would I have done it if I knew then what I know now? Yes.

I could not have done it on my own. Social change needs the courage of many. There were thousands in our campaign who showed that courage. I will name some. My team in parliament showed that courage in droves. They are my confidants, my advisers and my emotional support. Darelle Duncan, a warrior for women's rights, was by my side throughout. Julie Hamblin, Dr Philippa Ramsay, Professor Caroline de Costa and our gang of rebel doctors and lawyers, without whom this would have been an impossible journey. We all stood on the shoulders of women who had fought for abortion rights before us. We transformed the movement into a political inevitability.

I never expected to receive any accolades. It was nonetheless delightful to collect the feminist Edna Ryan Grand Stirrer Award of 2017, for inciting others to challenge the status quo.

Daring to shake up the system comes with risks: you put your reputation, your neck and your peace of mind on the line. I did all that, and I followed the best piece of advice I was given when I came to Australia from Pakistan: feel the fear and do it anyway. When you know it's the right thing to do, you just have to do it. And pay the price.

The criminalisation of abortion was a symptom of the patriarchy that infects our society. At the heart of the failure to decriminalise abortion for so long lay the profoundly patriarchal view that women and their bodies must be controlled. Violence against women continues in schools, universities, workplaces and in homes because dominant masculinity and male power remains the norm. I wonder if there is a single woman on this planet who has not experienced an unwanted sexual advance, be it verbal or physical, subtle or blatant? Young or old, white, Brown or Black, executive, teacher, student, political staffer, journalist or waitress, famous or completely anonymous—as women, no matter who we are, we are targets of bullying, harassment and sexual violence. We get so used to it that we've just brushed it off and moved on. But we've had enough. More and more women are speaking their truth. We deserve respect. We demand not to be harrassed, assaulted and raped. We will make decisions about our bodies. We are the ones to give consent. No one else. It's so good to see momentum building behind the push for an unambiguous standard in society that 'only yes means yes'. Respectful relationships and clear and direct sexual consent education in schools must start at an early age to prevent gender-based violence.

The economic, social and political oppression of women continues because patriarchy is allowed to flourish.

Just as anti-racism is a remedy for racism, so feminism is the antidote to patriarchy.

And just as patriarchy is powerful, so must be our feminism.

I know more than most the power of the patriarchy in silencing women. I know well the power of feminism too.

Most of my young adulthood in Pakistan was spent under the regime of military dictator General Zia-ul-Haq. Fuelled by religiosity and patriarchal customs, laws became even more regressive during his dictatorship. In particular, changes to the penal code which criminalised sexual relationships outside of marriage had very serious social and legal implications for women. But this growth in misogyny was matched by a rise in feminist activism.

I was surrounded by women who subverted patriarchy in many different ways. Some quietly, like my mother and her mother. Others more unabashedly, like my aunt. There was an unmatched camaraderie among these women. Their relationships were indispensable, profound and powerful. Their overt and covert rebellion against the dominant system made it easier for me to mark out my own path in life. Most of my female cousins are better educated than the male ones. Many are career women. They have worked as teachers, academics, chartered accountants, in advertising and in the civil service. Some have been working mothers. By and large, they all chose their own destiny. One of the cousins I looked up to most went on to become the first female deputy commissioner in Pakistan. It was their feminism that made me who I am.

In discussions on feminism, the role of men often comes under scrutiny. Should they be part of our feminist struggle? Can they be trusted to help break down the very system that advantages them? Can they truly be feminist?

Men are free to be feminists. But they have to spare us the performative and tokenistic feminism that is characterised by the wearing of a white ribbon or the right T-shirt, by putting a popular frame on a profile picture or by starting hashtags. Feminism is about us, not them. If men want to be true allies, they must be willing to put down the tools of patriarchy: power, dominance, control, coercion. They must listen, learn and—crucially—shut up. That means they need to be okay with staying behind the scenes and leaving the space wide open for women to take centre stage. It means not hijacking conversations on women's issues. It means calling yourself a feminist not only in spaces where it draws praise, but in the male-dominated spaces where it has a more challenging effect: the locker rooms, Cabinet meetings and boardrooms from which women are largely excluded.

During our campaign for reproductive autonomy, there were many men who stepped up but whose faces and names were never seen or read. They wrote letters, started petitions, helped tape up posters and took the photos, rather than squeezing themselves into the frame. They walked the walk.

One of these men was my husband.

Growing up, Omar was surrounded by strong, independent women like his mother and his aunts. One of his role models, his paternal grandfather, had been a strong ally of women. In the 1940s he established a school for girls in Lucknow, now a part of India. In the last years of the British Raj, he was becoming very concerned about the lack of educational opportunities for Muslim girls. He had been a highly respected Additional Chief Engineer of the Central Public Works Department, but was now paralysed and bedridden. Not deterred by his disability, he enlisted community support to organise the funding for a fee-free primary school. To make sure this school was not viewed as a charity project by the parents of prospective students, his youngest daughter moved to this new public school. His eldest daughter, Hameeda Bano, took on the role of headmistress.

The next challenge was to ensure that these students continued on to high school. One of the best ways to do this was to normalise young Muslim women's attendance at high school. The problem was that, at that time, many Muslim women used covered tangas, horse-drawn carriages, as transportation in order to observe purdah, or religious seclusion. Even if they were going to high school, no one could actually see them. Making them visible seemed like a straightforward solution, but it did require pushing the boundaries of societal customs. They did. His daughters and those of his friends started cycling to school and back. Other families now had the example, and the permission, they needed, and they followed suit.

Once the school was up and running, Hameeda Bano was offered a job at the government education department as Inspectoress of Schools. If she accepted, her first posting would require her to visit schools in rural areas and remote villages where access and safety posed real threats for a young woman. Encouraged and supported by her parents, she embraced these challenges. Her father bought her a small Ford car. For her security, her mother gave her a pearl-handled Mauser 0.25 semiautomatic pistol with a twelve-shot magazine. So started her career in education—a career that flourished and would peak when she became a university professor in Karachi, Pakistan. Now that is all-round badass feminism, and an amazing role model.

When I hear women say, 'Feminism is language of the past,' or 'It's not a useful term,' it breaks my heart. Feminism isn't an old-fashioned idea whose time has come and gone. If history has taught us anything, it's that feminism must remain in vogue all the time.

My Abbu and Ammi on their honeymoon in 1957.

Ammi and me at ten months old in 1964.

At ten months old on Abbu's motorbike with my two older brothers.

Aged five just after starting school in Pakistan in 1968.

My and Omar's wedding day in Lahore, August 1989.

Me with baby Osman in Pakistan with the orange VW, our first car.

Me with Osman and the two suitcases of our life in Lahore, outside the motel on Anzac Parade we stayed in after landing in Sydney.

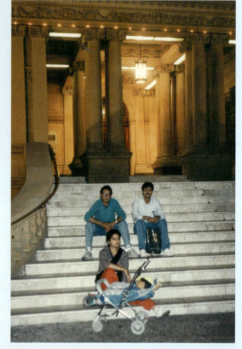

With Omar, Osman and a friend on Town Hall steps, seeing the sights on our first night in Sydney, March 1992.

Me and Osman washing the Datsun 120Y, 1992.

Our first trip to Canberra and parliament house, 1992. I could not imagine in my wildest dreams that I would be a senator one day twenty-six years later!

A photo Abbu took of Sydney Harbour Bridge in 1956 when he did his Master of Engineering in Sydney, one of his many photos and slides of Australia that we saw growing up.

Omar, Osman (sleeping in the stroller) and me in 1992 at the 60th birthday of the Sydney Harbour Bridge.

Accepting my Australian citizenship certificate at Randwick Council in 1994.

My Master of Engineering Science graduation at the University of New South Wales in 1994.

Osman, me, Aisha and Omar at my PhD graduation in 2000.

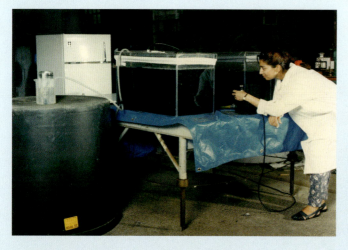

Me with one of my University of New South Wales PhD experiments: anaerobic digesters.

At work in Port Macquarie outside a stormwater project site.

My swearing-in to New South Wales Parliament in 2013. *Legislative Council of New South Wales*

Camping at Maules Creek in 2014 with Frontline Action on Coal to protest against clearing the Leard State Forest for coalmining.

Speaking at the Rally for Palestine at Sydney Town Hall, 2014.

Rallying for refugees, Port Macquarie, 2014.

One of the 'Love Letters to Mehreen'. Staying quiet wouldn't make the trolls go away, so we decided to fight back against the filth my office and I received online.

My high school netball team in 1978 when we won the interschool tournament. I am second from left and played Defence.

Playing for the 2015 New South Wales Parliament netball team.

Fighting the Stop Taxing My Period campaign with Subeta Vimalarajah and Senator Larissa Waters in 2015.

At Sydney's Mardi Gras Fair Day with Osman in 2015.

Speaking at the Rally for Greyhounds in Martin Place, Sydney, in 2016.

With Cosmo, an ex-racing greyhound who is now part of our family. Many greyhounds die on the track or are put down when they are deemed no longer useful to the racing industry.

Fighting coalmining on the rich farmland of the Liverpool Plains, 2016.

At a Stop Adani rally in Newtown in 2017.

Campaigning for abortion law reform at Cobargo Folk Festival in 2017.

Campaigning in Albury to decriminalise abortion and provide safe access for women.

My first speech in the Senate in 2018. *David Foote/Auspic/DPS*

Outside Al Noor Mosque in Christchurch in 2019.

Election night 2019 after winning in the Senate. *Freya Fullwood/The Greens NSW*

Knitting pouches for orphaned animals after the 2019–20 bushfires.

Speaking at the climate-change rally in January 2020 at Sydney Town Hall.

COVID-ready in Federal Parliament, 2020.

At the Black Lives Matter rally in Sydney, 2020

FEMINIST AS FUCK

In 2014, Julie Bishop, then Australia's first female foreign minister and only female Cabinet minister under the regressive Abbott government, declared at the National Press Club that she was 'no feminist'. It was a huge backward step. Feminism has and should change over time. Its application will vary in different contexts, cultures and communities, but denying the usefulness of it as a label plays into the demonisation of the concept, cultivated by the patriarchy and so-called men's rights activists (MRAs).

The rejection of feminism and the reluctance to embrace it perpetuates patriarchal ideas and structures. With toxic masculinity alive and well, there are enough people out there wanting to destroy feminism as it is. Let's not feed their appetite. Just like talking about racism brings out the racist trolls, talking about women brings out the MRA psychopaths. Sadly, there is simply no way to talk about feminism in Australia without being personally attacked and vilified.

When COVID-19 hit our shores, I was quick to point out in the Senate that women were on the front line of the crisis. The right-wing identity-policing media were as quick to ridicule me in response. In an article criticising my speech, Rita Panahi wrote in the *Herald Sun*: 'The identity politics-obsessed far-Left party won't allow a little thing like a global pandemic to get in the way of its hobby horses: toxic racial politics, intersectional feminism and anything that divides us into distinct groups based on factors beyond any individual's control.'[9] Tim Blair from the *Daily Telegraph* was quick to step in too: 'Nobody gives a damn about stupid woke causes in a time of global contagion, but priority-confused Greens senator Mehreen Faruqi is doing her very best to keep pointless gender grievances alive.'[10]

Only a few days after my speech in parliament, the United Nations released a policy brief—*The Impact of COVID-19 on Women*—which stated: 'Across every sphere, from health to the economy, security to social protection, the impacts of COVID-19 are exacerbated for women and girls simply by virtue of their sex.'[11] Since then, there has been widespread agreement about the undeniable disproportionate impact of the pandemic on women. Yet when I took a feminist stand, I was maligned and mocked for stating facts.

It took a century to reform abortion laws. Now we are told that, on current tracking, global gender parity is a century away.[12] At least five more generations of women will have their minds and bodies violated, they will be discriminated against and exploited in the workplace, and they will be denied equal representation.

We have fought and won many battles. There are always more to win.

Gaining the right to vote and run for parliament has not led to equal representation.

Women have joined the workforce in droves. We work hard. We pursue careers in every profession under the sun. Laws have been enacted for equal pay and equal opportunity. Still, we continue to be underrated and underpaid.

The prevalence of gender-based violence results in one in three women experiencing sexual or physical violence. Gendered violence kills one woman a week.

Women are more disadvantaged than men by war, poverty and climate change.

Australia's ranking in the Global Gender Gap Index has been steadily dropping for more than a decade.

The gender pay gap has hovered between 14 per cent and 19 per cent since the turn of the 21st century.

Older women are the fastest-growing cohort of people who are homeless.

The feminisation of poverty means women have less savings and less superannuation. They earn less, and their jobs are more insecure and more likely to be casualised.

Writing down these statistics is infuriating, as the huge disparities and their impacts sink in. And knowing that these numbers, although they reveal vast inequality, yet manage to conceal its full extent makes my blood boil. They don't show how the multiplicity of women are faring—for instance, First Nations women, migrant women, refugee women, women of colour, Muslim women, trans women and disabled women. These women and others who are made invisible in reports and in society simply fall through the cracks. Their voices go unheard.

Shockingly, life expectancy for Aboriginal women in Australia is still 9.5 years less than for non-Indigenous women.

Muslim women have become the most likely targets of retaliation in the aftermath of terrorist incidents. Following negative media attention on Muslims, reported abuse of Muslim women and women who 'look Muslim' increases.

Trans women of colour are much more likely to suffer multiple instances of sexual harassment than other women.[13]

Women know well that the journey for our rights is tough, long and full of dead ends and U-turns. The journey to parity for marginalised women is even tougher.

Waves of feminism have ebbed and flowed; the tide hasn't quite turned. Our predecessors pushed hard against the wall of patriarchy so that we could have a better life. They were able to smash through a few bricks here and there. Some of us have squeezed through those holes. Others are still hammering away. Some of the holes are bigger, weakening the structure. But the wall still stands.

I am tired of trying to dismantle the patriarchy brick by brick. I'm tired of being told to go to the back of the queue. I'm tired of waiting. I won't be waiting for another century. Neither should you.

Going forward, our feminism must be all-encompassing, here and across the globe. It is not an individual quest. Feminism isn't the exclusive domain of the left, or the white, or the privileged. It must be without prejudice and discrimination. It must be with and for all.

The campaign to decriminalise abortion taught me to ignore the 'established wisdom' that we must go slow, that our change should be incremental. It doesn't have to be that way.

Let's put down the hammer. Let's get in the driver's seat

FEMINIST AS FUCK

of a bulldozer to attack injustice with the same vigour that our enemies use to imprison us.

Let's knock down the wall of patriarchy once and for all. Let's not accept anything less.

4

MUSLIM, BROWN AND PROUD

—

In 2020, Senator Kamala Harris made history. She is the first woman, and the first Black, South Asian woman, elected vice president of the United States of America. Her victory speech acknowledged this breakthrough: 'Because every little girl watching tonight sees that this is a country of possibilities.'

It's true you can't be what you can't see. It warms my heart to see a part of me when I see her. In a political house of cards, where most of the cards are stacked against us, this was indeed a moment to celebrate. It was a moment to ponder. And reflect. That this possibility only became a reality more than 200 years after America's first presidential election is a glaring reminder of the lengthy, hard-fought struggles of women. Women of colour have been struggling harder for much longer.

This was also a time, I realised, to mull over my own country's history of gender, race and politics.

Australia has been plunging downward in gender equality for some time. On the World Economic Forum's Global Gender Gap Index in 2021, it fell to 50th position, having been fifteenth in 2006 and dropping another six points since 2020.[1,2]

The gender make-up of the Australian parliament is changing at a glacial pace. The racial face of our politics, too, has hardly shifted in the last 30 years.[3] It was only in the second decade of the 21st century that we got our first female prime minister, our first female Indigenous senator and our first female Muslim senator. Women who buck these trends contend with a culture of bias, aggression and harassment. Some are hounded by sexism and misogyny; others are subjected to intense racism.

Julia Gillard became the first female prime minister of Australia in 2010 and was quickly deposed in 2013. In her short time as the nation's leader, she faced incredibly sexist personal attacks from her opponents and in the media. She was often demonised for being unmarried and having no children. She was branded with disgustingly offensive labels: she was a 'witch,' a 'bitch' and 'deliberately barren'. Radio shock jock Alan Jones even proposed that she should be put in a sack, taken far out to sea and left to swim her way back. Gillard had to endure a running commentary on her appearance, her character and her competence to which no male prime minister has ever been subjected.

The attacks on women's credibility become more toxic for women of colour. We live life at the intersection of racism and sexism. The mingling of these two visceral forces multiplies the poison of hate many times over. I'm often asked to speak about how I respond to the prejudice I experience because of my racial and gender identities. Do I expose it? Do I call it out? How do I fight back?

The one thing we rarely talk about is the grinding effect this toxicity, and the effort it takes to push back against it, has on our lives. The toll it takes on our mental and physical health is immense. Trolls and haters have an uncanny ability to poke and prod at the scars and wounds which women of colour bring in a whitewashed, patriarchal world. It is an experience that is hard to explain. We are despised not just for who we are but also for what we look like and where we come from. We are hated for having the temerity to raise our heads above the parapet to join the public debate. These are rights that others take for granted.

Nova Peris, the former senator for the Northern Territory, was the first Indigenous woman elected to Federal Parliament in 2013. She left politics after a single term. It was years later, in 2020, that she revealed the intensity of the racism to which she had been subjected as a senator. It was a big factor in her decision not to return to parliament for a second term, even though her seat was a safe one.

'If not every day, every second day I would be attacked: by racist trolls, mail that was sent, phone calls . . . It was just horrific,' she said. 'I had death threats, the AFP were tracking down mail that was sent to me . . . If you are an Aboriginal person and you challenge the status quo, you are going to be attacked.'[4]

Her attempts to call out racism were met with even more racism. Nova's story is similar to those of other women of colour who are politicians in Western countries.

During his time as president of the United States, Donald Trump time and again targeted the four progressive Democratic congresswomen of colour known as 'The Squad'. He told them to go back to the 'broken and crime-infested places from which they came'.[5] Mocking Ilhan Omar, the first Somali-American elected to Congress, he said: 'She's telling us how to run our country. How did you do where you came from?'[6]

I see a lot of my own experiences in the attacks on these women. Since I joined the upper house of the New South Wales Parliament in 2013, the avalanche of messages sent my way echo these comments. The steady rise in gender and race hatred reached a crescendo after I delivered my inaugural speech as the first female Muslim senator in Australia five years later. I was not backwards in coming forward.

'The reality is that my presence in the Senate is an affront to some,' I said. 'They are offended that people of colour, and Muslims, have the audacity to not only exist but to open our mouths and join the public debate. Some politicians call us cockroaches. Some say we are a disease against

MUSLIM, BROWN AND PROUD

which Australia needs vaccination. Some, if they had their way, would ban us from making Australia our home. So it is with great pride that I stand here before you, unapologetically—a Brown, Muslim, migrant, feminist woman, and a Greens senator. I say "unapologetically", because if there is one thing people with stories like mine are asked to do constantly, it is to apologise for our presence, because we are not quiet enough, not respectful enough, not thankful enough, not Australian enough.'

I was showered with accolades for my truth-telling. The speech received 2.5 million views and was covered by *Al Jazeera*, the *Guardian* and newspapers around the world. It even made a cameo appearance in the ABC series *Total Control*, with Deborah Mailman's character studying it while pondering her own first speech in the Senate. Simultaneously, a horrible feeding frenzy of hate was unleashed on social media. Comments like 'Put your burka on—and shut the fuck up!', 'Deport the whining bitch' and 'Revoke citizenship and Deport' were some of the vile reactions on my Facebook page. Others said: 'Can someone shoot this bitch?', 'Going to be great bashing her', 'She needs to be stoned to death', and 'Put a bomb under her'.

It was later revealed by a *Guardian* investigation that I, along with the two first Muslim congresswomen in the United States, Ilhan Omar and Rashida Tlaib, was a target of a covert international plot to control some of Facebook's largest far-right pages to harvest Islamophobic hate for profit.[7] At the time of my first speech in the Senate, ten pages of this network launched a coordinated action, inciting their 546,000 followers to attack me for speaking against racism.

Facebook took down several pages and accounts which violated their policy, but only after being alerted by the *Guardian*. That's not good enough. The damage was done. The hurt inflicted. Even worse, some of these pages were still operating in 2021. Pages and groups that promote harassment are well known to social media companies, but are ignored in a way that 'real world' abuse and harassment would not be. Targets of abuse carry the burden of reporting each and every threat in the hope it will be addressed. From my experience, it takes quite a lot of abuse to violate Facebook's standards. One Facebook user wrote to me: 'Stay here and someone might do [us] a favour and put a bullet in your head'—and even that didn't offend their community standards.

My son Osman, then working for the ABC, had his personal phone number released by a prominent right-wing personality on Twitter. This doxing led to him receiving hundreds of racist messages, abusive phone calls and even death threats. It's hard enough when I am the subject of hate, but it was unbearable to see my son go through the anguish this caused him. It cut my heart up. I remember lying awake all night, my emotions oscillating between fear for Osman's safety and anger at politicians and the media who brush away our concerns as 'attention seeking' and 'hijacking' the public debate, or who classify hatred as 'the rough and tumble of politics'. Just because they are not subjected to it doesn't mean it doesn't exist.

Right-wing threats are all too often dismissed. Social media platforms continue to profit from the proliferation of hate speech. Media outlets continue to target racial and cultural minorities while they platform fascists and white nationalists. Politicians continue to normalise hate as they evade the subject of far-right extremism.

Most galling is the federal Coalition government's ongoing false equivalence between 'right-wing extremism' and 'left-wing extremism'. How many times have I asked ministers serious questions about tackling the growing threat of far-right extremism or the normalisation of white supremacy, only to be told that they condemn right-wing and left-wing extremism? The government counter-terrorism arrangements are, they tell me, ideologically agnostic. In February 2020, after the head of ASIO, Mike Burgess, warned of the rising threat of right-wing extremism in Australia, Peter Dutton told reporters it was important for security agencies to deal with threats from both right-wing and left-wing 'lunatics'.[8]

These responses are hard to listen to. Equating 'left-wing extremism' with 'right-wing extremism' is nonsensical. Mario Peucker and Jacob Davey studied empirical evidence to investigate if the radical left was a threat to our security. Nothing in their findings suggests radical (or extreme) left-wing movements in Australia currently pose any significant security threat.[9]

The reluctance to recognise far-right extremism without conflating it with other forms of supposed extremism gives a free pass to white nationalism. It contributes to hate incubating in society. It minimises racism and stops action that seeks to combat it. Yet it happens again and again in Australia, as if conservative politicians are competing with each other to see who can win this race to the bottom.

The white supremacists who stormed the Capitol building in Washington on 6 January 2021 drew widespread condemnation from across the globe. But in Australia, Michael McCormack MP, our Acting Prime Minister at the time, drew a false equivalence between this riot and the Black Lives Matter movement. Equating a group that assaulted democracy with a group that sought racial justice is disgusting and downright dangerous. It simultaneously diminishes the legitimacy of a racial justice movement and downplays the threat of fascism.

You wouldn't think McCormack's words could get any worse than this. They did. He then went on to claim that 'all lives matter', using a phrase that has become associated with white supremacy, far-right nationalism and racism.[10] The use of this abhorrent slogan further dismisses the significance of Black deaths in custody. It is also an attempt to harness votes. McCormack's National Party wants to win back people who, over the years, have become supporters of Pauline Hanson's One Nation (PHON) party. They want to tap into the fear, division and racism that lies beneath the surface of our nation's psyche and which has been inflamed by PHON, but also normalised by a segment of the mainstream political class who see advantage in courting racist votes.

When political leaders dog-whistle or openly fan the flames of racism, it draws support to them and widens their audiences. It sends a crystal-clear signal that bigotry is okay. Like clockwork, soon after McCormack's comments I received an email with the line 'All white lives matter'. It makes me sick to my stomach to think that the lives of Black, Indigenous and people of colour (BIPOC) are so easily traded away for self-serving politics. Trump may have gone, but Trumpism is alive and well in our country.

***

After the Christchurch mosque massacre in March 2019, I criticised the independent senator Fraser Anning for stoking anti-Islamic sentiment by blaming the attack on Muslim immigration. The Coalition's Peter Dutton, meanwhile, claimed the Greens were 'just as bad' as Fraser Anning for calling out white supremacy.[11] When I condemned the climate of hate contributing to such violence, I was questioned, attacked and constantly asked for proof. News Limited's *Australian* newspaper wrote that I was pursuing a 'spotlight moment of political nark and incendiary slogan bombing'.[12]

The report of New Zealand's 'Royal Commission of Inquiry into the terrorist attack on Christchurch masjidain on 15 March 2019' makes for highly disturbing reading. It details how an Australian man was radicalised and came to commit this horrific terrorist attack. It makes clear that the terrorist who murdered 51 Muslims began forming his 'extreme right-wing Islamophobic ideology' in this country from a young age, including by engaging online with far-right groups based in Australia.

The report details the man's associations with various Australian far-right groups, and his donations to extremist media organisations which have regularly been given platforms and crossed over into 'mainstream' politics and media in Australia. The actions of these groups extend far beyond the online world they inhabit. Two months after the Christchurch massacre, I decided to host an anti-racism forum in New South Wales' second-biggest city, Newcastle. Just days before the event was scheduled, we were forced to cancel it when the venue's management told us they had received threats of violence from far-right groups. Those two groups are mentioned in the Royal Commission's report.

The Christchurch attacks have left a permanent deep wound on me. It is a lingering sadness that has forever become part of me.

I had an opportunity to visit Al Noor Mosque and meet the community three months after the attack. I was invited by Shakti Community Council, a non-profit organisation serving migrant and refugee women of Asian, African and Middle Eastern origin. They had been providing frontline support to the families affected by the massacre. I remember pulling up outside the mosque and being shocked at the normalcy of the world around it: it's a modest mosque in the middle of a fairly nondescript suburban area. But as I walked into the prayer area, I felt the electricity of what had happened here.

This was the front door where the first victim was killed, a man who thought the killer was there to pray, and so had welcomed him. Here was the hallway the killer must have run down, leading to the prayer room where he killed worshippers indiscriminately. There was the carpark where he shot even more, before returning from his car with a reloaded gun to kill the wounded. The victims were as young as three.

I did my namaz and prayed for the dead in the hall in which they had been killed so brutally. I sat with the families of those who had been targeted and heard their trauma—a mother now without a son, a young widow, a fatherless child. Amid their immense grief, I felt their strength and determination to survive and rebuild their lives. I had hoped to lighten their load; instead, they helped me deepen my resolve to forge a path against hate.

Shakti had arranged a conference to discuss the elephant in the room: the role of white supremacy in the horror of Christchurch. It was called 'Let's Deal with It: A trans-Tasman conference towards racial equity'. When I had received the invitation, I had looked at the title of the event and thought how, if such a conference happened in Australia, it would inevitably have been set upon by the right-wing press, as happens here whenever race is discussed. At the conference, I was struck by the resolve in the room, which was filled with Māori and Pākehā women from all walks of life. I will not forget that. I will work to build that same strength in my country.

In 2020, I proposed the creation of an anti-racism portfolio for the Australian Greens so we could build public activism to address systemic racism and quash the far-right. Redefining our work to make anti-racism a core focus is pretty ground-breaking for a political party. I feel the heavy responsibility of this portfolio. Tackling racism is a big job, but I relish this work in partnership with Greens senator Lidia Thorpe, the first Aboriginal senator from Victoria, and so many in the community committed to building an anti-racist society.

On the plane home from Aotearoa (New Zealand) I couldn't help but think that if such an attack had happened in Australia, the response would have been much different. If 51 Muslims had been killed, would there have been a Royal Commission and a serious examination of right-wing extremism? Would our prime minister have behaved with the grace of Jacinda Ardern, who correctly understood that her role was to heal her nation, not poke at its scars?

The truth is Australia is yet to reckon with being the country that raised the Christchurch killer. We can't keep obfuscating the fact that this terrorist attack was 'driven by an extreme right-wing Islamophobic ideology'.[13] Far-right extremism is not only present in our country, it is growing.

It worries me deeply that there are clear and ongoing links between the toxic far right and elements of our mainstream media and parliamentary politics. Some do it openly, from centre stage. Others race-bait from the sidelines. Many just remain silent. They are all complicit in normalising hatred and white supremacy.

It concerns me that there are people in parliament who are not reprimanded for their racism and bigotry, and that those of us who do highlight it are quickly called to order. We are the ones who are questioned. We are the ones asked for proof. We are the ones attacked. While this attitude prevails in our national parliament, we as a country have little hope of tackling racism or terrorism.

The media, and in particular right-wing media, has played no small part in mainstreaming racism, Islamophobia and mistruths. They have offered a platform to fascists and Neo-Nazis, and given them unquestioning coverage. On the flipside, others have failed in their responsibility to critique white nationalists and politicians who whip up hate. The unwillingness to amplify the harm caused by racism has played right into their hands.

Sadly, some of our own media and politicians contributed to the 'sick political moment' that manifested itself in a violent insurrection at Donald Trump's encouragement on 6 January 2021. Media outlets, including 'our ABC', have platformed Trumpian fascists like Steve Bannon long after they were denied airtime overseas. Canadian right-wing figure Lauren Southern, who now lives in Australia, is a regular contributor on Sky News. Fox News and Sky News have spread misinformation on voter fraud in the United States. Some Australian politicians have promoted these same conspiracy theories, suffering no repercussions from their leaders.

Right-wing media has been the flagbearer for the dog-whistling and flagrant racism that fostered the toxic climate from which a white supremacist Australian terrorist emerged with military-grade weapons to slaughter people in peaceful prayer. None more so than News Corp. It is unquestionable that Murdoch media outlets publish harmful propaganda that fuels racism and misinformation, while also giving cover to white supremacists. Fanning conspiracy theories and stoking intolerance and racist abuse is a business model for them. Advertisers who profit from this monstrous platform of hate are accomplices. If they want to do something useful, they can walk away with their wallets.

The right-wing media is not simply opportunistic and profit-driven, it has an agenda. Its leaders know that its constant vilification of First Nations people, Muslims, Asians and refugees shapes public opinion and policy. It has encouraged the expression of negative sentiments towards these communities, which eventually turn into open hostility and abuse. It has aided and abetted the cruelty and inhumanity of a number of bipartisan asylum seeker policies: mandatory detention, offshore processing, and the locking up of refugees in hotels during the pandemic. These policies of deterring, detaining and deporting vulnerable people have resulted in unimaginable damage to thousands, including women and children. The racialisation of asylum seekers as Muslims has extended Islamophobic prejudice to them.

You've got to question why politicians give News Corp their time and voice at all. Progressive politicians appearing on the daytime programs of Sky News lend the network a credibility it doesn't deserve when its night-time trolls emerge. Their disgraceful and malicious agenda should be rejected altogether. Actively engaging with such media reinforces and encourages negative attitudes towards marginalised communities. Staying silent, likewise, keeps the hate afloat and increases its intensity. Not acting to stop this spread of racism harms the targets and delays social cohesion, and a failure to recognise this emboldens these abhorrent far-right groups.

In January 2021, almost 40 white nationalists gathered at Gariwerd (the Grampians) and nearby Halls Gap, openly taking photos of themselves lighting Ku Klux Klan–style crosses, yelling 'White power!' at people on the street and giving Nazi salutes. They are bolstered by the unwillingness of the political class to take real action, the politicians who decry the activities but then go on Sky News. You can't condemn racism and then, in a warm glow of self-congratulation, appear on racist TV. You can't meet racism halfway.

Let me be clear: any platforming of the far right and Neo-Nazis is a stain on the media. Some in the progressive media treat those of the far right as an academic curiosity, seeking them out (and even taking selfies with them) as a way of finding out how they think. There is a difference between critiquing these people and handing them megaphones or normalising their ideas. The problem is that even if most people turn away from watching it, at least some will be enticed to take the next step towards extremism. And that is how these movements cross from the periphery to the mainstream. This isn't a game. This isn't a theoretical study. For us, this is a fight for our lives.

***

The growth of the far right has been accompanied by a rise in Islamophobia, with girls and women the most likely targets. Charles Sturt University's 2019 'Islamophobia in Australia' report found that harassment of Muslims in public spaces guarded by security officers had jumped by 30 per cent since the last report, and racist attacks requiring hospitalisation had doubled.[14]

In my years of public life, I have been a witness to and a target of hate's exponential growth in Australia. The year after I became the first Muslim woman politician in Australia, we reached a new and disgraceful low when the federal parliament's presiding officers enacted new rules.[15] Muslim women wearing a burqa or niqab would be forced to sit in glass enclosures segregated from the public gallery if they visit the 'people's house' in Canberra. While that proposal didn't get very far in the end, the notion of policing Muslim women is still very much alive, whether it's putting us in boxes, shutting us up or curbing our thoughts.

Not a day goes by when I don't receive a hateful, abusive message on Twitter or Facebook. Others make phone calls;

still others send emails. Some even write letters. A man once sent me an extremely sexually explicit and abusive letter with a signature from his church. When I brought this to the church's attention, he sent me an apology explaining that he was upset because Turkey had invaded Greece. As I saw it, he wasn't sorry for writing the letter; he was sorry he got caught. What does Turkey invading Greece some 400 years ago have to do with me? Well, I am a Muslim, and Turkey is a Muslim state. So obviously I must be responsible for the actions of all Muslims throughout time. How bloody ridiculous!

If you are a Muslim migrant, where you come from will haunt you forever. Public demands to 'get out of my country' and 'go back where you came from' are familiar to all of us. If you are a woman, it gets worse. One contributor to the ever-growing pile of hate mail told me that 'Muslims are complete scum', before clarifying that 'Muslim women are even worse than the men'.

The more you speak up about these slurs, the more you get attacked. Accompanying the now predictable hatred are the haters' assumptions about why I speak out. It's to attract more loathing, they say, so that I can play the victim. Someone called my office to tell my staff I was a drama queen. Others accuse me of playing identity politics, using my gender, race and religion as weapons—as if these are not the constant subject of the abuse I receive. I admit, I don't shy away from saying things that others find controversial. But surely we can provoke conversations on controversial issues without descending into racism or sexism.

Accusations of 'playing identity politics' in order to cause division are designed to shut us down. Identity politics itself has become a maligned negative concept, as if people of a certain gender, race or religion use it to gain advantage in society. As if it's not the pervading racism and sexism that are the problems but the people railing against them. This completely ignores the lived reality of those who face systemic disadvantage because of these very attributes. Those claiming we play the 'race card' or the 'gender card' to get ahead, and even using the catchcries of 'cancel culture gone too far' or 'political correctness gone mad', have probably never felt the corrosive effects of discrimination, racism and insults that are meant to diminish, silence and control us.

If anything, those who use the term 'identity politics' as a weapon are the very ones most guilty of it. If anyone has benefited from their identity and played it to their advantage, it is the old white men who run this country, its companies and its institutions. It is ironic, too, that the people accusing me of playing identity politics are also the ones who cannot see beyond my race, gender and religion. No matter what the subject I might be speaking about, they will reduce it to my race and religion.

A racialised stereotype of Muslims is rife in society. In 1978, Edward W. Said eloquently laid out the concept of 'Orientalism', by which was meant the cultural characterisation of Muslims and Arabs as inferior (and the elevation of European culture as superior) in order to justify the colonialisation and subjugation perpetrated by Europeans.

MUSLIM, BROWN AND PROUD

'In newsreels or news-photos,' Said wrote, 'the Arab is always shown in large numbers. No individuality, no personal characteristics or experiences. Most of the pictures represent mass rage and misery, or irrational (hence hopelessly eccentric) gestures. Lurking behind all of these images is the menace of jihad. Consequence: a fear that the Muslims (or Arabs) will take over the world.'[16]

Not much has changed. We are viewed as conservative. Muslim men are portrayed as Middle Eastern, with beards and turbans, or as gun-toting terrorists. The caricature of a Muslim woman is one wearing a hijab or a burqa, which are taken as signs of oppression. Muslim women are presented as passive victims of male power, not free to make up their own minds.

At one end of the spectrum, this submissive depiction of Muslim women 'others' them in Western societies, and is seen as threatening and undermining Western values and cultural identity.[17] At the other end, Muslim women, along with women of colour, are exoticised and fetishised. We are reduced to mere objects of desire in some kind of warped colonial fantasy. White women have told me how beautiful my tanned dark brown skin is. In state parliament I was once told that a white MP used to call me 'butter chicken' because he liked my voice and accent. These are not compliments. This is cringeworthy, condescending infantilisation. Both stereotypes subjectify us in extreme ways. They rob us of our agency and individuality.

Muslim women are not a homogenous, identical set of people, but these narrow depictions wipe out the complexities, pluralities and histories of the different families, cultures and ethnicities we come from. Like other people of faith, Muslims come in all shapes and sizes. We have a variety of political views and values. We too deserve the benefit of individuality naturally afforded to others—but the reality, for millions, is a life muted by these negative (mis)representations.

While we are rendered invisible by this racialised stereotyping, the visibility of veiled Muslim women makes them easy targets of Islamophobic attacks, which usually spike in the wake of a terrorist incident. Women are targeted in shopping centres, in open public spaces and on public transport. The Islamophobia Register lists alarming details of the harassment Muslim women face.[18] A woman wearing a head scarf was tripped over by a man as she was walking with a toddler. A mother and daughter were rammed by a car in another alleged incident. A high school student reported being attacked by a classmate. Some Muslim women said they removed their head scarves in public for fear of being attacked.

Despite the abuse they received, Muslim women remain in the background of political responses. Politicians meet prominent men within ethnic and religious communities, round tables are held with these 'community leaders' and photoshoots are organised—but all too often women are glaringly missing. There is no shortage of Muslim women within the community who are well positioned to provide advice, yet very few are invited to become part of the national conversation.[19]

MUSLIM, BROWN AND PROUD

For me as a Muslim woman, this abuse, subjectification, stereotyping and exclusion is personal. Of course, politics and identity are inextricably entwined. The personal is political. Why shouldn't it be? I didn't suddenly appear on the Australian political scene from a vacuum. It wasn't that someone waved a magic wand and there I was, a replica of Western perceptions. Our past makes us who we are in the present.

Our identities are multilayered, dynamic and evolving. Our experiences are rooted in the socio-political contexts we've lived in. But these too easily get erased for a clickbait headline like this one, which I read in the *Daily Mail* in May 2017 following hearings of the NSW Parliamentary Inquiry into Human Trafficking: 'EXCLUSIVE: "Feminist" Muslim Greens MP defends arranged marriages and is "happy" hers was organised by her PARENTS—and says it's different from being "forced" to wed a man'.

My sin? Clarifying with a witness that a 'forced marriage' is not the same as an 'arranged marriage', and that millions of people are introduced to their partners through family connections before deciding themselves if they wanted to get married. Omar and I had fallen in love the day we met. Quite possibly, though, we wouldn't have met or got married without our families' involvement.

I think it's very unlikely that the *Daily Mail* journalists listened to the audio of hours of Legislative Council committee hearings. It still brings a wry smile to my lips when I think about who went running to the media when they heard me say it. Their world must be small and meaningless if a headline in the *Daily Mail* is a win for them.

It wasn't the first time the *Daily Mail* tried to pin me down with a dog-whistle headline. When they asked my views on halal slaughter, they were told I supported mandatory stunning of animals—something that was happening already in almost all halal slaughterhouses in Australia anyway. They decided to run some incredibly deceptive headlines, presumably in an attempt to drive a wedge between me and the Muslim community. They didn't, of course, mention in the article that I'm a vegetarian, and personally I don't think any animal should be slaughtered.

Some don't want me in Australia because I'm a Muslim. For them, my way of life is incompatible with modern Australia. Others tell me to stick to my religion and not to meddle in 'our way of life'. They don't want me to campaign for decriminalising abortion or legalising drugs. Either way, I'm accused of being divisive.

Honestly, I don't think I'll ever be Australian enough for some. Not even, as I wrote in August 2018, if I stood on Bondi Beach serving sausage sangers in an Akubra, draped in an Australian flag with a Southern Cross tattoo on my arm.[20]

I just don't fit the mould they have made for me. I am Muslim but I don't wear hijab. I'm from Pakistan yet I am progressive, and assertive. I wear shalwar kameez and I wear a hardhat too. I don't drink but I can swear like a drunk. These oddities, it seems, make me a sinister paradox.

That's when the shit really hits the fan. I'm damned if I do and damned if I don't.

***

When you disrupt the false, reductive portrayal of Muslim women, everyone is confused—the left, the right and those in between. I mean, who has ever heard of a progressive migrant Muslim woman of colour who speaks her mind? When strong perceptions clash with a contrary reality, the nuances and complexities are deliberately obliterated, or wilfully ignored.

When I was first elected to parliament, a prominent male Muslim leader expressed his wariness. He stated that being part of the Greens 'will be something that is likely to test her . . . we will be watching to see whether she will allow her beliefs as a Muslim to succumb to the party policy'.[21] He was, of course, referring to the Greens' position on LGBTQI+ equality.

It wasn't only his proposition that bothered me: his assumption that I would 'succumb' to party policy was really offensive. He expected I would be passive, as if I were a bystander without agency. It was actually the opposite. I joined the Greens *because* of social justice policies like marriage equality that reflect my values of compassion and dignity. Since then I've worked with members to make our policies more progressive: I want uni and TAFE to be fee-free; I want to legalise cannabis; I want to end commercial horse racing.

This man was not alone in his view. My continued support for marriage equality, which included co-sponsoring the cross-party marriage equality bill in the New South Wales Parliament in 2013, brought upon me the ire of friends and family back in Pakistan. I was told that 'Western' thinking had got to me. I'd been brainwashed. I'd lost my way and I would burn in the fires of hell for eternity. Some have disowned me. I've lost connection with some others.

But in the face of hostility, I did not shy away from public support for marriage equality. I never hid my views. During the height of the marriage equality debate in Australia in 2017 I wrote an opinion piece for *The Guardian*, clearly articulating why as a Muslim I was publicly and proudly voting 'YES', and so was my family.[22]

Perhaps most surprising is the flak I've copped from some within the Greens for being a Muslim. Honestly, it was the most unexpected form of insult, and really hurts. I've since talked to other women of colour and understand that the experience is not unique to me. Progressives have blind spots just like anyone else, from the 'brogressives' to the POEBIs (Progressive On Everything But Israel). Some harbour a deep mistrust of religion that spills over into racism without much prodding.

Just days after I moved into my Senate office in Sydney, my staff were called incessantly over a period of days by a Greens member who complained about some Muslims in his neighbourhood who had cleared their land unlawfully. He wanted me to personally apologise for the damage these people had caused to the environment. He claimed that I, as a Muslim, bore responsibility for their deeds. When we refused, he lodged a complaint with my state party.

Now, you would expect that such an unreasonable demand would be nipped in the bud. Not so. I was asked not only to respond to the complainant, but to meet him face to face to assure him that my religion had nothing to do with my decision. That I was always secular in my decision-making. He was happy to come meet me at my office, I was told. The fuck he was. Over my dead body would I give such assurances to such bigotry. My track record speaks for itself. I'm happy to be judged for my actions, not the actions of others.

I have become quite used to demands for an apology or condemnation for every act of terrorism by ISIS, as if I were somehow responsible for their atrocities, and then being attacked for not doing so. Is every Australian Catholic MP asked to condemn and apologise for every act of child abuse committed by Catholic clergy? Of course not. They shouldn't be. And I shouldn't be either. It is a no-win situation for me, though. If I were to apologise, it would create an expectation that I should do so for every crime committed by someone who happened to be Muslim. If I don't, I will be cast as a terrorist sympathiser.[23]

In fact, it wasn't the demand for a personal apology that shook me to the core, it was that some in my own party couldn't see his blatant Islamophobia. It shouldn't have surprised me. Over the years, I have experienced the consequences of this blind spot which some progressives have about religion and people of faith. I know of members who did not vote for me in a preselection contest because of that 'Muslim' thing, referring to the homophobic religious views associated with mainstream Islam, even though they knew well my strong advocacy for marriage equality and LGBTQI+ rights.

In my early days as an MP, when the hate was pouring in, some Greens colleagues, while sympathetic, told me to get used to it. They said they too had been vilified for our radical policy stances. They may have been trying to reassure me, but comparing racism with abuse that white people receive for a policy position was cold comfort. At best, their thoughtlessness ignored my experiences of racism; at worst, it minimised them.

In 1963, Martin Luther King drew attention to the way the white progressive establishment talked about standing in allyship with the African American struggle, but often served as a handbrake on the movement, its tactics and strategies. In his 'Letter from a Birmingham Jail', he wrote about being 'gravely disappointed with the white moderate'.[24] In the letter he noted that the 'shallow understanding from people of good will is more frustrating than absolute misunderstanding from people of ill will. Lukewarm acceptance is much more bewildering than outright rejection.'

I can relate to this. White progressiveness that refuses to recognise its own complicity in the system we are trying to overturn is damaging to an anti-racist movement. The rolling of eyes when I bring up racism (as if to say, 'Here she goes again'), the calls to 'take the high road' and just ignore the hate (as if racism isn't corrosive, but something that should roll off our backs), and most importantly, the inevitable reluctance to cede space to others are all signs of the white reluctance to give up the privilege they've had for centuries.

Often, white progressives will talk the talk, but when they have to reflect upon their own role, or let people of colour talk for themselves rather than talk for them, they suddenly forget how to walk the walk. Or, even worse, when their power is threatened, they try to take you down or reduce you to nothing more than an empty puppet, doing the dance of someone who is pulling your strings. They also reduce you to the stereotype of a Muslim woman without the agency to make her own choices. They always know better.

When I decided to run for the Senate, I was gravely hurt by the character assassination that came from people who were not pleased by my decision. I had considered them allies, even confidants, and held them up as shining examples of true progressives. Almost overnight there was a concerted effort to transform me from a solid left-wing MP to a lackey of those in the party viewed as less progressive. I was cast as a gullible and presumably brainless Brown woman who didn't understand what she was doing. I was ignored at rallies by people who just weeks before would have hugged me and thanked me for my work. Did it not occur to them that I had the right, in a democratic preselection, to put my name forward, as did any other member of the NSW Greens?

Wasn't this the grassroots democracy we had all been fighting for? Or does political tribalism trump all else?

The most stinging comment, written on Facebook by a Greens member, underscored for me the latent racism of some progressives. It said I should just wait another four years before launching my bid, so as to not cause a challenge to the sitting senator. To me, that read: 'Go to the back of the line, Mehreen.' Well, I refused.

I thought long and hard before running for the Senate. As a state MP, I had fiercely challenged structural racism, broken the long parliamentary silence on abortion, led campaigns to protect our precious environment, pushed for public and active transport and opposed the government's privatisation agenda. It was time to step up the fight in federal politics. The resurgence of the far right and the normalisation of the politics of hatred had me especially worried. I wanted to take my energy and activism to challenge those who enable racism face to face in the Senate. I wanted historically silenced voices to be heard in the highest office. If only those outride who were so quick to slander me had taken the time to talk to me, perhaps they would have understood.

For me, this was an unexpectedly harsh lesson in the cutthroat nature of politics. The sad thing was that it wasn't even a factional fight, as happens often in political parties. It taught me a few things. When it comes to power and privilege, few are willing to let go, even if it advances the marginalised. We still have some way to go in my own party, to say nothing of those outside who unreservedly drum up divisions, fuel racism and undermine progressive movements.

Yet it was equally a lesson in hope. There were enough Greens people who had championed my bid for the Senate. They helped with strategy and campaigning. Most of all, they provided me with the emotional support that convinced me I was worthy. In the end, a majority of Greens members did believe in my ability and agency, and I won the preselection with a big margin—I took 60.7 per cent of the vote, to be precise.

When I received the news, I was in Coffs Harbour speaking on preventing domestic violence at a public event. After a few very difficult months as I'd tried to reconcile myself to the hostility coming from some within my own party, I was overwhelmed by this show of support from grassroots members. In fact, whenever I meet members across New South Wales and Australia, I know there are more than enough people of goodwill in my party whose understanding is much deeper than the 'shallow understanding' Dr King wrote about. It is their commitment to walk the walk that gives me optimism for the future.

For years after coming to Australia, I ignored or kept quiet about the racism my family and I were subjected to. First, I thought it was me: I must have done something wrong. Then I gave the benefit of the doubt to the insulter, thinking that once they got to know me, they'd change their mind. Underlying these justifications of staying silent was my overwhelming desire not to make trouble. Life was hard enough after migrating here. Now I know it wasn't ignorance—it was racism. I wish I had spoken out then.

I wish I had challenged my employer when they offered me an entry-level engineering job, even though I had a master's and a PhD in engineering and years of experience. Instead, I accepted a job that was well below my level.

I wish I had questioned why I had to sit a written English exam as part of a job interview for a position of environmental engineer at a local council, given that I spoke and wrote fluent English. Instead, I sat the exam.

I wish I had said 'Fuck off' to the real estate agent who asked me three times if I was aware of the high rent of the townhouse I wanted to inspect, her voice getting louder each time. Instead, I smiled politely and took the keys that she was so obviously reluctant to hand to me.

I wish I had set up a meeting with my son's high school principal when another kid screamed at him to go back to Afghanistan. This happened soon after 9/11. My son was in Year 8 and was giving a speech at the school assembly. Instead, I let it go.

I wish, I wish, I wish . . . Instead, instead, instead . . . I do regret not calling out the racism then. I so wanted to fit in, to be an Australian, to be one of 'us'.

Staying quiet back then just delayed the inevitable 'othering' that came anyway when I did find my voice. It was simmering beneath the surface of 'multicultural Australia', where your Australianness is conditional. It is conditional as long as you keep your head down, your mouth shut. It is conditional on you remaining grateful for being let in. It is conditional on you agreeing with those who hold power. It is conditional as long as you assimilate and give up your own identity.

I find this version of multiculturalism merely skin-deep. Its value is measured only in the economic advantage Australia gets from migrants through our skills, food, culture and trade connections with our ancestral countries. There is no quid pro quo.

Australian multiculturalism requires that we have to justify our existence here by the currency of our contributions. But even that currency is limited. We are tolerated while we remain cogs in the wheels of the economy, doing the jobs that no one else will. This view was expressed clearly when former senator David Leyonhjelm thanked 'Australia's young brown men' for driving him in Ubers, delivering his pizza and serving him at his local 7-Eleven. He may have thought this was a virtuous speech, but to me it was patronising and condescending.

Migrant workers employed in 7-Eleven stores have been systemically exploited: they work in casual jobs under terrible conditions, and they are routinely underpaid and threatened. Many 'gig economy' drivers are migrants on temporary visas and international students. Poor industrial conditions and low wages make this work dangerous, as workers drive themselves to exhaustion, making just enough money to survive, while the companies they work for bank big profits. At the end of 2020, at least five food delivery drivers were killed on the road—four in Sydney alone.[25]

Governments can't wipe their hands clean either. Excluding these workers on temporary visas from welfare support during the COVID-19 pandemic forced more of them to continue working during a highly precarious time. If self-appointed white saviours really want to show gratitude, they could fight for the rights of these workers. We get platitudes, but too often issues of systemic racism and chronic labour exploitation are swept under the carpet.

If we bring our parents here, that becomes an economic drain on the country. We become a liability at times of crisis and are left to fend for ourselves. Politicians court us as voting blocs, but we disappear in parliaments. They've befriended us by enthusiastically sharing our food and culture, but we are really just photo opportunities during Diwali and Eid. They've taken what we offer willingly, but not given back.

If Australia is to truly become the 'greatest multicultural country', then we must recognise the intrinsic value of cultural preservation as an essential part of the fabric of the nation. We must understand that maintaining and enhancing individuals' connections to their culture and language enriches us all. And at the core of this change must be recognition and respect for the oldest culture in the world.

A multicultural country is anti-racist and feminist: racism and the patriarchy are systems designed to accumulate power and privilege. We can't just wish them away: their dismantling has to be deliberate.

I speak out on racism and sexism because it is the first step in the process of tearing down structures of white power that entrench inequalities. I don't do it to claim victimhood. I don't want sympathy. It doesn't make me feel good. I don't want others to feel bad. It is simply an expression of truth. It is voicing the experiences of others like me who don't have the public platform I have. It helps others speak out. I know what it's like not to have a voice. I will never be silenced again.

***

Receiving and exposing hate is exhausting. The vicious insults and threats grind me down. Over the years, I've tried many different ways to deal with the vitriol, from ignoring it to reporting it and highlighting some of the worst examples, sometimes with a touch of humour.

A year into my political journey, the abuse was becoming unbearable. Moderating the Facebook comments alone was becoming a full-time job for my staff. Abusive phone calls were taking a toll on our health. Something had to be done. Most people I confided in were completely unaware of the abuse, or were in total disbelief. Some, usually those who will never feel the sting of structural oppression, dismissed these online manifestations of racism as inevitable and ineffective. Well, they may have been inevitable, but they were damaging us. Ignoring them wasn't going to stop that. Nor would it stop them.

At a strategic planning day, my team and I decided that we shouldn't cop all this silently. We agreed that 'don't feed the trolls' may be heartfelt advice from allies, but for us it was not an option. Staying quiet wouldn't make them go away; in fact, it gave them exactly what they wanted: their voice, our silence. We decided to fight back. So we launched 'Love Letters to Mehreen', a comeback to the filth we got.

Every few weeks, we would pick a particularly hate-filled message (sadly, there were plenty to choose from) and respond to it in a humorous way. It was a mix of taking the piss and treating this racist rubbish for the crap that it was . . .

To Mitchell, who asked, *'How the fuck has a muslim been let into AUSTRALIAN POLITICS'*, I offered: *'Hi Mitchell, I know, right . . . one minute it's White Australia and then BAM!'*

When Trudy said, *'We don't need muslim sluts in government!'*, I replied: *'Worth a shot, I reckon, can't be worse than the current lot!'*

My response to Raymond's question—*'is that why these dirty paki Indian pricks are here taking aussie jobs because of this qant of a thing?'*—was: *'Dear Raymond, I'm guessing they aren't taking your job as chief spellchecker . . .'*

When Jamie expressed his disagreement—*'Mehreen I think we disagree on two key points and that's killing greyhounds to save them doesn't make sense and muslim immigration to Australia was the worse thing since small px'*—I had to be honest and say, *'Dear Jamie, I have a hunch we would disagree on more than that.'*

To Jack's confused comment *'Good looks is not enough. Swearing on the bible makes you an MP. Swearing on the quoran doesn't make anyone living here an Australian. Drain the swamp,'* I responded, *'I'm not sure what charm school you went to, but you sure have a funny way of flirting . . .'*

The Love Letters really took off. They struck a chord with people who had been on the receiving end of racist comments but had suffered in silence. It allowed people often oblivious to racist abuse an insight into being a woman of colour in public life. I think people really appreciated the sassy, tongue-in-cheek retorts. They could have a light laugh as well as witness the seriousness of the abuse.

An unexpected outcome of the Love Letters was the willingness of people to push back on the abusers on my Facebook and Twitter. They helped develop a community of supporters willing to back me up, which I took as an assurance that people really do care. Of course, it was also quite cathartic for me and my staff to take control back from the abusers. The project became so successful that we produced a series of mugs, which we sold to raise money for the Asylum Seekers Centre in Sydney.

A few months after launching Love Letters, I did an interview with the BBC about racism in Australia and the project. I knew there would be consequences. Sure enough, a few days later, there it was, a full-page attack piece in the *Daily Telegraph* with the headline 'Greens MP in a race to the bottom'. That was my punishment for dragging Australia's racist underbelly out of the shadows and into the light. The article now hangs on a wall in my office. It is a memento of the hate-driven politics of the right, which will always target you when you respond to bigotry and xenophobia. It is a visible reminder of the cost of speaking up. More than anything, it encourages me never to stay silent. The resistance to my presence only makes me louder and bolder.

While my journey into the Australian parliament was unexpected, when I entered politics I was certain that I would be myself. I am proud of my Muslim, Pakistani and Australian identity. I made a conscious decision to wear colourful Pakistani shalwar kameez as often as possible. It is part of who I am. It is part of my identity. Perhaps, most of all, the mischievous rebel in me wants to jolt politicians into seeing the world outside their periphery, which is not as pale, male and stale as it is inside. I didn't realise the full impact of my decision until I started getting messages like these from people of South Asian background from all around the world:

'I love it so much when you wear shalwar kameez in parliament. I see my reflection in you.'

'When I see you proudly wearing a Punjabi dress in the Senate, I know I'm represented.'

Representation, in all its forms, matters. It is important to be who you are.

MUSLIM, BROWN AND PROUD

I don't hold back. I tell it like it is. Perhaps that's one of the reasons politics has not been easy for me. No pathway into politics is ever easy, I imagine, but when the system is stacked against you because you look different, or because you are different, the obstacles multiply. We don't have role models to look up to. There were no politicians that looked like me. We have to jump through many extra hoops in our own political parties simply to validate our legitimacy. Then we have to prove ourselves to the electorate in ways that others never have to. I've had doors shut in my face. I've been told I have no right to be in Australian politics because I'm 'not even from here'.

Well-wishers have often said, 'Develop a thicker skin, Mehreen.' I tell them I don't want to grow a thick skin. I'd rather suffer pain and be disappointed when the going gets tough than lose my sensitivity and vulnerability. I don't want to become immune to the needs and feelings of the people I represent.

The idea that people like me, who are not seen as 'real' Aussies, should just get on with their work stoically and feign indifference to the volleys of abuse that come our way denies us our right to feel just like anyone else does. It is not good enough to tell us to grow a thick skin, or to ignore it and it will go away. It is not good enough to acknowledge the existence of racism and then shrug your shoulders and walk away. It is not good enough that we have lukewarm allies who are unwilling to let people of colour determine our own fate. It is not good enough to make excuses for racism, whether it is because people are ignorant, or because they are going through economic hardship. And it is definitely not good enough for people to use their privilege to sideline us while they speak on our behalf, no matter how great that makes them feel.

Young women of colour tell me how good they feel about seeing someone like themselves in parliament. Migrants tell me they hear their story in mine. Alongside these feelings, they express their hesitation about following in my footsteps for fear of being vilified the way I am. Why would you get involved in a system where you risk being routinely publicly shamed and stigmatised because of who you are and what you look like?

I'm here to tell you: we must take that risk. In order to change the face of Australian politics, we have to stop waiting for our turn. No one will roll out the red carpet for us. We must roll up our sleeves and get to work.

I want to make it easier for people like me to make the journey I've made. I want to smash down the doors that have been so tightly shut to us. I hope at least to push them ajar.

5

THREE DECADES AN ENVIRONMENTALIST

—

I start writing about the environment by acknowledging my deep-seated respect for the extensive histories, cultures and connection of First Nations people with nature. Many of us are now waking up to what indigenous peoples around the globe have known for thousands of centuries—the deep and dynamic connections between humans and their environment.

My own love affair with nature started early in my life. My favourite two weeks of most school summer holidays were spent in the Kaghan Valley, in the foothills of the majestic Himalayas. We would pile into Abbu's sky-blue Toyota Corona and head out to the mountains. From the valley we could see the tall, snow-covered peaks of Chogori (K2) and Nanga Parbat. It was here I walked on glaciers, drank clear sweet water from ice-cold rivers fed by the melting snow, and saw the sky reflecting from lakes so glassy that you couldn't tell where the sky ended and the lake began. I climbed mountain slopes dense with tall pine trees, a carpet of pine needles under my feet, and breathed in the crisp air laden with their scent.

It was here that I first bonded with nature. The scenery and smells seemed to become part of my DNA. If I close my eyes, I can see the snow and smell that fresh pine as if I was back in Kaghan. My childhood memories have not faded at all, and my love for nature has only become fiercer. The reckless ruining of the natural world makes me furious. I don't have the spirit of compromise when it comes to the environment.

Scientists tell us that even if we limit global warming to 1.5 degrees Celsius, more than 30 per cent of glaciers along the Himalayan mountain range, including in my beloved Kaghan Valley, will disappear by the end of this century.[1] Once the snow vanishes, so will the rivers it feeds, and the millions of people in Pakistan, India and other countries who rely on them for farming and food. Mighty nature won't disappear with a whimper, though. When the snow melts, it will first cause havoc by flooding rivers and lakes, bursting their banks. It will consume the habitat of the endangered Barfani cheetah, or snow leopard, who has survived the harsh conditions of these rugged mountains over millennia but may not live through human destruction of nature.

And the destruction and exodus have already started. Lives are being lost. Villages have disappeared. Communities of people who've lived, worked and played in the shadows of these majestic mountains are being uprooted, forced to start again in new places, their connection to land and water severed forever.

I fear that if we don't take radical action right now, those snow caps and glaciers on the Himalayas will disappear, never again to be experienced except in memory. The snow leopard will be gone. People and cultures will be gone.

The tragedy of the melting Himalayan snows is as real to me as the tragic mass fish kill in the Baaka (Darling River), near Menindee, a place I visited for the first time just a few years ago. I was in the far west of New South Wales in early 2019 just after hundreds of thousands of fish choked to their death. I saw stagnant rivers and cracked dry earth. I saw emaciated kangaroos trying to find shelter from scorching heat, poisoned after drinking the algae-ridden river water. I felt the 50-degree heat as I met with locals, themselves hot with anger at governments that have sided with the big corporate irrigators and turned a blind eye to the slow death of this precious ecosystem. I met with Barkindji elders who have been dispossessed of their water rights since colonial invasion, and could trace the destruction of the ecosystem right back to that moment.

At Menindee, science tells us, the lack of water, poor water quality and a fluctuation in water temperature resulting from extremely hot days followed by a cool change killed the fish. But behind the science of any crisis lies its politics. Inaction to tackle the climate crisis has exacerbated drought conditions and caused record high temperatures. Gross mismanagement, incompetence, overallocation of water and corruption have pushed the Murray-Darling river system to the brink of destruction. State and federal governments have turned a blind eye to blatant water theft by irrigators, which has robbed the river system of its lifeblood, the environmental flow of water that sustains the ecosystem. The town of Walgett in New South Wales was forced to rely for months on groundwater with sodium levels fifteen times higher than the drinking water guidelines specify because the rivers had run dry.[2] Aboriginal communities have been deprived of their cultural connection with water—indeed, their rights and the rights of nature have been completely obliterated—while the demands of big irrigators are fulfilled. The already miniscule Aboriginal water entitlements in the Murray-Darling Basin keep declining,[3] as First Nations voices have been shut out of water sharing discussions.[4]

The Murray-Darling stands as a prime example of the way nature is exploited across the globe. Over the years, it seems, as Earth's biodiversity dwindles, we are doomed to keep repeating our mistakes.

Time and time again we have seen the environment used and abused for what it can give us—minerals, coal, oil, gas and wood. But as with all things in life, whose air, whose water and whose land gets degraded as the earth is dug up, as ocean beds are drilled and forests are chopped down, depends on who you are and where you're from. Race, class and gender all play a part in the distribution of environmental impacts, with poor people, Indigenous communities, people of colour and women bearing a disproportionate burden of the environmental destruction.

The centrality of nature to life and the intersection of environmental, racial and social justice have driven me for most of my life. The year 1992 kickstarted my journey into environmentalism. Since then, I've lived and breathed the environment in my studies, in my teaching, in my engineering, in my work as a consultant and local government engineer, and in my politics.

I started my master's degree in water and waste management two days after I arrived in Australia. It was then that I met someone who has played an instrumental role in feeding my hunger to learn more about nature, and in nourishing my ability to protect it. Dr Ronnie Harding was one of my lecturers. She is a pioneer in environmental education. Ronnie started the Institute for Environmental Studies at UNSW a few months after I started there. It's where, a decade later, I got my dream job teaching environmental management.

A colleague and I co-wrote a book with Ronnie exploring the complexities and contestations of environmental decision-making. She taught me some valuable lessons about being true to myself and not fearing being challenged. For her, admitting to mistakes and not knowing the answer to every question asked in class were not weaknesses—that was part and parcel of how we learn. Above all, she helped me to realise the value of the knowledge others have, whether it is people's intimate knowledge of their local area, or traditional Indigenous knowledge built up over centuries, or knowledge acquired through research and inquiry. Many people will have known a teacher who lit a spark of passion in them, or rekindled a flickering flame to its full burning potential. For me it was Ronnie.

The year I migrated to Australia and started my postgraduate studies was also the year of the 1992 United Nations Conference on Environment and Development, dubbed the Rio Earth Summit. I was swept along by the promise of this mega conference, which aimed to bring the world together in a united purpose to protect the environment and those who depend on it. The new concept of sustainable development—which the UN defines as 'development that meets the needs of the present without compromising the ability of future generations to meet their needs'[5]—fit in neatly with my philosophy of environmentalism. The notion of reconciling economic development with environmental protection was appealing to me. I hoped that we would finally be on the road to addressing social, economic and environmental justice by recognising the needs of communities who had suffered the worst impacts while gaining little of the wealth from the Earth's exploitation. I was hoping, too, that the abuse itself would be reined in as we realised the unsustainable trajectory we were on.

Sadly, I underestimated the power of the capitalist system and the vultures within it who will rape and pillage nature for every last dollar it can add to the billions they have already accumulated. I overestimated the will of weak governments and greedy politicians hungry for political donations who so easily capitulate to vested interests. Three decades after the Rio Earth Summit, inequality between and within nations is rising, climate change is exacerbating and the environment is in steep decline. And 'sustainable development' has become the oxymoron its critics said it appeared to be from the very start.

The no-holds-barred neoliberal capitalist system of profit and wealth hoarding at the expense of the planet continues unabated. The global North's insatiable appetite for industrial and economic growth has rapidly depleted nature, and then the environment has been used as a dumping ground for the excesses of their rampant consumption. Greenhouse gases and toxic fumes spew endlessly into the air. Land, rivers and oceans become receptacles for poisonous waste from stuff we make and stuff we then throw away.

This relentless mistreatment of nature continues even as there is acknowledgement that its consequences should be addressed. However, how these consequences are addressed is narrow and simplistic. Environmental issues are framed as isolated bio-physical problems, and fixing them is by and large limited to technical solutions which only treat the symptoms, leaving the underlying causes to persist. Attempts to manage the environment by controlling the discrete symptoms of its degradation, while ignoring harder-to-fix 'wicked' problems like unbridled resource consumption and wealth accumulation, is only exacerbating both the environmental crisis and the inequality crisis.

My view is that unless we try to understand the complex and dynamic interactions between social and ecological systems, the uncertainties involved, and their moral dimensions and context-dependent nature, we are destined to keep going around in circles, misconstruing the problem and producing mismatched solutions.

After the historic Rio Earth Summit, hopes were high as key agreements like the Convention on Biological Diversity and the Framework Convention on Climate Change (a precursor to the Kyoto Protocol) were set up. It felt like the world was getting its shit together. The principles of intergenerational and intragenerational equity, conservation of biodiversity and the precautionary principle were institutionalised in the legislation and policies of nations around the world. Back then, Australia was leading the pack. We added the term 'ecological' to 'sustainable development' to ensure that environmental needs remained the focus. We quickly enacted laws and agencies to protect nature.

Embarrassingly, we have now become laggards. I was made acutely aware of this shame when I attended the 2012 United Nations Conference on Sustainable Development, known as the Rio+20 Earth Summit. I longed to recapture some of the hope of its predecessor two decades earlier. When other attendees found out I was from Australia, they asked me why we were still arguing about whether climate change was real or not when the rest of the world had moved on and was debating what strategies would best mitigate global warming, or better prepare us for its consequences. I really had no explanation other than to acknowledge the wilful ignorance of our decision-makers, who had not accepted the science and were unwilling to make any change.

More recently, Australia's lack of ambitious action on climate lost us an invitation to speak at the Climate Ambition Summit in late 2020. This snub from the international community did not, however, spur Prime Minister Morrison into any serious action to cut carbon emissions; rather, he brushed it off by dismissing the importance of the summit.[6]

Even worse than lagging behind, we have become blockers. In 2019, at the United Nations Climate Change Conference (COP25) in Madrid, Australia tried to block global climate action by insisting on using Kyoto carry-over credits to meet its Paris Agreement climate targets.[7] Attempting to use these credits in this way is like a student insisting that they can use anything above a pass mark in one subject to compensate for lower marks in another, and therefore pass both. It doesn't quite work like that. Australia was the only country trying to use this dodgy accounting trick rather than committing to real action.[8] The government only agreed to drop these carryover credits when it was sure it wouldn't need them—not because it had a concrete plan to reduce emissions, but because catastrophes like the drought and COVID-19 had largely done the work of emissions reduction.

TOO MIGRANT, TOO MUSLIM, TOO LOUD

I'm not surprised by Australia's reversal from leader to laggard. In 2018 we got a prime minister in Scott Morrison who not only brought a hunk of coal into parliament, but brought the coal lobby right into his inner circle by appointing a former deputy CEO of the Minerals Council of Australia and Rio Tinto's lead lobbyist as his chief of staff. What a victory for the fossil-fuel lobby, while the planet cooks and burns.

The fossil-fuel industry has waged a decades-long misinformation campaign to prevent climate action, with the likes of Exxon and Shell hiding the effects of carbon pollution from fossil fuels in the 1980s.[9] Now that environmental concern is rising among the public, corporations continue with business as usual, only with much more sophisticated 'greenwashing', expensive advertising that diverts attention from their environmentally destructive practices and breaches of environmental laws.[10]

We often think about natural disasters as 'acts of god'. But they aren't always. In many cases they are acts of mankind, and specifically of greedy corporations. The acceleration in the severity and intensity of natural disasters is directly linked to the anthropogenic climate change driven by carbon pollution, to which corporations have been the major contributors. As *Newsweek* noted in 2020, 'A report from Carbon Majors . . . found that just 100 companies since 1988 were responsible for 70 percent of the world's greenhouse gas emissions.'[11] Many of these corporations not only knew they were contributing, but actively discouraged climate action to protect their profits. We shouldn't shy away from labelling them as environmental vandals.

If there is one example of corporate brutality that illustrates the lengths an unrestrained profit-obsessed corporation will go to, it is the human and environmental damage caused by US company Union Carbide to the people of Bhopal, India. On 3 December 1984, 40 tonnes of toxic gas leaked into the atmosphere from the Union Carbide pesticide plant. Amnesty International estimates that at least 7000 people died in the first three days, and about 25,000 have died since. Another 500,000 have lingering health problems. More than three decades on from this industrial disaster, the polluted air and groundwater are still poisoning the people of Bhopal. Gas-exposed victims are more likely to die from diseases such as cancers, lung and kidney disease, women have been particularly adversely affected, and many children whose parents and even grandparents were exposed that fateful night are affected by disabilities.[12]

After fighting tooth and nail, this American multinational paid out US$470 million in compensation. This paltry sum translated to only US$2200 per victim and completely ignored intergenerational impacts.[13] The site remains unrehabilitated and the company refuses to accept liability. The CEO was wanted on homicide charges by the Indian government, but the US government refused to extradite him. He died at age 92 in a Florida nursing home. Union Carbide was bought out, then merged and remerged to become part of Dow Inc., a company now worth tens of billions. While long-term environmental generational damage and trauma for thousands of people continues, there has been little accountability for those responsible for the deadly consequences, or justice for the victims.

It's no wonder we are in the midst of ecocide. The environment is being killed. It is being done deliberately. This destruction is not an aberration or a one-off. It is systematic, and it happens again and again. The killers know full well the amount of human, environmental and economic wreckage they are leaving behind, but they are willing to gamble that the money they make will protect them from the worst effects—a luxury not extended to most of the world's population.

I for one have decided not to take this lying down.

**

By the time I finished my master's degree in 1994 I knew I wanted to be fully armed as a warrior for nature. I moved straight on to a doctorate in environmental engineering. I did my PhD in the Cooperative Research Centre (CRC) for waste management and pollution control at UNSW. I found my people at this place. It was a mini-UN, with researchers from Jordan, China, Sweden, Germany, India and more. I made ever-lasting friendships. It was these friends and the endless cups of coffee we shared that helped me get through the tough technical puzzles and the emotional highs and lows that a PhD brings, especially when you're doing it with two young children, one of whom was born midway through my research. This place was my haven for five years.

The CRC Program was set up by the Hawke/Keating government in 1991 to improve and strengthen collaboration between research organisations like universities and industry. It was conceived against the backdrop of a decline in Australian industry and manufacturing in the 1980s, with the aims of boosting innovation and diversifying the economy, which had been largely dependent on resource extraction and agriculture.[14] We didn't quite get there: 30 years on, Australia is still grappling with the loss of manufacturing, as we've mourned the end of car manufacturing and the closure of Newcastle's steel industry, and with them the painful loss of thousands of jobs.

COVID-19 has brought into sharp focus the need to reboot Australian manufacturing. If done right, a sustainable manufacturing sector can offer good wages and decent jobs that value workers. It can open new frontiers in regional Australia and the chance for a just transition from polluting and dangerous work in the coal industry to work that has a more caring purpose for people and the planet. New opportunities can range from micro factories and social enterprises to large-scale advanced manufacturing.

The authors of the research report *Beyond Business as Usual: A 21st Century Manufacturing Culture in Australia* explain the importance of building a more just and environmentally sustainable manufacturing sector which provides decent jobs in an inclusive society and production with a small ecological footprint.[15] They provide existing examples of social enterprises, cooperatives, public companies and private companies that are using these values to manufacture quality products, provide employment and serve the interests of the public and the environment.

For me as an engineer, the prospect of remaking manufacturing while simultaneously addressing sustainability is exhilarating. As a politician, I know genuine leadership and political will is needed to underpin a manufacturing renaissance that will reject the past mistakes of corporate centralisation and market-driven visions to put the public, workers and the environment at the heart of any enterprise.

The CRC program was not quite the panacea for boosting industry, but for me it did provide the opportunity of a decent stipend and work as a research assistant. I was thankful for that as I donned my floppy hat and stepped on stage to receive my PhD degree as my four-year-old daughter, nine-year-old son and husband proudly watched on.

Knowingly or unknowingly, we had all made sacrifices. My daughter was just four months old when she started part-time childcare at the centre I had helped set up. I would go there a few times a day to breastfeed her. There was always frozen breastmilk I had pumped the night before, in case I couldn't make it there in time. My internal struggle between what seemed like two competing priorities—my responsibility as a mother and my ambition/passion as an individual—was ongoing. Looking back, I don't think I would have, or could have, done anything differently, except perhaps not study. I've never reconciled the guilt I've carried for being the mother who wasn't always there for her children, because many times that void was filled by my husband or the wonderful early learning and childcare workers for whom I will be eternally grateful. We try to do our best in the situations we are in. Only time shows us if we have succeeded.

After completing my PhD, I was tempted to stay on and find a job teaching at uni. After all, that had been my dream. But as a student I'd benefited most from those teachers who had experiential knowledge of the theories they taught, compared with those who only knew the theory. I had formed a strong view that to be a good teacher, you needed practical experience in those areas you were lecturing in. And so, reluctantly but resolutely, I extricated myself from the comfort of my familiar uni life to launch myself into unknown territory—what my husband described as the real world. So began my career in consulting and local government.

The experience I was seeking in environmental management was delivered in spades, first at Port Macquarie-Hastings Council and then later at Mosman Council. It was in these community-focused workplaces that I was able to put into practice the principles of ecological sustainability I'd studied.

I was the first environmental engineer ever hired at Port Macquarie Council, and had the flexibility to make the role my own. And I did not miss the opportunity, I can tell you. The sheer variety of work—from stormwater reuse projects to rainforest rehabilitation, from environmental education to estuary management, from environmental art festivals to cycling infrastructure—meant my cache of real-world experience expanded quickly. My work took me all around the Mid North Coast, enabling me to explore the natural beauty of the coast and the hinterland. For me, the science and engineering have always been the easy bits. Their application and interaction with the social and natural systems to improve lives and the environment is the real challenge.

It might be a cliché to say that councils are the level of government closest to the people, but it is true. Working with the community became a central plank of my professional ethos. Involving people in environmental decisions was fulfilling in so many ways. I now know that solutions, or resolutions, to the many wicked challenges we face today will come only through collective decision-making, through debate and deliberation among people who hold a diversity of views. And we have to navigate our way through these conflicting views, by facilitating open dialogue and clarifying values and views, not hiding from them.

The people I worked with shared their local knowledge generously. They were also willing to learn from the expertise of others. Most of all, I loved that the community had engaged in decisions that affected them and their surrounds, and their contributions had enhanced the outcomes.

As the saying goes, all good things come to an end, and so did this role. If you are lucky, sometimes even better things come along. And I was: a lecturing job in sustainability and environmental management at UNSW came up.

THREE DECADES AN ENVIRONMENTALIST

When people hear about my environmental journey and professional career in sustainability, they nod knowingly and say, 'Ah, now I understand why you joined the Greens.' I love that my party is seen as synonymous with environmental care. But it is frustrating that we are pigeon-holed as a single-issue party that only cares about one thing—the environment. That's not how I see it.

I have always seen the environment as so much more than 'one thing'. I don't see social and environmental problems as discrete. When you live with nature, you start to see it as a system with many interacting parts, which cannot be detached. The unprecedented fires, floods and droughts unfolding across the world as a result of human-induced global warming, and the devastated communities and environments left in their wake, shows just how inseparable anthropogenic and ecological processes are. Every aspect of our lives affects our environment, and every aspect of the environment affects our lives.

The reality is that the environment is at the beginning and end of everything. That's why philosophies that elevate the 'rights of nature' resonate with me. I want to protect the environment for its intrinsic value, not just for what it can give us. Nature was here long before we arrived. We must learn to live as a part of nature, not apart from it.

By contrast, the very human-centric Western worldview holds that we humans have a 'right to nature'. It is galling to me that humans' exertion of our superiority over the environment makes it a mere means to satisfy our ends. Where

I see magnificent trees to be hugged and protected for glossy black cockatoos and powerful owls, developers see highrise buildings flashing with dollar signs. Where I see beautiful bush resplendent with koalas, kangaroos, eastern water dragons and grey-headed flying foxes, greedy corporations see logging and mining profits. Where I see opportunities to connect with nature, hear the birdsongs and enjoy the sounds of the rainforest, governments beholden to vested interests see the cash flowing from political donations. But the value of nature cannot be monetised. It must be taken beyond the limits of economics and into the spheres of justice and morality.

The environment is resilient, but we've stretched it beyond its limits. Nature has had enough. It is biting back, and its wrath is impacting humanity indelibly.

Shouldn't protecting nature, then, be the ultimate act of selfishness? It seems counterintuitive to take a human-centric approach that harms people. After all, if our wellbeing, indeed our survival, depends on the purity of the air we breathe, the availability and quality of the water we drink, and the health of the soils which grow the food we eat, shouldn't we be nourishing the environment, not killing it? The disconnect between our actions and their consequences seems illogical—until you figure out whom the actions are benefiting and who is bearing the consequences.

It is the rich and powerful, and mainly white people, who profit from the abuse of the environment, while poor people and people of colour suffer disproportionately. Unjustly, those facing the first and worst impacts of environmental degradation did not contribute substantially to the problem either. To make the injustice worse, those who reap the benefits from nature's destruction also have the means to shield themselves from the effects of their handiwork. As the crisis worsens, it is creating a climate and environmental apartheid, where the privileged can afford to adapt while the marginalised are left to contend with the burdens.

The environment might be the most obvious connection that led me to the Greens, but the truth is I was motivated to join the party because of its focus on social *and* environmental justice, both in Australia and around the world. I saw the Greens as the only political party outspoken on justice for First Nations people, migrants and refugees in this country, and for people of colour and marginalised communities beyond our borders. These are the communities that are facing severe racial, economic and environmental inequalities.

I am so tired of hearing that 'nature does not discriminate'. Sure, there are no natural boundaries between society and the environment, but geopolitical boundaries do divide the world into the global South and the global North. These arbitrary lines drawn by colonialists in London, Paris and Washington have been the genesis of so many international conflicts and humanitarian disasters, and of the environmental racism borne by those who live in the global South. These patterns of systemic discrimination continue, as the impacts of climate change, natural disaster and pollution fall disproportionately on them. Climate breakdown, in particular, looms large on the landscape of global inequality.

Pacific Islanders have water lapping at their doorsteps. Their homelands are sinking as their very existence is threatened by sea level rise, flooding and coastal erosion. The world is cooking as global warming causes temperatures to rise. In 2015, extreme heat killed 800 people in Pakistan.[16] Entire villages have been swept away by waters gushing down from melting glaciers. Droughts, floods, fires and hurricanes have intensified across the world, but without doubt the impact on poorer nations is far greater. These places are much more vulnerable to natural disasters because they lack sufficient essential services, the resources for preparedness and the capacity for recovery, which further exacerbates the impact.

And women are at the front line of these disasters. They are more likely to die or be injured. During the 2004 Asian tsunami, three times as many women than men died.[17] Gender-based poverty and inequality magnifies the impacts of disasters such as these for women and girls. Women are often not taught survival skills like swimming or climbing, they have lower mobility because they are generally the primary care-givers for their families, and cultural constraints often decrease their ability to escape and reduce their access to shelter and health care. Following disasters, women are usually at higher risk of being placed in unsafe, overcrowded shelters, as they lack economic power in the form of savings, property or land.

In rural areas, women and girls are usually responsible for fetching water and collecting traditional fuels such as firewood for their families. With environmental degradation, these already time-consuming and physically draining tasks now take even longer, as they have to search further afield for resources. As a result, women and girls have reduced time for education, learning other skills, earning money, engaging in politics and other public activities, perpetuating the cycle of disempowerment. While women carry a disproportionate burden of a deteriorating environment, their voices go unheard as they are often excluded from decision-making.

Environmental racism isn't only inflicted on countries of the global South, of course—it is also replicated within the boundaries of nations. In Western countries, BIPOC populations are much more likely to live near hazardous waste sites, contaminated land or in neighbourhoods where they are exposed to high levels of air pollution, all of which negatively affect their health and wellbeing.[18]

Young Ella Kissi-Debrah is one tragic face of this injustice. Her life was cut short at age nine when she died in London in 2013. An inquiry in 2020 ruled that air pollution was a cause of her premature death. Ella had lived her whole life near roads that had high traffic, exposing her to excessive nitrogen dioxide emissions, which induced and exacerbated her severe asthma.[19] When Hurricane Katrina hit the US Gulf Coast in 2005, it was poor Black people living in the low-lying flood-prone areas who bore the brunt of the destruction.[20]

TOO MIGRANT, TOO MUSLIM, TOO LOUD

The water crisis in the city of Flint, Michigan, has been called the worst example of environmental injustice and racism in recent US history.[21] In a city of predominantly Black residents, the disaster that led to the poisoning of the city's water supply was left unattended for years. As a cost-cutting measure in 2014, the appointed administrator switched the city's water supply to the industrially contaminated Flint River, which lacked sufficient treatment to guard against corrosion of the city's lead pipes. For years residents' water was laden with dangerous levels of lead, and there was little to no political action despite pleas from locals about health concerns. Residents organised, they held protests and public meetings but were ignored. *The Guardian* reported on the immense toll of the water crisis: 'the rashes, the hair loss, the ruined plumbing, the devalued homes, the diminished businesses, the homeowners who left the city once and for all, the children poisoned by lead, the people made ill or killed by Legionnaires' disease'.[22] In 2020, civil proceedings culminated in a settlement worth more than US$600 million for the victims of the water crisis, and criminal investigations resulted in nine officials being charged over the deaths in 2021. But how can any settlement or conviction truly compensate for the human and environmental tragedy?

In the 1950s, the British government was given permission by the Liberal Australian prime minister Robert Menzies to conduct nuclear bomb testing in Maralinga, South Australia, leaving vast areas of land highly contaminated with radioactive carcinogenic chemicals.[23] The Maralinga Tjarutja people living on country have paid the heavy price of this experiment, which was part of Britain's effort to develop nuclear weapons. Their land and water were poisoned, they were blinded and harmed by the radiation and left with ongoing health problems, which continue even after the land has now been decontaminated and returned to them as its rightful owners.[24]

Such destruction is not a thing of the past. In 2020, Juukan Gorge, a 46,000-year-old Aboriginal site of deep historical and cultural significance, was blasted by Rio Tinto to mine iron ore in Western Australia.[25] Our weak environmental laws allowed this crime to be committed.

The history of environmental racism also taints the Western conservation movement. As white settlers ejected indigenous tribes and mobs from the land they colonised, some of that land later became national parks.[26] The first national park in the United States was created through the expulsion of indigenous people and the rural poor.[27] Even the mainstream environmental movement has largely ignored environmental justice by focusing intensely on biodiversity preservation at the expense of affected communities. Elizabeth Yeampierre, co-chair of the Climate Justice Alliance, articulates this when she criticises this movement, which was 'built by people who cared about conservation, who cared about wildlife, who cared about trees and open space . . . but didn't care about black people'.[28]

Modern environmentalism has used people of colour as scapegoats for environmental problems, especially when it comes to rising population. In Australia, environmental racism also targets migrants. This has emerged both from the conservatives and within the progressive environmental movement itself. We migrants are blamed for everything from traffic congestion to land clearing. We are told by those on the right of politics that Australia's infrastructure can't cope because there are too many migrants. We've become easy targets to hide the lack of planning by governments. The sustainable population cheerleaders want to keep us out because, apparently, the environment is being destroyed to accommodate us. At a 'Politics in the Pub' event on 'population and environment', the environmentalist on the panel (someone I knew, by the way) was concerned that when migrants came from poor countries where they have a small ecological footprint to rich countries like Australia that have a much larger footprint, they start contributing much more to environmental destruction.

What racist, skewed and perverse logic! After the discussion, that panellist approached Omar and me to assure us that we were not the migrants he was referring to. We were fine. We were the 'good', environmentally aware migrants. The hide!

The obsession with Brown and Black women's fertility is another thinly veiled racist attempt by environmentalists to blame others for the ecological crisis we are in. This is dangerous, and plays straight into far-right conspiracy theories like 'the Great Replacement', which inspired the Christchurch killer who massacred 51 innocent Muslims while they were at prayer.[29]

Is it really us migrants and people of colour who are vandalising the environment? The reality is that the ecological footprint of an Australian is more than nine times greater than someone in Bangladesh, six times more than a Pakistani, and five times greater than someone in the Philippines or Indonesia.[30] In effect, people from these countries are actually subsidising the extravagant lifestyles of those in Western countries as they cannibalise the planet and its resources. Sustainable populationists should look in the mirror before they start looking to shift the blame.

∗∗∗

The devastating climate-induced bushfires of the Australian summer of 2019–20 should have been a wake-up call. Climate scientists made it clear that climate change has made such fires at least 30 per cent more likely[31] (and probably much more). If we remain on this trajectory, around one-third of the world, including communities in Australia, will suffer Sahara Desert–like heat within half a century. Still the Morrison Coalition government refused to awaken from their climate stupor. The bushfires consumed 33 lives, more than 2000 homes and many more livelihoods. One of the lives lost was that of my dear friend Daintry Gerrand's sister, Julie Fletcher, of Johns River. In Daintry's own words, this is what was lost:

The farm was Julie's peaceful space. Family and friends, past and present, enjoyed this tranquil tidal reach of the Stewarts River, the finger of agricultural land bounded by river, by lake and national park estate. Julie's death was a traumatic event—she lost her life to an apocalyptic combination of fire and wind.

My family and I were some of those friends who had enjoyed Julie's peaceful place. It was deeply heartbreaking to visit the remains of the home their dad had built with his own hands and ingenuity. It was still tranquil, but I can never forget the tumult of what had occurred there. It lay there in the piles of rubble and ashes. This is what the climate crisis looks like.

The fires engulfed more than 12 million hectares of land and killed more than a billion animals. Australia already has an unenviable record on mammalian extinctions. Thirty-five per cent of all global mammal extinctions have been in post-invasion Australia. The first mammal to go extinct because of climate change, the *Melomys rubicola*, is a little-known rodent-like mammal which lived on the Australian island of Bramble Cay. If we are not careful, the well-loved koala may be the next.

In New South Wales, if we keep going down the current path of land clearing, koalas will be extinct by 2050. It's scary to think that in my lifetime the only koalas we might see will be in a museum. It reminds me of the cuddly koala soft toy that sat proudly on our living room mantelpiece in Lahore.

THREE DECADES AN ENVIRONMENTALIST

It was a hopeful reminder that one day I might see the real thing. And I did. In fact, at our home in Port Macquarie it wasn't unusual to see one in our front yard, or hear a group of them grunting away at night. Those days are long gone. Every time I go up there now, instead of coming across a koala I see the jarring appearance of more and more fibreglass koalas adorning the streets and open spaces of Port Macquarie. This trail of one-metre-high, beautifully painted 'Hello koalas' is part of a tourism promotion. I find it rather vulgar that as the koala capital of New South Wales is losing real koalas, more fake ones are popping up.

The koala is often peddled as the iconic Australian species—it regularly adorns our international tourism campaigns—but irresponsible and greedy government decisions have pushed it to the brink. Land clearing for infrastructure, agriculture, property development and mining always seems to get the green light, at the expense of the environment. It doesn't have to be this way. We can create jobs, make life better for people and protect the environment. When weighing environmental and economic interests, the balance always tips in favour of money and profit. Approvals for bulldozing animal habitat and connection corridors are justified by a promise to protect bushland somewhere else.

All this is done under the false promise of the greatest con job in environmental regulation: biodiversity offsetting, which is no more than an accounting trick to justify destruction of nature. The biggest scam in this legal destruction of the environment is just that—the destruction of precious bush. Under this scheme, even if one piece of habitat is protected, another is killed. The net result is biodiversity loss, and it's often irreversible.

Moreover, it is not possible to assure that biodiversity in two locations is the same, or even equivalent in quality. Biodiversity offsets are often not even established before the environment is ruined. Leaked documents show that offset plans for the M7 toll road in Sydney haven't been delivered, even fifteen years after the road opened to traffic.[32] Other massive toll road projects in Sydney—WestConnex and NorthConnex—were not even required to secure offsets before endangered ecological communities were destroyed. Environmental offsets selected for the controversial Western Sydney Airport at Badgerys Creek had already been earmarked for environmental protection.[33] This double-dipping of offsets is an ongoing problem which makes a mockery of the practice. In a climate-constrained world, the destruction of bushland and the pretence of compensating for it is nothing short of criminal. But big developers and big mining companies have been given this get-out-of-jail-free card while the environment gets a death sentence.

Nature's destruction is happening at a local level when suburban bushland is chopped down to make way for a toll road or a high-rise building. For the environment it's death by a thousand cuts as the laws meant to protect it are weakened, and loopholes are left open or bypassed. Climate change, the global manifestation of this indiscriminate abuse of nature, has shot us into the Anthropocene era in the 21st century.

How did we get here?

There is no doubt that the stunning decline of the Australian environment correlates with the abysmal environmental record of European colonialism. Two centuries of colonisation have wrecked the millennia of care of country by First Nations people. We have become a deforestation hotspot of the world. It is undeniable that at the core of the climate crisis is Western extractive capitalism's incessant need to be fuelled by the spoils of nature's destruction. It views indigenous communities as backwards for living in harmony with, rather than exploiting, nature. And it has falsely entrenched itself as the only paradigm for human progress: growth at all costs. These costs have been paid by the colonised, while the benefits are gathered by the colonisers.

The story of the industrialisation of the global North cannot be separated from colonialism. The imperial colonisers ruthlessly extracted natural resources from the colonised countries to fill their coffers and feed their power and greed.[34] Their wealth was built with the resources and labour of the colonised peoples. This extractive capitalist relationship is always predicated on taking. In South Asia, it was primarily the taking of resources. In Australia, it was the bloody possession of land and culture.

The legacy of colonialism is devastating. Take British India (which included present-day Pakistan), where Britain drained a total of nearly $45 trillion during the period 1765 to 1938. That is seventeen times more than the total annual gross domestic product of the United Kingdom today. In Australian terms, that is 34 times the size of the total Australian economy.[35]

It is tempting to think of colonialism as something of the past, something no longer relevant, but the deep depravity of what it wrought may never be repaired.

In many ways, colonialism has merely transformed into extractive and exploitative global corporations that control vast swathes of the world. As Arundhati Roy says: 'Capitalism is the new empire. Capitalism run by white capitalists.'[36]

The injustices of colonialism and imperialism haven't ended. They are ongoing in the grossly unfair neoliberal trade and debt systems. They are ongoing in the incessant, self-interested attempts to control complex geopolitical conflicts in Iraq, Afghanistan and the Middle East, arrogantly ignoring that the root cause of these conflicts lies in the original Western interventions, and the economic and environmental injustices they wreaked.

They are ongoing as Australian governments hand out millions in Asia-Pacific foreign aid contracts to companies accused of 'sophisticated' bribery of public officials in those regions in which they operate.[37] They are ongoing in the way aid is viewed as advancing the national interests of countries providing development assistance, or as charity, and not as reparations for injustices of the past.

Too often foreign aid has been used to subsidise Australian

business. Too often it has ended up in the pockets of Australian companies, rather than with the people it was supposed to help. Too often aid is viewed and distributed through the lens of the 'white saviour industrial complex', which wants to feel good about helping others while obliterating the agency of those they are helping and framing them as a problem that needs to be solved. Teju Cole, who coined the term, said in a tweet: 'The White Savior Industrial Complex is not about justice. It is about having a big emotional experience that validates privilege.'[38]

I want us to reimagine foreign aid as an issue of global justice, not as a way to validate white superiority. Not as a way to further our own national ambitions, but as a way to right historic wrongs. Not as a way to further our greedy trade interests, but as a way to build communities in parts of the world that have been left destitute.

For example, TransAfrica, the United States' oldest African American human rights organisation, has advocated for slavery reparations for many years. Its president, Nicole Lee, has said: 'Countries that profited from slavery should pay reparations separate and apart from their role as donors.' Lee prefers that reparations remain its own issue, separate from aid, because its goals are different. 'Aid is important, given present circumstances, but reparations call for a deeper understanding of what is owed.'[39]

It really does take some deep thinking to recognise that inequality is not a natural phenomenon. Poverty is not an accident. Uruguayan author Eduardo Galeano recognised this, 'Poverty is not written in the stars; underdevelopment is not one of God's mysterious designs.'[40]

Just like environmental exploitation and destruction, keeping people in poverty is planned and it is deliberate. We are not poor because we were lazy or primitive. We are not poor because we lacked innovation or morals. We were, and are, cut off at the knees by the colonialists many still celebrate. Reparations for these damages is a debt owed, not a favour bestowed.

The climate debt owed by the global North to the global South only strengthens the case for reparations. Millions of people around the world who have been dealing with the climate crisis for some time don't have the luxury for us to play political football with climate change policy. They need, and deserve, action. Australia must play its part and provide reparations to affected countries and communities, commensurate with its historical and ongoing contribution to the problem. Once our coal exports are counted, we are the world's sixth-largest contributor to climate change. Every tonne of coal we ship out brings us and our neighbours one step closer to the climate precipice.[41]

Continuing to rely on fossil fuels for energy is simply not an option from an environmental or a human rights lens. If climate change continues unabated—and perhaps we have already passed the tipping point—the rich will retreat to their enclaves while the poor bear the brunt of hellish temperatures, extreme weather and the breakdown of society. We absolutely need to reduce carbon emissions rapidly if we are to have any hope of salvaging a remotely habitable world in the future, but the current trajectory of the transition to renewable energy has me torn. As an engineer, I have no doubt that transition to renewable energy must be at the heart of the great decarbonisation. But as someone who wants to change the world, I am fearful of missing the window of opportunity for us to do that in a way that tackles the root causes of injustices.

I am fearful because I'm starting to see familiar patterns of power and privilege emerge in the green economy. There is a reluctance to tackling intersectional injustices and inequalities alongside overhauling our energy systems. What is the point of simply replacing one source of energy with another if the exploitation of the planet and its peoples continues?

***

Many in the environmental movement have bought into the myth that the 'green billionaires' are here to save the world. I don't think they are. The Elon Musks, Michael Bloombergs, Jeff Bezoses and Bill Gateses and their like are simply about amassing wealth and power. This is what billionaires have always done. They are driven by profit. The environmental movement needs to understand what Erik Loomis said so succinctly: 'After all, a green capitalist is still a capitalist, who wants to profit off paying workers as little as possible.'[42]

The world cheers when people like Larry Fink, CEO of the world's largest asset manager, Blackrock, says in his annual letter to investors that the transition to renewable energy presents a 'historic investment opportunity', but we ignore the fact that Blackrock invests in pipelines that displace indigenous communities, in the deforestation of the Amazon, and in companies that make the bombs that kill children all over the world.

We can't turn a blind eye to the fact that companies that are building the renewables revolution are acting like companies always do, with disregard for the environment, workers' rights and human rights. A survey from the Business and Human Rights Resource Centre found that none of the top renewable energy companies around the world was fully meeting its responsibility to respect human rights, as defined by the UN Guiding Principles. It also found that 'when it comes to attacks on human rights defenders, the violation of indigenous people's rights and child labour, the renewable energy sector is the third-worst, coming in only behind the mining and agribusiness sectors'.[43]

There is a real risk of 'climate colonialism' locking away from communities in the global South land which is purchased by the North as carbon offsets. Poor countries cannot simply become 'offsets' to allow business as usual for climate culprits.

It is becoming increasingly clear that Western nations that overconsume massively disproportionate quantities of natural resources and have a footprint many times larger than those in the global South don't intend to change their ways even as they tackle climate change. Complex socio-political dimensions of environmental problems remain unaddressed, as do power structures like racism, sexism, neoliberalism and capitalism.

These are uncomfortable truths for the climate movement. Their focus remains, by and large, on technological solutions. Rapid transformation to renewable energy is the mantra. Fossil-fuel corporations are the enemy. I don't disagree with that—but I want more.

Equity must become the central plank of the environmental and climate justice movement. It must tackle the ecological crisis, but it must also confront the real challenge of overcoming racism, white supremacy and the structural inequalities within the environmental movement that have resulted in very different ecological realities for those living in the global North and the global South, for people of colour and for indigenous peoples across the world.

Let's not trade off justice for urgency. There's no need to. We can chew gum and walk at the same time. Let's not use the arguments against intersectionality that we've used before to justify leaving some people behind for the so-called greater good. Over and over, systemic power imbalances result in the same marginalised people being left out and behind. We must do better than that. We must demand better of ourselves. Otherwise, we are just projecting the injustices of the past into the future. Tinkering around the edges of an age-old embedded system that has helped accumulate wealth and power for the few at the expense of the many is not good enough.

To put it simply, the environmental movement must decolonise. That means transforming white-majority-led, white-majority-issues campaigns into an intersectional struggle that incorporates an understanding of and commitment to eradicating colonialism, structural racism and the other forms of systemic oppression that lie at the heart of our ecological crisis.

In addition to my fundamental commitment to justice, decolonising environmentalism is a very personal struggle for me as a woman of colour who grew up in Pakistan, once a colony of the British Empire, and later migrated to Australia, a state built on stolen land. I know that colonialism by its nature is exploitative, extractive and deliberately provokes differences between communities in order to fulfil its divide-and-rule mentality, which has subjugated people so successfully. It has left a trail of destruction, division and resentment wherever it was inflicted.

As people with colonial histories, we have internalised this destruction and oppression. We think of ourselves as the problem and look to white people to solve it. The story of Tarbela Dam in Pakistan is a classic example of this legacy of colonialism. It is the story of social and cultural displacement and dislocation.[44] One of the many conflicts created after the partition of British India was that of water rights. Rivers that flowed into Pakistan had their source in India and required an agreement between the two nations on how the water would be distributed in order to avoid future disputes. This led to the Indus Water Treaty which was brokered by the World Bank. As part of this deal, Tarbela Dam was built on the Indus River. It was funded mainly through a loan from the World Bank. The project was led by Italian, German, French and Swiss companies. It may have solved an immediate problem in the short term, but it caused long-term environmental damage and social injustice.

Thousands of acres of productive land were submerged, never to be used for farming again in a country that relies heavily on agriculture for income. More than a hundred villages were destroyed, and tens of thousands of people were displaced, dislocated and dispersed from their social networks and cultural roots, with little compensation or resettlement. Bibi, whose village was drowned when the Indus was dammed, cried as she told of her predicament: 'People see endless blue water in the lake of Tarbela that ensures light and prosperity to many people in this country, but all I see is blood of 120 villages. This is the cost of development that a whole generation of district Haripur was made to pay.'[45]

Yet Tarbela Dam is proudly touted in Pakistan as the largest earth-fill dam in the world. It's a trophy project, a World Bank experiment, and an unmitigated disaster.

People of colour are talked about, but not talked with or listened to. These are the very people who are most affected by climate change and environmental degradation. They have solutions too. They are put on the covers of the annual reports and brochures of environmental NGOs as proof of their 'charity' work, but they're not in leadership roles within their organisations, where they could be in charge of decisions that affect them. Their disproportionate environmental burdens might be acknowledged, but their calls for resources and reparations go unheard.

Decolonising environmentalism is about bringing in the people who have been historically locked out of conversations, not ignoring or erasing them. In 2020, Ugandan climate activist Vanessa Nakate was cropped out of a photo published by media, not identified in another, and identified wrongly in yet another; the other four climate activists, all white women, didn't suffer the same fate.[46] When Black and Brown faces and voices are rubbed out from the climate movement, it's environmental racism. Stop. Just stop.

Environmental history is not a single story. We must deconstruct that story. We must start telling and hearing other stories which are not predicated on the conquering of nature and of people of colour. Their voices and experiences can break down dominant white narratives. To do that successfully, we, as people of colour, have to start by decolonising our own minds. We need to throw off the subconscious shackles of colonialism, which tell us that we are not as worthy as white people. It may not be easy because so many of our minds have been captured by the dominant narrative of white supremacy, but it must be done.

I am endlessly grappling with the question of whether our movement is up to the monumental task of reshaping the way the world works, where improving conditions for the marginalised and for people of colour is a condition for climate solutions. Where we look to protect Mother Earth while simultaneously ending racial and social injustices. Or are we stuck just fiddling around the edges, embracing whatever greenwashing comes our way as a win? I worry that we are not up to this task yet, although I know that we can be.

This has to change.

The most powerful campaigns I have seen have been born in the living rooms of homes or the local pub, or simply during a chat on the phone or a yarn under a tree. They haven't come out of the boardrooms or Slack channels of the big environmental NGOs that dominate the landscape of environmentalism. More than once I have seen these big NGOs come in and take over a local grassroots campaign in an attempt to 'professionalise' it. A social movement that doesn't look like the community can't expect much buy-in from the community. It's the plain truth that at the forefront of almost every environmental organisation—the Greens included—is a white man. And we sit back and wonder why non-white communities aren't interested in what we have to say? We must build cross-racial, cross-class solidarity. We must centre the voices of indigenous people and people of colour.

Here's the thing. We cannot address global inequality without addressing racism and privilege, and without improving the condition of workers and how we treat each other. We cannot save the planet without ending the excesses of capitalism and neoliberalism. We cannot lift people out of poverty without addressing the extractive relationship that rich countries and corporations still have with the global South, which gives them open slather to rake in ever-growing profits.

Let's call a spade a spade. We are in deep shit. We don't have the time to work our way out of it gradually. Something radically different is needed. NOW.

There is a view among many environmentalists that the best hope for change may come out of a crisis. As I'm writing this book, the world is in the middle of a pandemic. COVID-19 has ravaged the world with disease, death and loneliness, savagely reminding us how closely our wellbeing is linked with the health of the environment. As industry shut down and the economy slowed, air pollution, including greenhouse gas emissions, plummeted.

Stories of bluer skies and breathable air emerged from all over the world. My mother, who was in Lahore at the start of the pandemic, told me her asthma had dramatically improved. She was breathing much easier. She saw stars in the night sky for the first time in decades, because the shield of smog that had cloaked it for so long lifted. She had never seen so many different species of birds in her garden.

It shouldn't take a crisis, let alone death and devastation, to jolt us into action. But if that is what it takes, then the deadly moment is here. It's a moment for us to show courage and draw on our wisdom, to learn from our past mistakes and make different choices now, before we have no choices left at all.

THREE DECADES AN ENVIRONMENTALIST

My two children often point the finger at me, telling me my generation is to blame for the world we're in today. One beset by climate-induced droughts, fires, floods and heatwaves, one with a deep inequality gap and rising racism. This is the world we've made for them. The generational corruption of a rampantly extractive capitalist society has brought us to where we now are.

I can't deny this hard truth. I can't hide away from the fact that young people today are faced with the possibility of being the first generation in memory to be worse off than their parents.[46]

I know that on top of the stress of economic pressures, their mental health and wellbeing is impacted by the climate anxiety they carry. But it is these very young people who give me hope as well. They are not accepting a doomsday scenario. They are staunch in the face of a government that is trying to suppress dissent. They want us to be accountable for our decisions, and responsible for protecting their future.

Young people do not buy into the bullshit of 'change is incremental', or 'we must work within the system to change it', or 'be less activist'. They actually give a shit. They are demanding and taking radical action. They are rightfully challenging and shattering the misconception that they are smashed-avo-loving, money-wasting, lazy and entitled. They have stepped up for each other and their communities— both online, on Instagram, Twitter and TikTok, and out on the streets, with the climate strikes, women's marches and the

TOO MIGRANT, TOO MUSLIM, TOO LOUD

Black Lives Matter protests. They are showing us how it's done and how things can change. Young people, particularly women of colour, are pushing through to take their place at the front and centre of these movements.

Rather than reprimanding them, blaming them for getting locked out of the housing market and misrepresenting them, let's support them as they attempt to undo some of the damage done by our generation. I owe it to them to use my position and platform to support them in speaking out and turning things around. What's needed is a revolution, on their terms. I'm ready to be a part of it. It's the least I can do.

EPILOGUE: IS IT ALL WORTH IT?

—

It's March 2021. I am devastated. I'm embarrassed. I'm angry and I'm pissed off.

My workplace, the Australian parliament—the house of the people—has been exposed as a house of violence where women are bullied, harassed and assaulted. A lid on sexism, misogyny and sexual assault has been lifted since Brittany Higgins courageously shared her story. Everyone on the outside now knows what many on the inside knew. The revelations and allegations of sexism and harassment just kept coming. I've been ashamed to work there. My skin has crawled with disgust every time I've walked in. It's hard to imagine how survivors of sexual violence must be feeling, their trauma deepened by the deflection, denial and obfuscation of the Morrison government.

I've had it up to here with women being viewed through the lens of their relationship to someone—a mother, a daughter, a wife, a sister. That makes us anonymous. It renders us invisible. We don't need to be tethered to a man for other men to not rape and harass us. We deserve to be respected for who we are in our own right. Full stop.

When thousands of angry women gathered outside parliament demanding justice, rather than showing a semblance of respect and leadership by coming out to listen to their stories, messages and demands for justice, the prime minister instead, from inside the comfort of his chamber, effectively told us we should be grateful we were not 'met with bullets'. How demeaning. How appalling. This is really hard to stomach. This tells women: *You are not heard. You are not believed. You should just shut up and get on with it*. Dangerously, it tells men: *You don't need to hear the message*.

It takes immense courage to speak your truth in a world where the perpetrators have the power and the influence. Women of colour know what that feels like. We are silenced every single day. We face the double whammy. We are silenced because we are women. We are silenced because we do not have the right skin colour. It's hard enough for any woman to speak up about bullying and harassment—for us it's even harder because of who we are. There is layer upon layer of power, privilege and hierarchy above us that we have

IS IT ALL WORTH IT?

to push through just to raise our heads—and then we have to muster further courage to speak up.

I'm so thankful that parliament is having its reckoning. Many women MPs, past and present, are speaking out about the harassment they've endured. But I can't help but wonder whether these stories would face the light of day if they did not affect the privileged. If this kind of abuse is happening to middle-class white women, imagine what is happening to those who are infinitely more exposed: the young hospitality workers who are sexually harassed in a bar or cafe, the vulnerable migrant cleaners working in insecure jobs who become easy bullying targets, the sex workers who face violence and harassment because their occupation is stigmatised. Many are people of colour. People in the community and in parliament whose stories and experiences are uninteresting to the political and media establishment. My heart yearns for the gaze of the investigators to pierce into those corners of our society, which are barely spoken about.

I know that my workplace drips with white power and privilege. I know that men occupy the corridors, cafes and chambers like they are omnipotent. I know that the name 'senate' has its roots in a Latin word meaning 'old man'. Really, that tells you all you need to know about this place.

The Australian parliament looks nothing like the world I live in. It is a lonely place for a migrant, Muslim woman of colour. It's not just the faces in parliament that matter but how the business of parliament is done. It's no secret that our parliaments are aggressive workplaces where shouting matches and sledging are the norm. You are just expected to develop a thick skin and act 'like a man'. If you don't, then you are written off or sidelined. You are forever pushing uphill to prove your worth—to be heard, to be reached out to, to negotiate with, to be friends with. You end up walking the emotional tightrope between being 'a cold-hearted bitch' and 'hysterical'.

I have worked in many places in my professional engineering career. Most of them have been dominated by white men, but none of these places were anything like parliaments, where you are laughed at, berated or considered so different that the only way colleagues can relate to you, or even talk to you about policy, is through other white people. They prefer to engage with versions of themselves. Instead of taking the opportunity to redress the power balance and have your back, sometimes even 'allies' use the opportunity to court their own relationships to influence the agenda and feel more powerful.

At other times the prejudice is apparent in condescending remarks like 'Oh, what a beautiful traditional dress you're wearing,' or being pleasantly surprised at finding out I am a civil engineer. Some days I could scream with frustration.

***

I'm under no misapprehension about the fact that I'm an outsider in this political bubble. In fact, I wear it as a badge of honour, in so far as my being here heralds a much-needed

IS IT ALL WORTH IT?

change in the make-up of representation. But being an outsider shouldn't mean you are shut out. It shouldn't mean you are laughed at almost every time you talk about sexism and racism in the chamber. It shouldn't mean that colleagues on the opposite side can tell you to go cook with cow dung like a million families on the subcontinent do, when you criticise their exuberance for expanding coalmining in a climate-constrained world. It shouldn't mean you get accused of using terrorist tactics in the chamber just for objecting to being misrepresented. Just because you don't conform with long-held practices shouldn't mean you are cast out altogether. The constant struggle of being who you are in a structure that fails to acknowledge difference, let alone respect it, has been intensified by the spotlight currently shining on the toxic culture of parliament. It has become quite overwhelming.

The moment you bring up racism and sexism publicly, or even confide quietly to a close colleague, you brace yourself. For the eye roll, for the other person to immediately provide a defence of the perpetrator. To be told that maybe you're being too sensitive. *Surely you're reading too much into it . . . they couldn't possibly mean that. I've never experienced that kind of behaviour from them, so maybe you've misunderstood their intention . . .* This sends you into a spiral of self-doubt, and sometimes you're the one who ends up apologising. On the other hand, you become overly grateful to the people who believe you and empathise with you, almost to the point of feeling indebted to them because they are such a rarity.

TOO MIGRANT, TOO MUSLIM, TOO LOUD

The amount of emotional energy we expend when confronting racism can sometimes be more than when experiencing it. We start policing our own behaviour to not be too loud, too ungrateful, too outspoken, so we can avoid further racism and sexism. And that's the very intention of oppressors. As Toni Morrison said, 'The function, the very serious function of racism is distraction. It keeps you from doing your work. It keeps you explaining, over and over again, your reason for being.'[1]

At this moment, I can't help but think: *Do I really want to be here?*

I'm reminded of questions people have asked me over the years.

Is it all worth it?

If you had to live your life again, would you change anything?

Would you choose a different path?

Questions people ask so easily.

Questions I don't have easy answers for.

Questions I often dismissed, but which suddenly have sharp pertinence.

These days, I think more about our decision to migrate from Pakistan to Australia. COVID-19 travel restrictions have plunged me into the uncertainty of not knowing when I'll see my mother or brothers or sister or daughter again, none of whom live in Australia. I've never been much of a life planner, but even if I had been and carefully filled out an Excel spreadsheet (I am an engineer, after all!) with all the pros and cons of coming to live here, the ramifications of

IS IT ALL WORTH IT?

a global pandemic wouldn't have been on it. No one could have predicted that.

Neither could I have envisaged being a politician in Australia. Nor foreseen the hate and racism that would be thrown at me once I was. I couldn't have known how infected society here was with the same sexism that I had struggled with in Pakistan. If I had known, would that have stopped me from moving here, or joining politics? Can you know these things until you experience them?

If I had known that I would be attacked just for having an opinion and saying it, a right which is afforded to many others who live here, would I have stayed quiet, head down, grateful for the opportunities my new country provided for me? Would my life be easier if I had? Would it be better? Would it be different?

So many questions. Not many answers.

But here's the thing. I've only lived my life. It is what it is. I've never had the luxury to reflect on the possibility of another life. This one took over.

None of the big decisions I made—moving countries, moving cities, having children, changing jobs, joining politics—was taken lightly. Each was made within the context of that moment in time, with the information available to us at the time. Omar and I would often allay any apprehensions we had about the final decision by convincing ourselves that we would make it work, or that most decisions could be undone. If we didn't like life in Australia, we could move back. If our move to Port Macquarie didn't work out, Sydney was always there. If politics was not for me, then I had my profession to fall back on. In hindsight, this is easier said than done. At the time, though, it was a safety net that gave us permission to make mistakes.

At times the momentum of circumstances thrust me in one direction or another. Sometimes you just go with the flow and see what's in store for you. I think not having rigid, long-term life plans has allowed me to bend easily with the twists and turns of life. I've blown with the winds of change at times, and at others I've stood in their way to protect what I hold precious from being damaged. I've never regretted my openness to being flexible, even when I've been scared of where I might end up. I've felt the fear and done it anyway. Looking back, some may have been life-changing moments but I didn't know at the time how much of my and my family's life they would change, or how.

I still find it amusing that it was in 2004 in Port Macquarie, the conservative National Party's heartland, that I joined the Greens. I'd lived in the inner west of Sydney—what's now called the Greens' heartland—for years, but the thought of joining the political party, even though I voted for them, never crossed my mind. Perhaps it was the slower pace of life in a small town that gave me the space and time to think beyond the day-to-day struggle. Perhaps it was in reaction to the lack of political debate in town that I actively sought out political people, and it was a time when my sense of the injustice being done to refugees and their harsh treatment by Australia was heightened. Perhaps it was fate that

IS IT ALL WORTH IT?

brought me in touch with the handful of Greens members in the area. One night around our dinner table, I found out that almost all of my six or seven guests were Greens members. It was meant to be! The next day I joined the Greens.

I didn't have any aspirations of becoming an MP. I relished my work as an engineer. Actually, the thought of becoming a politician never even crossed my mind. I would have quickly dismissed it if it had. I mean, what possibility was there that a Brown, migrant, Muslim woman could be in parliament. There wasn't a single person like me in any parliament in Australia! Not in my wildest imagination could I have envisioned myself there, even if I wanted it. Even years after being elected to the New South Wales Parliament, I would pinch myself while I sat in the upper house to make sure it was real, because it still felt so surreal.

Joining a political party was a big step for me. I wasn't game enough to do it on my own, so I dragged my then fourteen-year-old son and his best friend along to join with me. All I wanted was to support a political movement whose values and actions aligned with mine. It wasn't until years later, after we'd moved back to Sydney, that the notion of political representation entered my thoughts. I had my arm twisted by members of my local Greens group to run as a candidate in Heffron at the 2011 New South Wales election. Heffron was the southern Sydney seat of the Labor premier of the state, Kristina Keneally, who by a twist of fate is now my colleague in the Senate. Anyway, it was the safest Labor seat in parliament, and the

Greens had no chance of winning it. Really, that was the only reason I agreed to run!

We Greens in New South Wales run a candidate in every seat at state and federal elections, because it is an opportunity for us to engage the community in political discussion and give voters an alternative to Labor and the Liberals. We refuse to accept corporate donations, which means running campaigns on shoestring budgets with a focus on grassroots power. My campaign team of volunteers decided on door-knocking as the centrepiece of our community engagement strategy. And that is what lit the spark in me—what showed me that public service as an MP was something I really could do.

As daunting as it is, I find door-knocking the most enjoyable part of campaigning. The privilege of opening someone's front gate, knocking on their door and then having the opportunity to chat about what they want the world to be is enthralling to me. Of course, not all conversations are deep and meaningful, but door-knocking restores my faith in humanity. And the responses I've had from those whose doors I've knocked on—most of them, anyway!—has shown me that their trust in politics and politicians goes up a notch as well.

While I've had a few doors shut in my face—by people who want to have nothing to do with the 'socialist Greenies', or with someone like me 'who isn't even from here and should have nothing to do with our politics', or both—by and large people are nice. They are happy to have a chat if

IS IT ALL WORTH IT?

they have time, they take your flier, they tell you what they think needs to change, hoping you will make it an election issue, or they politely tell you, 'No thanks.' I've had invitations to come into people's kitchens to have a cup of tea, I've been offered a glass of iced water on a hot day, and someone even gave me a plant when I mentioned it was one of my Abbu's favourites. Campaigning doesn't get better than that.

So many people told me it was the first time a politician had knocked on their door in decades. This surprised me. No wonder politicians are disconnected from people's day-to-day lives. No wonder people feel taken for granted as political parties retreat from society and become more focused on the pure pursuit of power.

I'm often knocking on doors until the ban on political campaigning kicks in the evening before election day. I find it intoxicating. It is a unique but simple opportunity to meet and listen to community members directly, unfiltered, without the gatekeeping of interest groups. It's a chance to introduce your own ideas face to face rather than through social media or mass emails. These conversations have the potential to change hearts and minds, of people on either side of the door. I realised how easy I found talking with people on so many topics. I realised my life experiences over a couple of decades had provided me with the skills to relate to most people: I was a migrant, I had survived on the dole, I had worked in local government, as an academic and as an engineer, I had lived in the big city and in a small town. These conversations were exciting. I could understand people's needs and wants. I could use my experience to bring the community and their desires into the fold of political decision-making. I decided I could do this, and do it well.

We didn't win Heffron in 2011, but we increased the Greens' vote. State-wide, Labor lost the election to the Libs in a landslide. Kristina Keneally resigned soon after, and I ran again in the 2012 Heffron by-election, increasing the Greens' share of the vote. My already whetted appetite made me hungry to contest a winnable seat. When the time came, I was ready. The rest, as they say, is history. I joined the New South Wales Parliament in 2013, becoming the first Muslim woman to enter any parliament in Australia.

It did change everything.

I was thrust onto the public stage. I have never shied away from rocking the boat, but challenging the status quo of established power requires every ounce of energy you have. I diverted my emotional energy from family and friends to the project of change-making. I had less and less time with my children, my husband and my friends, unless they too were part of my political world. I didn't realise the extent to which it would impact my life and that of my immediate family.

My husband worked full-time and long hours, but now also took on most of the responsibility of running the household. Takeaway dinners became the norm (the one thing Omar can't do is cook!) and old friends slowly started drifting away. Looking back, I see I could have done some things differently. I could have tried harder to prioritise family and friends more

IS IT ALL WORTH IT?

over my work. I should have tried harder. But at the time I felt the huge load of responsibility. I wanted to make my party, my supporters and my community proud of me.

It was so unusual for someone like me to be in parliament that I didn't want them to regret their choice of me as their representative. As an outsider, I felt an overwhelming urge to prove that I was good at what I was doing. I didn't want to be the case study of a political party choosing a minority candidate, and that candidate letting them down. My reputation was at stake, but so was the reputation of community members with a similar background to mine. If I failed, their journeys into the political world might be much harder. I didn't have the luxury to make mistakes.

And, of course, I had not anticipated the extra pressure of having to prove my worth every step of the way and facing the backlash of racism. I find it very hard to draw the line between work and home. That line has always been blurry in my life—I was often on my living room floor writing my PhD thesis as my two kids ran around me; this gave me the time I needed the next morning to do canteen duty at Osman's primary school. I'm still learning to better prioritise life and work. Yet now my children are grown up and some friendships are irreparably broken.

***

Where you end up in life and what you do there is important, but for me, how you get there and how you do what you do there is even more so. In politics, more often than not, people convince themselves that it's the ends that matter, and they justify whatever means will get them those ends. Political parties do dirty deals to get support for their legislation. Politicians make promises to woo voters, promises they never intend to keep. Political candidates do the numbers, stack branches and smear their competitors to try to win that coveted number 1 spot in a winnable seat.

It matters how you get a bill to become law. Legislation should not be developed within the narrow mandates of the party of government, but with transparency, accountability and genuine public engagement.

It matters how elections are won. Not through pork-barrelling, not through promises that will never see the light of day, not through corporate donations which give the 'anointed few' undue power and influence, but through debating and deliberating on ideas in the public domain, in the view of the people who will be affected, by having convictions and being bold enough to argue and defend them but also by listening and being open to shifting your position.

It matters how candidates are selected to run for an election. Preselections through party machines or based on 'boys' club' networks or a 'do anything it takes to win' mentality chew up good people and spit them out. So many MPs have walked the well-trodden and familiar career path of coming up through the Young Labor or Young Liberal ranks, to become political staffers or lobbyists, then politicians themselves. There is very little opening for ordinary people to engage with those processes.

IS IT ALL WORTH IT?

It really does explain the blandness of our current political representatives as well. Julie Bishop claimed that the Liberal Party's 'big swinging dicks'[2] tried to thwart her career, and similar people exist to some extent across the whole political landscape. If these white, arrogant, entitled men are not trying to block and undermine you, they sure as hell won't lift a finger to support you, nor will they step aside and make space for women and other underrepresented groups. Even if they talk the talk of injustices, sexism and racism towards marginalised groups, they stop short when it comes to walking the walk. I've seen and heard too many examples of this from every side of politics, including my own. We should be more open to talking about this honestly, and not hide for fear of the criticism we'll get if we do.

To me, integrity is everything. Once you compromise on integrity, you are left flailing, lurching from issue to issue, whether it's chasing votes, preselection or legislation. A moral grounding doesn't mean you are infallible—heck, I'm far from it—but it does mean you are open, honest and critical about what you do, how you do it and who you do it with. Otherwise you are in danger of becoming the emperor with no clothes.

Even when we are committed to doing good, how we do it matters. As hard as it may be, we must interrogate how we do good. Questions like 'Why am I doing what I am doing? For whose benefit? With whom? How?' need to be asked repeatedly. We must remain acutely aware that we are there to challenge power and change its locus from the corridors of parliament to the streets of our suburbs. We must constantly remind ourselves that power draws people into its fold, no matter how virtuous their intentions. People get sucked into the wheeling and dealing. It's not all that hard to convince yourself that being in the tent is better than not being there at all, because at least you are slowly chipping away from the inside. But the tent can soon become a pretty cosy place, and people can spend decades chipping away without making much difference at all. Perhaps, if we critically reflected more, parliamentary debate would be less banal and toxic, and more an actual contest of ideas.

Being advocates for social and environmental justice doesn't mean we know all the answers, and it doesn't mean we know better than anyone else—and especially those experiencing injustice. Having good intentions doesn't give us a pass on accountability. The reality is that although we may have a burning desire to create solutions for others, these are meaningless and frankly won't work unless we work *with* the people these solutions are intended for, not simply on their behalf. That also means listening to and hearing those who have different views and interests to ours. This is not the shortest route, nor the most straightforward or easiest one. We must venture outside our comfort zone to reach out and reach across the divides of politics and political differences. I've found that when we take the risk of moving beyond our bubble, we have more in common with 'the other' than we think.

IS IT ALL WORTH IT?

The growing tendency to rely on focus groups to find out what an 'ordinary' person wants and then deliver it completely misses the point. Deep and complex issues will not be resolved by pitching to the centre, the left or the right. The recent history of voting in the United States and Europe has shown us that these paradigms have been shattered anyway. The success of populist politicians and anti-establishment parties surprised even pollsters. Politics, political positions and political allegiances are no longer set in stone; they have become more fluid. It seems that many people are no longer motivated by whole political ideologies, and are inclined to vote on issues that resonate strongly with them.

In this age of hyper-information, the messiness of politics has become even more scrambled. I think the existing bases of the old parties are shrinking and shifting. This has opened up an opportunity to talk with people who no longer fit into these traditional voting categories, but who are fearful about their futures and are looking for someone to solve their problems. It may be easier to cash in on the wave of discontent by pointing to immigration policies as the cause of rising inequality, unemployment, even terror attacks and environmental degradation, rather than the more difficult causes: neo-liberalism, corruption, racism and discrimination. Parties such as One Nation prey on people's anxieties not by offering genuine solutions but by manufacturing enemies against whom voters can direct their anger and frustration. These merchants of hate whip up hysteria against migrants, Muslims and minorities to get themselves elected. We, too, need to engage with a broader audience and provide an alternative that responds to their fears and insecurities without appealing to humanity's base instincts. Venturing outside the safety of our echo chamber to encourage genuine democratic engagement has the capacity to challenge and persuade people to change.

I joined the Greens because of the party's propensity to push boundaries rather than chasing votes or accolades. Decriminalising and legalising drug use, winning marriage equality and ending live exports were not popular issues when we brought them to the political agenda, but they were issues worth fighting for. I went from Greens supporter to member to state MP and then senator because I retained my faith in the grassroots nature of the party that empowers members. The first state council meeting I attended, soon after I joined the party, demonstrated the genuinely democratic decision-making that has become the trademark of the NSW Greens. It is both revered and criticised by people inside and outside the party. I was delighted by this devolution of power, whereby members deliberated on policy, on the allocation of funds, on the party's priorities. After hearing so much about the 'faceless men' and centralised decision-making of other parties, the openness of the discussions and the commitment of Greens members to achieving a consensus-based outcome was refreshing.

I want to expand this style of decision-making within the Greens. One way for us to do that is by democratically

IS IT ALL WORTH IT?

electing our leadership by a membership vote. The current system—a closed-door process that is done and dusted in a day, run by MPs who are themselves aspiring to be leaders—is highly unsatisfactory, especially for a party founded on the principle of grassroots democracy. The COVID-19 crisis has revealed in no uncertain terms how quickly autocracy can become normalised, while people's democratic rights and civil liberties fall by the wayside. At the start of the pandemic, Australian citizens and permanent residents who were mostly Australian Chinese were quarantined in a mining camp and on Christmas Island, while the rich and famous could completely avoid even hotel quarantine. In Melbourne, thousands of people in nine public housing towers were locked down under heavy police guard without notice, a punitive measure imposed on no other area with an outbreak.[3] The Victorian ombudsman found this action by the government put at risk the health and wellbeing of many people, and was a breach of human rights law.[4] This reveals how far we still are from the notion of equality between the vulnerable and the powerful.

This gives us even more reason to push for more democracy, not less. We can lead by example and demonstrate our commitment to participatory grassroots decision-making, rather than entrenching power and privilege. Giving members the right to vote for their party leadership will empower them, and will go some way to rebuilding the trust people have lost in democracy, in political parties and in politicians.

TOO MIGRANT, TOO MUSLIM, TOO LOUD

I want us to be better. A party that claims to challenge the establishment cannot then reinforce the entrenched order. We can be parliamentary megaphones of the people at the same time as challenging the broken system in which we work. I acknowledge that's not an easy task, but no one ever said solving interrelated complex problems was easy.

People tell me this 'isn't the way things are done'. They tell me, 'Mehreen, this is the world of politics—it's different from the real world.' But isn't that the very problem? I want politics to resemble the real world, both in how it looks and in how it operates. Why should we keep perpetuating a 200-year-old colonialist system and culture that violently dispossessed First Nations people of their land? That oppression and racism continues. It has expanded to envelop asylum seekers and migrants of colour. It makes no sense to persist with a system that inflicts such harm on so many—unless you're one of those who benefit from it.

Perhaps I am too idealistic. But if being idealistic means being unrelenting on matters of integrity, if it means trying to see the best in people, it if means believing that politics is not a game or a career, that power should lie with the people, not with the politicians who serve them, and that things can change, then I am an idealist.

Why shouldn't we strive for a world where everyone is treated with dignity and respect? A world where our lives are seen as having equal value, no matter where we are from, what we look like, or what our bank balance, postcode, religion, sex, gender identity are?

IS IT ALL WORTH IT?

I am by nature a trusting person. I trust others and hope they feel they can trust me. I'm used to taking people at face value. I'd rather confront conflict than avoid it, and would rather directly approach someone to resolve an issue than go behind their back. Politics has made me more cynical, and more cautious. I have been bitten by people betraying the trust I've placed in them. I've been punished for being honest and open. It is hard to work in an environment where you constantly have to watch your back, no matter where you are or who you're with—in parliament, in community meetings, with the media, sometimes even with your own colleagues. It was a big leap from engineer to politician. Going from a profession that ranks at the top of the list for ethics and honesty to one that sits near the bottom was a shock to my system.

But I refuse to lose my idealism. I want to remain who I am. I want to be who I am. I've found my voice. I'm not going to shut up or let up.

***

I am who I am because of the many influences on me and my experiences of life. I count myself lucky to have shared my life with people who have moulded, loved and supported me.

My Ammi showed me many things, told me many things and didn't tell me many other things. She showed me how to be kind, generous, big-hearted and resilient. She taught me to cook, knit and sew, then generously told me that the student had surpassed the teacher many times over. I've knitted pouches for joeys after the summer bushfires of 2019–20. I've sewn facemasks to keep us safe during the pandemic.

Cooking has become one of the joys of my life. While I was on unpaid maternity leave after Aisha was born, I even dabbled in large-scale cooking. I made hundreds of gulab jaman for our food stall at the inaugural 'Festival of the Moon' in Sydney Park in 1996. My son and I have done cooking demonstrations at the Wauchope Farmers Markets. I make videos and share the recipes my mum handwrote for me when I was moving to Australia. I cook for friends and family, for pleasure, for raising money for charity and as an antidote to relieve the stresses of political life.

My culinary journey has evolved through my life. In Lahore, I baked the odd cake, fried chips and helped Ammi in the kitchen at times. In Australia, I started cooking her recipes and others from cuisines around the world. The more I cooked, the more adventurous I became. My cooking style and ingredients became more intricate. I upgraded in a few years from salmon mornay to chicken tagine, slow-cooked chilli lamb shoulder and thrice-cooked chips. When I became a vegetarian, I discovered a whole new world of food and rediscovered some oldies. Samosas made from scratch, baby eggplants with tamarind, chickpea and lentil curry, fried cauliflower with hummus and pine nuts and carrot halwa became the order of the day. I've started pickling olives that come off my olive tree, and preserving

IS IT ALL WORTH IT?

lemons straight after harvesting them from the bush next to my front door.

I like challenge and creativity when cooking. I am game enough to attempt any recipe that takes my fancy, and to embellish it. Possibly the hardest recipe I've made is Adriano Zumbo's eight-layered V8 vanilla cake from the final week of season two (I think) of *MasterChef*. It took me two days to complete this masterpiece—one to source the ingredients and accoutrements, and another to cook and assemble. It was delicious, and made more so by sharing it with family, friends and work colleagues. The burn marks on my arm, acquired while taking the cake layers in and out of the oven, are now the only reminder of that herculean effort.

Cooking for my family of four, for guests when they come to stay, for my team and volunteers, and for dinner parties and lunches gives me the deep satisfaction of nourishing people. I enjoy good dinner-table conversation like anyone else, but what makes me happier is when this conversation happens around a table resplendent with food I've cooked for others to enjoy.

I'm so grateful to my Ammi for passing on this joy of cooking for people. While she taught me and told me many things, there were some she didn't tell me. She did not tell me there were any limits to what I wanted to achieve. She did not tell me that I should not or could not push boundaries and challenge convention. She did not tell me I wasn't enough on my own—that I needed a husband or children to be a complete woman. She did not tell me that I should be a stay-at-home mum to my two young children rather than doing a master's and a PhD. In fact, she came over to help us out through the most difficult period, so I could finish my research. I can't thank her enough.

But I'm not so grateful for some other things she didn't tell me. She never really told me what menstruation was. When I was around ten years old, she did tell me to let her know if I noticed any brown stains on my undies. Luckily for me, Year 7 human biology came to the rescue—before the brown stains did! Ammi never told me how painful childbirth could be. When I was pregnant with my first baby, my gorgeous son Osman, she told me that she had all her four babies without pain relief and it had not hurt at all. And I believed her. It hurt so much that it took me six years to muster the courage to have my second child, my beautiful, amazing daughter Aisha. I may never forgive my Ammi for this lapse in information giving, but I love her to bits nonetheless. She helped me believe in myself.

My Abbu was crystal-clear on honesty and integrity. For him there were no grey areas here. I've set the same high bar for myself. Oh, and he also told me civil engineers could do everything and anything. I took that to heart too. It was my engineering that helped me see right through the bullshit in the New South Wales government's transport projects. The tentacles of the WestConnex toll road have spread all over Sydney.[5] My first opinion piece, published in the *Sydney Morning Herald* in October 2013, systematically analysed

IS IT ALL WORTH IT?

the flaws in the government's backing of this '21st century road'.[6] It didn't, and still doesn't, stack up on transport, financial, environmental or social grounds. The toll it has taken on people and the environment that came in its way is irreversible. That was just the start of unpicking the major debacles in New South Wales transport agenda—the massive cost blowouts, the privatisation of public transport, the illogical ripping-up of existing trainlines, and the stripping from core government departments of engineering expertise; it's a long list. Ammi tells me how proud Abbu would have been if he were alive to see this.

My husband has always cheered me on from the sidelines. He has stood beside me and behind me, but never in front of me. He has always had my back. He has given unconditional love and encouragement. My politics and especially my outspoken criticism of the New South Wales government has no doubt hampered his career. We've joked about whether he should change his family name (which I added to mine after we got married) when bidding for engineering work. Omar often tells me that God broke the mould after he created me. Mostly it's a compliment, but sometimes my stubbornness gets the better of him. When the chips are down, his glass is always full. He's shown me how to find the bright side of any challenge. He's been frustrated by my drive (or obsession, as he calls it) to work myself to the ground. On days the pressure becomes too much for me to get out from under the doona, he's sat by me until the storm has passed. On nights I've broken down sobbing, he's held me until my tears have dried up and my racking body is still again.

Many people I've met along the way have given me the courage to defy the odds. Fahima Khala (Aunty) is one of them. She was one of the first women to study dentistry in Pakistan. I met her in Sydney, where she, her husband and three children had moved. Unable to find a job in Sydney in the early 1970s, she moved to Broken Hill for a year. After that, she worked in the School Dental Service in Victoria, travelling to remote schools to provide dental health services. Her story is one that defies the stereotype of a Brown Muslim woman in every way, shape and form. She worked in her profession even though it took her away from her husband and children. She lived by herself and travelled to rural areas. What a role model!

Would I be someone different if I lived my life over? Perhaps. I did once dream of being an actor. During the long summer school holidays in Lahore, I'd write plays and then round up my friends in the neighbourhood to perform them for our parents and extended families. My inspiration often came from the books I had read or the TV shows I'd been watching, such as Enid Blyton's *Famous Five*, *The Lucy Show* (and yes, I played Lucille Ball) and *Star Trek*. I guess those performances weren't a complete waste, as some of those dramatic skills do come in handy for a politician!

I could have been a sportswoman if there had been a professional track for women in sport at the time I was playing netball at school, cricket in front yards and driveways, and

IS IT ALL WORTH IT?

table tennis on our verandah. I think it's too late now to go down that route. I did try, though. In my late 30s I took up soccer. I reckoned that if both my kids could do it, so could I. Well, I couldn't. It was a harsh lesson—in more ways than one. Firstly, the coach would not let me play if I didn't wear shorts, something I had never worn and was quite uncomfortable wearing. Then, during my third training session, I injured my ACL and underwent an arthroscopy to contain the damage. Sadly, that was the start and end of my soccer career.

Looking backwards to help yourself become a better person going forward is important, but you can't really change the past. Learning life as you live it, interrogating it while you have the chance to change and be changed, is a precious gift. That's much more valuable than looking back and drowning in the regret of what ifs.

***

Would I have moved to Australia knowing what I now know? Maybe, but maybe not. I suppose this response will make my detractors hopeful that I might comply with their demands to 'piss off back to the shithole I came from'. I'm going to gleefully dash their hopes: I'm not going anywhere. Whether they like it or not, this is now my home. I'm staying put. Sucked in.

For most of my time in Australia, I've felt that I've fitted in and got on with life. I never felt the incompatibility between my culture and religion and the broader Australian society that prompted One Nation's Pauline Hanson to call for a ban on Muslim immigration. As more time has passed, I've been able to move between my two cultural identities quite fluidly—sometimes they've merged into a new one, replete with a mishmash of both. Most migrants I know are the same.

Yet there has been a deliberate attempt to make us feel we don't belong. The Cronulla riots of 2005 were a shock to many, and a reminder of the ugliness of racism in Australia. Former prime minister John Howard's comment in an interview on Channel 9—'As many people know, I'm not an overwhelming fan of the doctrine of multiculturalism'[7]— reinforced the ongoing reminders from conservative politicians about the 'failures' of multiculturalism. When then Minister for Immigration and Border Protection Peter Dutton said about asylum seekers, 'They won't be numerate or literate in their own language, let alone English. These people would be taking Australian jobs, there's no question about that,'[8] it further demonised refugees as people who couldn't fit in here and who should be feared.

It didn't always feel like this. I've often spoken about feeling quite welcome when I moved here with my husband, my big hoop earrings and my big hair, with my toddler son in tow. But years of anti-refugee, anti-Muslim, anti-immigrant sentiment has fomented a climate of hate which systemically targets and 'others' people like me. Australia has become a place where my belonging is questioned every single day. I can't just brush it off every single time. I can't say it doesn't hurt. I can't honestly say I may have been better

IS IT ALL WORTH IT?

off somewhere else but I have to seriously ask the question: is it all worth it?

Some days, it's easy to slip into futility. It's easy to think you are alone in a 'David and Goliath' struggle. It's easy to lose hope. Those moments are, however, fleeting. There is hope all around me. In the community, among Greens members, at gatherings in friends' homes, at protests in the streets, in shopping centres where I meet people who tell me they love what I stand for, and appreciate the unapologetic defiance they see in me. They tell me they admire my strength and resilience. Young women of colour tell me that because they see someone like them in parliament, they believe their path into politics or public life will be easier.

Just the other day, while I was shopping for a lipstick in Sephora at the Pitt Street Mall, a young man visiting Sydney from Taree came up to me and told me how much he loved the work my office did, and how I stood for everything that is dear to him and his partner. I feel blessed to be supported and loved in this way. Frankly, it's these people who keep me going. If I'm having some positive impact on people's lives, then it does make it all worthwhile.

In these moments, the heat of racism dissipates and the weight of aloneness lifts. I know I'm not on my own. I remind myself of the wonderful people I've met because I do what I do. People from every walk of life, at rallies, in women's shelters, in abortion clinics, in camping grounds and bus stops, on polling booths—people who have opened up their homes and hearts to me. The committed, dedicated, extremely bright people in my team and the volunteers who come in and out of our office every day working for climate justice, expanding the rights of workers, free public education and providing a home for all.

I remind myself too of the young people I meet who give me the best hope for the future. They are intelligent, articulate, full of purpose. They are radical activists. They have no qualms about taking to the streets for refugees, with First Nations people, for action on climate.

I remind myself of the thousands of people I haven't met but who I know are part of our collective movement for climate justice, gender equity and racial justice. Environmentalists who are not deterred by politicians slamming them for being 'selfish' and 'disgraceful' for protesting to scale back fossil fuels. Animal rights activists who are not daunted by being labelled 'vigilantes' and 'terrorists'. Unions and their members who are not afraid to stand up to big business and governments to fight for workers' rights. Those who join hands in solidarity to provoke systemic change for racial equity and are not deterred by police intimidation. I know I am not alone.

Ultimately, I am part of Australia and Australia is part of me. I want us to be the best we can be. In my first speech to the Senate, I explained my vision for Australia:

> I see an Australia that looks beyond its borders, not as a nation hungry for resources and cheap goods, not as a nation suspicious or fearful of others and not as an ally of

IS IT ALL WORTH IT?

a war machine but as a friend of people who are fighting oppression, marginalisation and injustices wherever they may be. We look beyond our borders as a proponent of democracy and human rights everywhere, not just where it is politically expedient. We look to international peace, to justice in Palestine, to welcoming refugees.

I see an unashamedly feminist country where the patriarchy is dismantled, where access to abortion is unambiguously legal, where the safety of women is of the utmost importance and violence against women is confronted as the crisis that it is. But gender equality is not just going to happen. Equality must be the law, and corporations that refuse to pay women the same as they would a man should be penalised.

I want to see an Australia where the voices of Indigenous women, trans women and women of colour are heard, not silenced, an Australia where the fruit of our labour is enjoyed, not exploited, where workers have power, unions are strong and no one has to work four jobs just to make ends meet.

I see a place where climate change is more than a political football, where the economy is working for the people and the environment, where the environment is seen not as diametrically opposed to the economy but as inextricably linked with it. A thriving environment is essential for our wellbeing.

I see a society that cares for animals, where greyhounds like my beautiful Cosmo are safe and happy in homes instead of being pushed to their limits and killed on racetracks for gambling, a society where we would never tolerate the inhumanity of live exports or factory farming and where our native species are safe from the threat of extinction.

At the very core of this Australia must be justice for First Nations people.

I am here to fight for this future.

I see an Australia embracing new ideas, knowing full well that old approaches have failed us. We are capable of unlearning and relearning by genuinely reflecting on the past, so we can do things differently—but only if we make that choice.

The documented and undocumented history of the many 'moments' in time has a lot to teach us. The Civil Rights movement, the women's movement, the environment movement have signified progress to a more equal world. Yet many were left behind in those struggles. Others did not make it to the pages of penned history; their stories are untold and unsolicited. Often it is the select few who make the front pages. Often they are powerful. Often they are men. Often they are white.

I get a bit tired of hearing that 'the climate crisis is upon us—we must act now'. The climate crisis has been upon so many in the world for some time now, another peril added to the existing injustices they already contend with because they are poor and marginalised. And just because

IS IT ALL WORTH IT?

the climate crisis is now recognised by progressives as an existential threat doesn't change the lived realities of others. Many in the community are rightly more concerned about their next pay cheque, the education of their children or the violence and abuse they are enduring in an unequal society. The truth is, these struggles are inextricably linked. Their resolutions must be ours too. We won't win unless we fight for collective justice.

Sarah Jaquette Ray writes:

> The prospect of an unlivable future has always shaped the emotional terrain for Black and brown people, whether that terrain is racism or climate change. Climate change compounds existing structures of injustice, and those structures exacerbate climate change. Exhaustion, anger, hope—the effects of oppression and resistance are not unique to this climate moment. What *is* unique is that people who had been insulated from oppression are now waking up to the prospect of their own unlivable future.[9]

Let's wake up to a clear-eyed view of history. It's time to move forward by reflecting, interrogating and correcting the mistakes of the past. We can't continue a piecemeal approach to outrage that lurches from one issue to the next. We can't just get rid of one lot of politicians only to replace them with others who look and act the same. We can't keep reproducing the same systems of power that have silenced, exploited and oppressed people. These old systems must be changed.

Calling yourself an environmentalist, a feminist or an anti-racist and being one are completely different things. It's not enough to say, 'I'm an environmentalist,' if you don't make racial justice central to the struggle for climate justice. It's not enough to say, 'I'm a feminist,' if you're going to ignore the struggles of Indigenous women, women of colour and trans women. It's not enough to say, 'I'm anti-racist,' if you don't step aside to make space for people of colour.

We are in a moment in history. Let's make sure our rage doesn't disappear into the abyss of untold history or an unchanged future.

This is a moment to be thoroughly pissed off. To speak up. To be loud. To disrupt. To dissent. To organise. To mobilise.

Let's act in solidarity with those who have been screwed over for centuries by colonialism, patriarchy and capitalism.

Let's do so by building a movement that restructures power and privilege to unwind centuries of entrenched injustices.

Let's do so with the hope that things can change. Because they can.

ACKNOWLEDGEMENT AND GRATITUDE

—

I acknowledge the traditional custodians of the land that I live on, the Gadigal people of the Eora Nation, and pay my respects to elders past and present. Sovereignty of this land was never ceded. It is, always was and always will be Aboriginal Land. I recognise that there can be no social or environmental justice without racial justice, and there can be no racial justice without First Nations justice.

When thinking about writing a memoir, I always felt writing my own story was a bit indulgent and superfluous. What could I say that would interest people? What value does my story have? I guess, this hesitation is part and parcel of the shattered confidence I live with as a Brown, Muslim, migrant woman in a place whose systems and institutions marginalise so many of us. But people like me are also part of the fabric of Australia. Our stories should be told, our voices should be heard.

In my life there are so many people who love, support, encourage and push me (in a good way!) to do what I do. This book too would not have happened without them.

My Ammi and Abbu have instilled in me values of honesty, plain speaking and truth telling.

My Ammi has always gone out of her way to help whoever needed it. Her compassion knows no bounds. Ammi was the fact checker and brains trust for my stories of growing up in Pakistan. But much more than that, she has loved and supported me in whatever I wanted to do in life, whether she agreed with it or not.

My Abbu passed away in 2004. He has left an example of uncompromising integrity for his children to follow. I hope I can live up to his standard.

My husband Omar is the love of my life. Since migrating to Australia where we have no family, we've only had each other to rely on. He has never let me down. My engineering career, my politics and this book have only been possible because of Omar.

My children Osman and Aisha who I am so proud of. They have graciously accepted their mama's work commitments even when it has meant an absence from their lives many times. Thank you for your constructive criticism which has kept me grounded (hopefully). I know that I am a better person because of both of you.

Osman, my son, whose boldness in pushing boundaries

ACKNOWLEDGEMENT AND GRATITUDE

with such aplomb motivates me every single day. Bouncing ideas with him always reveals new angles I hadn't thought of. I'm in awe of his capacity to grasp and unpack complex ideas with such clarity.

Aisha, my courageous daughter with whom I've debated and discussed so many ideas on feminism and racism over Facetime. I have so much admiration for her insights and knowledge of contemporary thinking, and the strength of her values. I can't wait to see you and hug you once international travel starts again.

Matt who was my chief of staff for seven years. He left our team in early 2020 for other adventures but enthusiastically offered to be my sounding board and adviser for this book. He remembers things I've hidden away in the recesses of my mind. He read, re-read and read again (and again) my draft chapters to give such honest and detailed advice. This book is much better for it. Then, he was game enough to also help out with the photoshoot, photo selection, publicity and anything else needed to finish the book. Matt is a true gem and his generosity, patience and intellect is unsurpassed.

Vythehi, who boosted my morale every time she provided feedback on each chapter. Telling me all the things she had enjoyed, then providing incredibly useful feedback which has improved my storytelling immensely. On top of this, Vy provided fantastic ideas for the book cover and then the saris for the backdrop. I will never forget the Facebook live Vy did with me from her mum's place with the dozens of saris laid out for me to choose from.

My team, past and present—Maliha, Mich, Max, Belinda, Emma, Tamara and Nat. I am so lucky to have such talented and committed people working with me. I can only do my work because of their fearless advice, loyalty and support.

Jane Palfreyman sowed the idea of this book in my head and heart, and convinced me that my story was worth telling. She has encouraged me from start to finish, and all the way through this book writing journey. It has been such a privilege and a pleasure to work with her and the team at Allen & Unwin.

I'm inspired and buoyed by the courage and commitment of Greens members and supporters in New South Wales and across Australia, the hundreds of people I've met through the years and the tens of thousands of others who I've joined on the streets. You keep the spark of hope and change burning bright.

Thank you from the bottom of my heart for your love, support and trust in me.

In love and solidarity,

Mehreen

NOTES

Chapter 1

1   Luke Henriques-Gomes, 'Robodebt: government to refund 470,000 unlawful Centrelink debts worth $721m', *The Guardian*, 29 May 2020, www.theguardian.com/australia-news/2020/may/29/robodebt-government-to-repay-470000-unlawful-centrelink-debts-worth-721m.

2   Peter Gottschalk, 'Who are Pakistan's Ahmadis and why haven't they voted in 30 years', *The Conversation*, 8 August 2018, theconversation.com/who-are-pakistans-ahmadis-and-why-havent-they-voted-in-30-years-100797.

Chapter 2

1. David Crowe, '"Highly problematic for public trust": Australian political donations revealed', *Sydney Morning Herald*, 18 January 2021, www.smh.com.au/politics/federal/highly-problematic-for-public-trust-australian-political-donations-revealed-20210117-p56up0.html.
2. NSW Parliament, Public Accountability Committee, *Report 8: Integrity, efficacy and value for money of NSW Government grant programs* (First report), March 2021, www.parliament.nsw.gov.au/lcdocs/inquiries/2606/Report%20No%208%20-%20Public%20Accountability%20Committee%20-%20NSW%20Government%20grant%20programs%20-%20First%20report.pdf
3. Lucy Cormack & Alexandra Smith, 'Premier says pork barrelling "not illegal" as she defends council grants program', *Sydney Morning Herald*, 26 November 2020, www.smh.com.au/national/nsw/premier-says-pork-barrelling-not-illegal-as-she-defends-council-grants-program-20201126-p56i6d.html.
4. Anne Davies, 'Berejiklian concedes $140m grant scheme was pork-barrelling, but says "it's not unique to our government"', *The Guardian*, 26 November 2020, www.theguardian.com/australia-news/2020/nov/26/berejiklian-admits-140m-grant-scheme-was-pork-barrelling-as-approval-documents-revealed.
5. Nick Wiggins, 'Queensland Government pushes for change as tree clearing increases', *ABC News*, 7 August

NOTES

2016, www.abc.net.au/news/2016-08-07/tree-clearing-report-queensland-laws-jackie-trad/7698474.

6   Elise Klein, 'Why is the government trying to make the cashless debit card permanent? Research shows it does not work', *The Conversation*, 12 November 2020, theconversation.com/why-is-the-government-trying-to-make-the-cashless-debit-card-permanent-research-shows-it-does-not-work-149444.

7   Elise Klein, 'There's mounting evidence against cashless debit cards, but the government is ploughing on regardless', *The Conversation*, 1 November 2019, theconversation.com/theres-mounting-evidence-against-cashless-debit-cards-but-the-government-is-ploughing-on-regardless-123763.

8   Amelia Adams, 'There's been a major win for expectant mothers with changes to pregnancy discrimination laws in NSW', *9 News*, 9 December 2017, fb.watch/4Jef8Wky66/.

9   Eryk Bagshaw, 'Parliament is no more diverse now than it was in 1988 as political staffer ranks explode', *Sydney Morning Herald*, 19 January 2019, www.smh.com.au/politics/federal/parliament-is-no-more-diverse-now-than-it-was-in-1988-as-political-staffer-ranks-explode-20190116-p50rol.html.

10 Gerry Stoker, Mark Evans & Max Halupka, *Trust and Democracy in Australia: Democratic Decline and Renewal*, Democracy 2025, December 2018.

Chapter 3

1   Christine Forster & Vedna Jivan, 'Abortion law in New South Wales: Shifting from criminalisation to the recognition of the reproductive rights of women and girls', *Journal of Law and Medicine*, Vol. 24.
2   National Advocates for Pregnant Women, 'Executive Summary: Paltrow & Flavin, "Arrests of and forced interventions on pregnant women in the United States (1973–2005): The implications for women's legal status and public health', *Journal of Health Politics, Policy and Law*, 25 January 2013, www.nationaladvocatesforpregnantwomen.org/executive_summary_paltrow_flavin_jhppl_article.
3   'Australian Abortion Statistics', Children by Choice, www.childrenbychoice.org.au/factsandfigures/australian-abortion-statistics.
4   Kate Aubusson, '"My body was a political stalemate": NSW has the abortion law debate it has been avoiding for 100 years', *Sydney Morning Herald*, 23 June 2016, www.smh.com.au/healthcare/my-body-was-a-political-stalemate-nsw-has-the-abortion-law-debate-it-has-been-avoiding-for-100-years-20160622-gpp2ns.html.
5   Christine Forster & Vedna Jivan, 'Abortion law in New South Wales: Shifting from criminalisation to the recognition of the reproductive rights of women and girls', *Journal of Law and Medicine*, Vol. 24, p. 856.
6   NSW Parliament, Abortion Law Reform (Miscellaneous Acts Amendment) Bill 2016, Second Reading,

NOTES

      11 August 2016, www.parliament.nsw.gov.au/bill/files/2919/2R%20Abortion%20Law%20Reform.pdf.

7   Lonergan Research, 'Public views on Abortion—NSW', prepared for The Greens NSW, September 2015.

8   NSW Parliament, Abortion Law Reform (Miscellaneous Acts Amendment) Bill 2016, Second Reading, 11 May 2017, www.parliament.nsw.gov.au/Hansard/Pages/HansardResult.aspx#/docid/HANSARD-1820781676-73360.

9   Rita Panahi, 'In tough times the Greens can still make us laugh', *Herald Sun*, 26 March 2020, www.heraldsun.com.au/news/opinion/rita-panahi/rita-panahi-in-tough-times-rely-on-the-greens-for-a-laugh/news-story/0a9130392ba0d778db5448294c34f7fe.

10   Tim Blair, 'Only One Tune, and They're Still Playing It', *Daily Telegraph*, 27 March 2020, www.dailytelegraph.com.au/blogs/tim-blair/only-one-tune-and-theyre-still-playing-it/news-story/2d220a6afc5f9076c2457d4f67b96bf5.

11   United Nations, *Policy Brief: The Impact of COVID-19 on Women*, 9 April 2020, p. 2, www.unwomen.org/-/media/headquarters/attachments/sections/library/publications/2020/policy-brief-the-impact-of-covid-19-on-women-en.pdf.

12   World Economic Forum, *Global Gender Gap Report 2020*, 2019, www3.weforum.org/docs/WEF_GGGR_2020.pdf.

13   Lydia Feng, 'Australian study finds risk of sexual assault and violence significantly higher for trans women of colour', *ABC News*, 26 June 2020, www.abc.net.au/news/2020-06-26/study-finds-high-sexual-assault-rates-for-trans-women-of-colour/12395226.

Chapter 4

1   World Economic Forum, *Global Gender Gap Report 2021*, WEF, Geneva, 2021, www3.weforum.org/docs/WEF_GGGR_2021.pdf.
2   World Economic Forum, *Global Gender Gap Report 2020*, WEF, Geneva, 2020, www3.weforum.org/docs/WEF_GGGR_2020.pdf.
3   Eryk Bagshaw, 'Parliament is no more diverse now than it was in 1988 as political staffer ranks explode', *Sydney Morning Herald*, 19 January 2019, www.smh.com.au/politics/federal/parliament-is-no-more-diverse-now-than-it-was-in-1988-as-political-staffer-ranks-explode-20190116-p50rol.html.
4   Nova Peris, speaking on *Q&A*, ABC TV, 1 March 2020.
5   'Donald Trump tells US congresswomen to go back to where they came from', *ABC News*, 15 July 2019, www.abc.net.au/news/2019-07-15/trump-tells-us-born-congresswomen-to-go-back-to-home-countries/11308368.
6   Matthew Choi, '"She's telling us how to run our country": Trump again goes after Ilhan Omar's Somali

roots', *Politico*, 22 September 2020, www.politico.com/news/2020/09/22/trump-attacks-ilhan-omar-420267.

7   Christopher Knaus, Michael McGowan, Nick Evershed & Oliver Holmes, 'Inside the hate factory: How Facebook fuels far-right profit', *The Guardian*, 6 December 2019, www.theguardian.com/australia-news/2019/dec/06/inside-the-hate-factory-how-facebook-fuels-far-right-profit.

8   Katharine Murphy & Amy Remeikis, 'Dutton says "leftwing lunatics" must be dealt with as ASIO warns of far-right threat', *The Guardian*, 25 February 2020, www.theguardian.com/australia-news/2020/feb/25/dutton-says-leftwing-lunatics-must-be-dealt-with-as-asio-warns-of-far-right-threat.

9   Mario Peucker & Jacob Davey, 'Does Australia's radical left pose a security threat? What the empirical evidence tells us', *ABC News*, 15 December 2020, www.abc.net.au/religion/does-the-radical-left-pose-a-security-threat-to-australia/12987240.

10 Karen Stollznow, 'Why is it so offensive to say "all lives matter"?', *The Conversation*, 13 January 2021, theconversation.com/why-is-it-so-offensive-to-say-all-lives-matter-153188.

11 Michael Koziol, '"It's a disgrace": Peter Dutton says the Greens are as bad as Fraser Anning on massacre', *Sydney Morning Herald*, 18 March 2019, www.smh.com.au/politics/federal/it-s-a-disgrace-peter-dutton-

says-the-greens-are-as-bad-as-fraser-anning-on-massacre-20190318-p51510.html.

12 'Mainstream Australia is grieving, not politicking', *The Australian*, 19 March 2019, www.theaustralian.com.au/commentary/editorials/mainstream-australia-is-grieving-not-politicking/news-story/3aad09f19cfa7a1fc4685e90c3df4f60.

13 *Report of the Royal Commission of Inquiry into the terrorist attack on Christchurch masjidain on 15 March 2019*, Vol. 1, Parts 1–3, 26 November 2020, christchurchattack.royalcommission.nz/assets/Report-Volumes-and-Parts/Ko-to-tatou-kainga-tenei-Volume-1-v2.pdf.

14 Charles Sturt University, 'Islamophobia continues in Australia: 2019 report', 18 November 2019, news.csu.edu.au/latest-news/islamophobia-continues-in-australia-2019-report.

15 Mehreen Faruqi, 'Mehreen Faruqi: Muslim women don't need glass cages—or glass ceilings', *Crikey*, 3 October 2014, www.crikey.com.au/2014/10/03/mehreen-faruqi-muslim-women-dont-need-glass-cages-or-glass-ceilings.

16 Edward W. Said, *Orientalism*, Vintage, New York, 1978, p. 226.

17 Aparna Hebbani & Charise-Rose Wills, 'How Muslim women in Australia navigate through media (mis)representations of hijab/burqa', *Australian Journal of Communication*, Vol. 39 (1), 2014, pp. 87–100.

NOTES

18 Amy Greenbank, 'Islamophobic abuse mostly directed at women wearing headscarves while shopping, study finds', *ABC News*, 18 November 2019, www.abc.net.au/news/2019-11-18/muslim-women-enduring-most-islamophobia-in-australia/11708376.

19 Mehreen Faruqi, 'Instead of yelling at us, ask Muslim women to join the discussion', *Sydney Morning Herald*, 25 November 2015, www.smh.com.au/opinion/ask-muslim-women-to-join-the-conversation-instead-of-yelling-at-us-in-the-street-20151125-gl79eg.html; Mehreen Faruqi, 'It's time to remember our history-making female Muslim leaders – and to join them', SBS, 22 February 2018, www.sbs.com.au/topics/voices/culture/article/2018/02/22/its-time-remember-our-history-making-female-muslim-leaders-and-join-them.

20 Mehreen Faruqi, 'I'm heading to the Senate and there's not a damn thing Fraser Anning can do about it', *Junkee*, 15 August 2018, junkee.com/mehreen-faruqi-fraser-anning/171636.

21 'Muslim Green set for tough test', *The Australian*, 8 April 2013, www.theaustralian.com.au/national-affairs/state-politics/muslim-green-set-for-tough-test/news-story/7720c74e9f389313f5332c7cdc5d822e.

22 Mehreen Faruqi, 'As a Muslim, I'm proud to support marriage equality', *The Guardian*, 18 October 2017, www.theguardian.com/commentisfree/2017/oct/19/as-a-muslim-im-proud-to-support-marriage-equality.

23   Martin Luther King, Jr, 'Letter from Birmingham Jail', 16 April 1963, letterfromjail.com.
24   Mehreen Faruqi, 'I know the actions of Isis are #NotInMyName, and I won't be pressured to apologise for them', *The Guardian*, 25 September 2014, www.theguardian.com/commentisfree/2014/sep/25/i-know-the-actions-of-isis-are-notinmyname-and-i-wont-be-pressured-to-apologise-for-them.
25   Naaman Zhou, 'Family of Uber Eats rider killed in Sydney files workers' compensation claim in test for gig economy', *The Guardian*, 8 December 2020, www.theguardian.com/australia-news/2020/dec/09/family-of-uber-eats-rider-killed-in-sydney-files-workers-compensation-claim-in-test-for-gig-economy.

Chapter 5

1   Damian Carrington, 'A third of Himalayan ice cap doomed, finds report', *The Guardian*, 4 February 2019, www.theguardian.com/environment/2019/feb/04/a-third-of-himalayan-ice-cap-doomed-finds-shocking-report.
2   Lorena Allam, 'Walgett's water crisis: NSW considers options after "concerning" sodium levels found', *The Guardian*, 22 January 2019, www.theguardian.com/australia-news/2019/jan/22/walgetts-water-crisis-nsw-considers-options-after-concerning-sodium-levels-found.

NOTES

3   Lana D. Hartwig, Natalie Osborne & Sue Jackson, 'Australia has an ugly legacy of denying water rights to Aboriginal people. Not much has changed', *The Conversation*, 24 July 2020, theconversation.com/australia-has-an-ugly-legacy-of-denying-water-rights-to-aboriginal-people-not-much-has-changed-141743.

4   Bradley J. Moggridge & Ross M. Thompson, 'Aboriginal voices are missing from the Murray-Darling Basin crisis', *The Conversation*, 31 January 2019, theconversation.com/aboriginal-voices-are-missing-from-the-murray-darling-basin-crisis-110769.

5   UN Environment Programme, 'Frequently asked questions', www.unep.org/explore-topics/sustainable-development-goals/why-do-sustainable-development-goals-matter/frequently.

6   David Crowe & Nick O'Malley, 'Morrison not expected to speak at global climate summit', *Sydney Morning Herald*, 10 December 2020, www.smh.com.au/politics/federal/morrison-shrugs-off-need-to-speak-at-global-climate-summit-20201210-p56mgg.html.

7   Bevan Shields & David Crowe, 'Australia drops plan to use Kyoto credits to meet Paris climate target', *Sydney Morning Herald*, 5 December 2020, www.smh.com.au/politics/federal/australia-drops-plan-to-use-kyoto-credits-to-meet-paris-climate-target-20201204-p56ko3.html.

8   Graham Readfearn & Adam Morton, 'Australia is the only country using carryover climate credits, officials

admit', *The Guardian*, 22 October 2019, www.theguardian.com/environment/2019/oct/22/australia-is-the-only-country-using-carryover-climate-credits-officials-admit.

9   Benjamin Franta, 'Shell and Exxon's secret 1980s climate change warnings', *The Guardian*, 19 September 2018, www.theguardian.com/environment/climate-consensus-97-per-cent/2018/sep/19/shell-and-exxons-secret-1980s-climate-change-warnings.

10 Bruce Watson, 'The troubling evolution of corporate greenwashing', *The Guardian*, 21 August 2016, www.theguardian.com/sustainable-business/2016/aug/20/greenwashing-environmentalism-lies-companies.

11 Basit Mahmood, 'There are 100 companies responsible for climate change, activist says', *Newsweek*, 8 September 2020, www.newsweek.com/climate-change-xr-extinction-rebellion-fossil-fuels-climate-greenhouse-gasses-emissions-1530084.

12 Hannah Ellis-Petersen, '"Bhopal's tragedy has not stopped": The urban disaster still claiming lives 35 years on', *The Guardian*, 8 December 2019, www.theguardian.com/cities/2019/dec/08/bhopals-tragedy-has-not-stopped-the-urban-disaster-still-claiming-lives-35-years-on.

13 Apoorva Mandavilli, 'The world's worst industrial disaster is still unfolding', *Atlantic*, 10 July 2018, www.theatlantic.com/science/archive/2018/07/the-worlds-worst-industrial-disaster-is-still-unfolding/560726.

NOTES

14 See David Noble et al., 'Desperately seeking innovation nirvana: Australia's cooperative research centres', *Policy Design and Practice*, Vol. 2, No. 1, pp. 15–34.

15 Katherine Gibson et al., *Beyond Business as Usual: A 21st Century Culture of Manufacturing in Australia*, Institute for Culture and Society, Western Sydney University, 2019.

16 Peter Hannam, 'Extreme heatwave days already hitting poorer nations more than rich', *Sydney Morning Herald*, 5 March 2017, www.smh.com.au/environment/climate-change/extreme-heatwave-days-already-hitting-poorer-nations-more-than-rich-20170303-guq7jl.html.

17 Geordan Dickinson Shannan, 'Women worse off when it comes to natural disasters', *The Conversation*, 7 January 2014, theconversation.com/women-worse-off-when-it-comes-to-natural-disasters-21717.

18 Harriet A. Washington, 'How environmental racism is fuelling the coronavirus pandemic', *Nature*, 19 May 2020, www.nature.com/articles/d41586-020-01453-y.

19 Sandra Laville, 'Air pollution a cause in girl's death, coroner rules in landmark case', *The Guardian*, 17 December 2020, www.theguardian.com/environment/2020/dec/16/girls-death-contributed-to-by-air-pollution-coroner-rules-in-landmark-case.

20 Reilly Morse, *Environmental Justice Through the Eye of Hurricane Katrina*, Joint Center for Political and Economic Studies, Health Policy Institute,

Washington DC, 2008, inequality.stanford.edu/sites/default/files/media/_media/pdf/key_issues/Environment_policy.pdf.

21 Jim Erickson, 'Five years later: Flint water crisis most egregious example of environmental injustice, U-M researcher says', *Michigan News*, 23 April 2019, news.umich.edu/five-years-later-flint-water-crisis-most-egregious-example-of-environmental-injustice-u-m-researcher-says.

22 Anna Clark, '"Nothing to worry about. The water is fine": how Flint poisoned its people', *The Guardian*, 3 July 2018, www.theguardian.com/news/2018/jul/03/nothing-to-worry-about-the-water-is-fine-how-flint-michigan-poisoned-its-people.

23 National Museum of Australia, 'Defining Moments: Maralinga', 13 March 2020, www.nma.gov.au/defining-moments/resources/maralinga.

24 Samantha Jonscher & Gary-Jon Lysaght, 'Maralinga story to be told through eyes of traditional owners affected by Britain's atomic bomb testing', *ABC News*, 1 July 2019, www.abc.net.au/news/2019-07-01/maralinga-retelling-the-story-of-britains-atomic-bomb-testing/11249874.

25 Samantha Hepburn, 'A 46,000-year-old Aboriginal site was just deliberately destroyed in Australia', *The Conversation*, 27 May 2020, theconversation.com/rio-tinto-just-blasted-away-an-ancient-aboriginal-site-heres-why-that-was-allowed-139466.

NOTES

26 Nicolas Brulliard, 'This land is their land', National Parks Conservation Association, 8 October 2020, www.npca.org/articles/2742-this-land-is-their-land.

27 Julian Brave NoiseCat, 'The environmental movement needs to reckon with its racist history', *Vice*, 14 September 2019, www.vice.com/en/article/bjwvn8/the-environmental-movement-needs-to-reckon-with-its-racist-history.

28 Beth Gardiner, 'Unequal impact: The deep links between racism and climate change', *Yale Environment 360*, 9 June 2020, e360.yale.edu/features/unequal-impact-the-deep-links-between-inequality-and-climate-change.

29 Leslie Root, 'Racist terrorists are obsessed with demographics. Let's not give them talking points', *Washington Post*, 19 March 2019, www.washingtonpost.com/opinions/2019/03/18/racist-terrorists-are-obsessed-with-demographics-lets-not-give-them-talking-points.

30 See data.footprintnetwork.org.

31 Pallab Ghosh, 'Climate change boosted Australia bushfire risk by at least 30%', *BBC News*, 4 March 2020, www.bbc.com/news/science-environment-51742646.

32 Lisa Cox, '"It's an ecological wasteland": offsets for Sydney toll road were promised but never delivered', *The Guardian*, 10 February 2021, www.theguardian.com/environment/2021/feb/10/its-an-ecological-

wasteland-offsets-for-sydney-tollway-were-promised-but-never-delivered.

33   Lisa Cox, '"Development should stop": Serious flaws in offsets plan for new western Sydney airport', *The Guardian*, 17 February 2021, www.theguardian.com/environment/2021/feb/17/development-should-stop-serious-flaws-in-offsets-plan-for-new-western-sydney-airport.

34   Lawrence Wood, 'The Environmental Impacts of Colonialism', Honours thesis, Bridgewater State University, 17 December 2015, core.ac.uk/download/pdf/48835717.pdf.

35   For discussion of this work by Columbia University economist Utsa Patnaik, see Jason Hickel, 'How Britain stole $45 trillion from India: And lied about it', Coalition for the Abolition of Illegitimate Debt, 31 December 2018, www.cadtm.org/How-Britain-stole-45-trillion-from-India.

36   Arundhati Roy & Avni Sejpal, 'How to Think About Empire', *Boston Review*, 3 January 2019, bostonreview.net/literature-culture-global-justice/arundhati-roy-avni-sejpal-challenging-%E2%80%9Cpost-%E2%80%9D-postcolonialism.

37   Christopher Knaus & Nick Evershed, 'Australia handed out millions in aid contracts to company accused of bribery', *The Guardian*, 12 July 2018, www.theguardian.com/australia-news/2018/jul/13/australia-

NOTES

handed-out-millions-in-aid-contracts-to-company-accused-of-bribery.

38 Teju Cole, 'The White-Savior Industrial Complex', *The Atlantic*, 21 March 2012, www.theatlantic.com/international/archive/2012/03/the-white-savior-industrial-complex/254843.

39 Pooja Bhatia, 'Should we think of foreign aid as reparations?', *Ozy*, 18 September 2013, www.ozy.com/news-and-politics/should-we-think-of-foreign-aid-as-reparations/1301.

40 Eduardo Galeano, *Open Veins of Latin America: Five Centuries of the Pillage of a Continent*, Monthly Review Press, New York, 1997.

41 Lucy Percival, 'Global emissions from Australian carbon exports dwarf any domestic cuts', *Renew Economy*, 3 May 2019, reneweconomy.com.au/global-emissions-from-australian-carbon-exports-dwarf-any-domestic-cuts-36990; The New Daily, 'Australia becoming a global emissions superpower, report warns', *New Daily*, 8 July 2019, thenewdaily.com.au/news/national/2019/07/08/australia-climate-emissions.

42 Erik Loomis, 'Why labor and environmental movements split—and how they can come back together', *Environmental Health News*, 18 September 2018, www.ehn.org/labor-and-environmental-movements-merge-2605763191/a-history-of-alliance.

43 Tim Ha, 'Exploitation rife among firms mining minerals for renewables, electric vehicles: Report', *Eco-Business*,

5 September 2019, www.eco-business.com/news/exploitation-rife-among-firms-mining-minerals-for-renewables-electric-vehicles-report/.

44 Rabih Azhar, 'Resettlement in new environment and its impacts on socio-cultural values of the affecters: A case study of Tarbela Dam, Pakistan', *Journal of Geography and Natural Disasters*, S6: 009, www.longdom.org/open-access/resettlement-in-new-environment-and-its-impacts-on-sociocultural-values-of-the-affecters-a-case-study-of-tarbela-dam-pakistan-2167-0587-S6-009.pdf.

45 Lead Scotland, *The Displaced: In the Footnotes of Development*, www.lead.org.pk/hr/attachments/Compandium/02_Social_Economic_Rights/The_Displaced.pdf.

46 Kenya Evelyn, 'Outrage at whites-only image as Ugandan climate activist cropped from photo', *The Guardian*, 26 January 2020, www.theguardian.com/world/2020/jan/24/whites-only-photo-uganda-climate-activist-vanessa-nakate.

47 Danielle Wood & Kate Griffiths, 'Generation gap: ensuring a fair go for younger Australians', Grattan Institute, 18 August 2019, grattan.edu.au/report/generation-gap/.

Epilogue

1 Toni Morrison, 'A Humanist View', Black Studies Center public dialogue, Part 2, Portland State

NOTES

University, 30 May 1975, www.mackenzian.com/wp-content/uploads/2014/07/Transcript_PortlandState_TMorrison.pdf.

2 Erin Lyons, 'Julie Bishop says group of "big swinging d**ks" tried to thwart her career', *Perth Now*, 9 March 2021, www.perthnow.com.au/politics/federal-politics/julie-bishop-says-group-of-big-swinging-dicks-tried-to-thwart-her-career-ng-de8ed889bdda6280337479920966a0ed.

3 David Kelly, Kate Shaw & Libby Porter, 'Melbourne tower lockdowns unfairly target already vulnerable public housing residents', *The Conversation*, 6 July 2020, theconversation.com/melbourne-tower-lockdowns-unfairly-target-already-vulnerable-public-housing-residents-142041.

4 Matt Woodley, 'Melbourne public housing lockdown breached human rights: Ombudsman', *News GP*, 17 December 2020, www1.racgp.org.au/newsgp/clinical/melbourne-public-housing-lockdown-breached-human-r.

5 Deborah Snow & Matt O'Sullivan, 'WestConnex: The toll road that broke Sydney', *Sydney Morning Herald*, 23 March 2021, www.smh.com.au/national/nsw/westconnex-the-toll-road-that-ate-sydney-20210323-p57d9y.html.

6 Mehreen Faruqi, 'Ideology runs over logic in the drive to build WestConnex', *Sydney Morning Herald*, 21 October 2013, www.smh.com.au/opinion/ideology-

runs-over-logic-in-the-drive-to-build-westconnex-20131020-2vuv7.html.

7   AAP, 'Integration can prevent terrorism, says former PM John Howard', *9 News*, 21 September 2014, www.9news.com.au/national/integration-can-prevent-terrorism-howard/b42a6c3a-5414-4278-856c-9ee0b8d57a27.

8   Latika Bourke, 'Peter Dutton says "illiterate and innumerate" refugees would take Australian jobs', *Sydney Morning Herald*, 17 May 2016, www.smh.com.au/politics/federal/peter-dutton-says-illiterate-and-innumerate-refugees-would-take-australian-jobs-20160517-goxhj1.html.

9   Sarah Jaquette Ray, 'Climate anxiety is an overwhelmingly white phenomenon', *Scientific American*, 21 March 2021, www.scientificamerican.com/article/the-unbearable-whiteness-of-climate-anxiety.

INDEX

1990s recession 15

Abbott, Tony 2, 66, 91, 133
Abbu (father) 242, 243
  academic career 13
  Colombo Plan scholarship 6
  integrity 21–2, 242
  learning, focus on 62
  Master of Engineering 6
  Sydney, love for 6
ABC *Four Corners*
  'Making a Killing' 70
  Total Control 143
ability equality 5
Aboriginal land rights
  Mabo decision 10
  terra nullius 10
  theft of land 44
Aboriginal people
  Appin massacre 44
  health 11
  justice, agitators for 47–8, 250
  life expectancy, shorter 11, 135
  prejudice against 10
  prison representation 11
  Stolen Generation 44
  systemic racism against 10
Aboriginal water rights 180
abortion
  access to safe and affordable 104–5, 116, 126
  anti-choice campaigners 113–14
  Crimes Act provisions 114
  decriminalisation *see* abortion, decriminalisation
  District Court ruling in 1971 108, 110, 114, 116
  doctors refusal to perform 115
  exclusion zones outside clinics 113, 118
  intimidation at clinics 113–14
  late-term 122

medical abortion by telephone 125
public hospitals 115, 124, 126
rural peoples lack of access 104, 108, 116, 124
abortion, decriminalisation 84, 99, 108, 126, 136
  aims of Greens bill 117
  anti-choice campaigners 113
  attempts to block bill 101–3, 113, 123
  campaigning in the community 119
  community views 118
  End12 movement 113
  Greens bill 99, 117, 120
  other states, legislation in 120
  professional bodies endorsement of bill 124
  rejection of bill 121, 126
  Women's Abortion Action Campaign (WAAC) 104
activists 85
  abortion decriminalisation, for 104, 118, 119
  frustrations of 90
aged care funding 12
Ahmadiyya religion
  Ahmadis, persecution 24–5
  establishment 24
  non-Muslim declaration in Pakistan 25
Air China 79
air pollution 197, 216
Al Jazeera 143
Al Noor Mosque 148–9
Ammi (mother) 6, 13, 28, 239–40, 241–2
Amnesty International 187
animal cruelty *see* greyhound racing
animal extinctions 202–3
animal welfare laws, advocating for 2

Anning, Fraser 147
Anthropocene era 205
Anti-Discrimination Act 1977
  pregnant employees provision 83, 84
Ardern, Jacinda 150
arrival in Sydney 1992 1, 8–9, 29
  first car 34
  first friendships 30, 31
  jobs, difficulty finding 16, 18
  loneliness 28–9
  new discoveries 33
  post as main communication form 29
  social welfare 18–19
  welcome, feeling of 40
Asia-Pacific aid, characterisation of 206
Askin, Bob 45
asylum seekers 41, 246
  demonisation of 92, 246
  indefinite detention 12, 92
  policies, inhumane 152
aunt (feminist) 14, 89
AusAID scholarship 26
Australia
  action on climate 184–5
  animal extinctions 202–3
  Asia-Pacific aid, characterisation of 206
  climate change contribution 208
  ecological footprint of each Australian 201
  environment destruction since colonisation 205
  equality, lack of 10, 12
  expectations pre-arrival 7, 11
  extremists, threats posed 145
  female prime minister, first 7
  first impressions 9
  manufacturing, loss of 189
  proportion of people born overseas 90

INDEX

white colonisation of 11, 199
widening of inequality gap 12
The Australian 147
Australian Army Reserves 37
Australian Christian Lobby 122
Australian High Commission
    Pakistan 15
Australian Lawyers for Human
    Rights 125
Australian national anthem 11
Australian Parliament
    Canberra after-dark scene 47
    Senate, becoming member of 46
    workplace culture, exposé
        219–22
'Australianness' 42

Baaka (Darling River) 179–80
Baird, Mike 69–70, 72, 75, 76,
    122
Bannon, Steve 151
Bano, Hameeda 131–2
Barkindji people 179
Bentley 85
Berejiklian, Gladys 45
    abortion decriminalisation bill
        122
    Daryl Maguire relationship 45
    grant funding rort 52
Bezos, Jeff 209
Bhutto, Zulifikar Ali 24–5
bias in the labour market 16
Bible 5
bigotry, flourishing of 40
Biodiversity Conservation Bill 2016
    impact three years after
        commencement of Act 60
    nature of 59
    passage of Bill 60
biodiversity offsetting 203–4
BIPOC (Black, Indigenous and
    people of colour) 147, 197,
    205

Bishop, Julie 64, 133, 233
Black Lives Matter 146, 218
Blair, Tim 133–4
Bloomberg, Michael 209
Bollywood 31
Bonny Hills 38
Brisbane River 3
British India 30
    education for Muslim girls in
        131
    India-Pakistan wars 30–1
    partition 25, 48, 212
    religious persecution in 26
    wealth taken by British 205–6
Budget, 2014 89
Burgess, Mike 145
bushfires
    2019-2020 201–2
    increased severity 60, 201
Business and Human Rights
    Resources Centre 210

Canberra 47
the Canberra bubble 90, 222–3
cannabis, decriminalisation 161,
    236
Cape York 37
capitalism 206, 216
'caring work'
    casualisation and underpayment
        33
    feminisation of labour 33
cashless debit card scheme 68–9
    First Nations people,
        disproportionate impact on
        68
casualisation of staff 67
Catholic Church 122
Centennial Park, Sydney 14
Centre Alliance party 67, 69
Centrelink robodebt 19
Charles Sturt University
    'Islamophobia in Australia' 154

childcare
　cost and accessibility 33
　COVID measures 33
　essential service, as 33
　free and funded, advocating for 33
　juggling work/study and 190–1
　UNSW, campaign for 32
Christchurch mosque massacre 147–9, 200
　Al Noor Mosque 148–9
　Royal Commission into 147–8
　white supremacy and 149
Christian Democratic Party 109, 110
citizenship
　Australian 42
　renouncing Pakistani 3, 41
Climate Ambition Summit 2020 185
climate change
　agitators for 47, 48
　Australian action on 184–5
　Australian contribution to 208
　bushfires, increased severity of 201
　climate apartheid 195
　global warming 178
climate debt, reparations for 208
Climate Justice Alliance 199
coal seam gas mining 76
coal, transitioning from 76
Coalition Party
　grants funding, rorting 51, 52
　migration commentary 41
Coffs Harbour 38
Cole, Teju 207
collective action, power of 92
Colombo Plan 6
colonisation
　assets and wealth taken by colonisers 205–6
　Australia, of 11
　decolonising 54
　divide and rule mentality 212
　environment, destruction of 205
　legacy of 32, 205–6
　multi-national corporations as the new 206
　reparations for 207, 208
　self-interest of colonisers 54
community campaigns 118, 119
community consultation 58
compassion 4, 58, 85, 161
Convent of Jesus and Mary, Lahore 8
Cooperative Research Centre (CRC) 188–9, 190
Cormann, Mathias 89
corporations as the new colonialists 206
corruption 235
　New South Wales history of 45
　Pakistan, in 21–2, 48
　pork-barrelling 51
　resignations from NSW Parliament 50
　'sports rorts' 51
　systems allowing rise of 95
Cosmo the greyhound 77–8, 79, 80
counter-terrorism 145
COVID-19
　cleaner skies and 216
　digital connectivity 29
　free childcare 33
　health during 29
　isolation from family 28, 224
　lockdown of public housing tower residents 237
　quarantine requirements, inequities 237
　social security payments 19
　temporary visa holders 93, 170
　women, impact on 133, 134

INDEX

Cronulla riots 2005 246
'cultural fit' 16, 27
cyclical incumbency 94
cyclists, compulsory ID 80

Daily Mail 159, 160
Daily Telegraph 134, 174
   gambling industry, revenue from 73
Davey, Jacob 145
de Costa, Caroline 127
deaths
   Aboriginal persons in custody 11
   women, violence against 10, 135
decolonising 54
   environmental movement 212, 214
deforestation in Australia 205
Delta Airlines 79
democracy 92
   participation in 93
democratic satisfaction, declining 91
Dharawal people 44
disabled persons and public transport 80
discrimination 235
driver's licence disqualification reform 80, 81–2
Duncan, Darelle 127
Dutton, Peter 145, 246

ecological footprints 201, 210
Edna Ryan Grand Stirrer Award of 2017 128
emails, abusive 2, 5, 155
emissions reduction and Australia 185
engineering profession
   male domination 10, 63
   migrant engineers, obtaining jobs 16, 18

environment, use and abuse of 180–1
   carbon pollution 186–7
   greenwashing 186
   profiteers from 194–5
   Rio Summit, since 183
   Sydney road projects 204
   symptoms, attempts to fix 183
   Union Carbide, Bhopal gas leak 187–8
environmental activism 181, 192–4
   decolonising 212, 214
   equity as central plank of 211
   justice for communities and 199
   NGOs 215
   structural inequalities in 211
   young people and 217–18
environmental decision-making 181
   people of colour, no role in 214
environmental legislation and conventions 45
   Climate Ambition Summit 2020 185
   Climate Change Conference (COP25) 2019 185
   Convention on Biological Diversity 184
   Framework Convention on Climate Change 184
   Kyoto Protocol 184, 185
   Paris Agreement 185
   Rio Earth Summit 1992 182, 183, 184
   Rio+20 Summit 184
   weakness of legislation 199, 204, 205
environmental racism 195
   BIPOC people bearing brunt of 197–9, 205
   blame, for and migrants 200

climate colonialism 210
reparations for 208
within nations 197
Exxon 186

Facebook
racist communications on 3, 143
standards before post removal 144
FaceTime 29
Family Planning NSW 125
far right-wing extremism 145, 146, 148
2021 Grampians white nationalists gathering 153
'the Great Replacement' conspiracy 200
growth of 150
Faruqi, Aisha 3, 28, 242
civil engineering degree 63
Faruqi, Mehreen
Bachelor of Engineering (Civil) 13
career outside politics 46, 54–5, 56–7
childhood 6–7, 13–15
cooking 240–1
cross-cultural adaptation 12–13
Edna Ryan Grand Stirrer Award of 2017 128
engineering work 54–5
environment *see* environmental activism
ethnic minority groups, reception by 96
geotechnical studies 22
Greens members, criticisms from 162–3, 166–7
Lahore *see* Lahore, life in
languages 12
lecturing position UNSW 192
life decisions, making of 225–6
marriage 23
Master of Engineering Science (UNSW) 10, 18, 26, 181
Muslims, criticism from for joining Greens 161–2
nature, love for 177–8
PhD Environmental Engineering 27, 188, 190
political career *see* political career
pride in Pakistani heritage 42
reasons for leaving Pakistan 21–2
schooling 8
shalwar Kameez, wearing of 174
Faruqi, Omar 9, 15, 22, 230, 243–4
Corps of Engineers in the Army Reserves 37
Datsun 120Ys 34
marriage 23
Master of Civil Engineering (Oregon) 22
Mehreen, meeting 22
near drowning, Sussex Inlet 37
paternal grandfather and aunt 131
taxi driving 18, 31
workplace harassment, Pakistan 24
Faruqi, Osman 9, 22, 28, 31, 144, 242
fear, cultivation of 92, 122, 235
feminism 104, 105
changing of 133
inclusivity 105
intersectionality and 107
lack of diversity in 107–8
men, role of 130–1
Pakistani women, among 129–30
patriarchy, as antidote for 129
Fink, Larry 209
First Nations justice, agitators for 47–8

INDEX

Fletcher, Julie 201–2
Flint, Michigan water supply 198
focus groups 235
Foetal Personhood Bill *see* Zoe's Law
Foley, Luke 72–3
  greyhound racing 73, 76
food delivery drivers 169
foreign aid
  Asia-Pacific in, characterisation of 206
  global justice issue, as 207
  reparations, as 207
  'white saviour industrial complex' 207
fossil-fuel industry
  climate action, misinformation campaign 186
  political donations 51
friends
  first Sydney 30, 31
  Pakistan, in 39
  Port Macquarie 38

Galeano, Eduardo 207–8
gambling industry
  greyhound racing ban 73, 74
  power of 73, 76–7
Gates, Bill 209
gender equality 5, 106, 134
gender identity equality 5
gender neutral language 118
gender pay gap 135
gender stereotypes 63
generational corruption 217
geographic divides 12
geopolitical boundaries and inequality 195–6
Gerrand, Daintry 201–2
GetUp 119
Gillard, Julia 2
  first female prime minister 7, 140

  sexism and misogyny towards 10, 140
Global Gender Gap Index
  Australian drop in rank 135, 140
government, distrust in 91
grandmother, walks in Jinnah Gardens 13–14
Grant, Troy 75, 76
green billionaires 209–10
greenhouse gases 183, 186
Greens Party
  2019 federal election 94
  anti-racism portfolio, creation 150
  attraction to 195
  candidates in every seat 228
  corporate donations and 51, 228
  democratic decision-making 236
  joining 226–7
  leadership, election of 237
  LGBTQI+ equal rights 4, 35, 161
  speaking out on issues 85, 86, 195
greenwashing 186
Greenwich, Alex 105
GREY2K animal welfare organisation 78
greyhound racing
  adoption of dogs 77, 79
  animal cruelty 71–2, 77
  'Don't Fly With Me' campaign 79
  export of dogs to China 78–9
  killing of dogs 72, 77
  NSW ban 69–76
  overturning ban 75–6, 78
  public popularity of ban 74
Greyhound Racing Australia 70
Griff, Stirling 64, 69
Groth, Anna 115
The Guardian 143, 144, 162, 198
Gundungurra people 44

habitual traffic offenders scheme 80–1
Hadley, Ray 74
halal slaughter 160
Hamblin, Julie 116, 127
Harding, Dr Ronnie 56–7, 181–2
Harris, Kamala 139
health funding 12
Herald Sun 133
Higgans, Brittany 219
Higher Education Loan Program 65
Himalayas and climate change 178–9
Hockey, Joe 89
homelessness 12, 19
  older women 135
horse racing, advocating for end of commercial 161
hospitality of Lahoris 21, 40
House of Representatives
  no proportional representation voting system 94
Howard, John 91
  'aspirational battlers' rhetoric 91
human rights
  attacks on defenders of 210
  COVID-19 lock down of housing tower residents 237
  renewable energy sector and 210
  UN guiding principles 210
humanities courses 61, 63
Hurricane Katrina 197

identity politics 156
Independent Biodiversity Legislation Review 59
Independent Commission Against Corruption (Federal) 52, 95
Independent Commission Against Corruption (NSW) 50
India (Hindustan), creation of 25

India-Pakistan conflicts 30–1
individualism, rise of 91
Indus Water Treaty 212–13
inflexible work arrangements 63
Institute of Environmental Studies (UNSW) 56–7, 181
integrity 21–2, 233, 242
International Women's Day Breakfast 106–7
Invasion Day 48
ISIS 163
Islam, tenets 24
Islamophobia 151, 152, 154
  burqa or niqab, wearing of 154
  harassment of Muslims, increase in 154
  jihad, fear of 157
  Muslim women, attacks against 154, 155, 158

Jahangir, Asma 88
Jinnah Gardens, Lahore 13–14
job insecurity 12
Job-Ready Graduates Bill 2020 61–2, 67–8
  impact of, projected 64, 65
  Senate inquiry, reference to 65
Johns River 38
Johnson, Boris 91
Jones, Alan 74
  Julia Gillard comments 140
justice 4, 47, 161, 181, 194, 195
Juukan Gorge destruction 199

Kaghan Valley 177–8
Kashmir, 2019 airstrikes 31
Kaye, Dr John 55
  greyhound racing 70–1
Keating, Paul 15
Kelly, Craig 17
Keneally, Kristina 97, 227, 230
Khala, Fahima 244

INDEX

King, Martin Luther 164, 167
  'Letter from Birmingham Jail' 164
Kings Cross 34, 35
Kissi-Debrah, Ella 197
koalas 60
  land clearing and extinction of 202–3
Kumar, Kishore 31

Labor Party
  abortion decriminalisation 102, 124
  greyhound racing ban 73, 75–6
  political donations, acceptance 51
Ladbrokes 73
Lahore, life in
  extended family in 14–15, 36
  family life in 6–7, 13–14
  hospitality of Lahoris 40
  house guests, continual 39
  Jinnah Gardens 13–14
  migration from 1992 1
  visits from father's Australian colleagues 6
Lake Cathie 38
Lambie, Jacqui 64, 65, 69
land clearing
  bushfires and 60
  koala extinction and 202–3
  NSW legislation 59, 60
  Queensland legislation 59
'Land Clearing Laws' *see* Local Land Services Amendment Bill 2016
law enforcement
  Aboriginal people, prejudice against 10, 44
Leard Forest 85
Lebanese Muslim migrants 41
Lee, Nicole 207

Leyonhjelm, David 169
LGBTQI+ rights
  criticisms from Muslims for supporting equality for 161
  Greens Party position 4
  injustices towards 44
  support for, reasons 4
Liberal Party 233
  deregulate university fees, attempt to 66
  greyhound racing ban and 74
  political donations, acceptance 51
  universities, treatment of 66
lobbyists 52–3, 95
local government 192
Local Land Services Amendment Bill 2016 69
  impact three years after commencement of Act 60
  nature of 59
  passage of Bill 60
loneliness 28–9
Loomis, Erik 209
'Love Letters to Mehreen' 172–3

McCormack, Michael 146, 147
Macdonald, Ian 17
McHugh, Michael 71, 72
McKenzie, Bridget 51
Macquarie, Governor 44
Macquarie Street 44
Maguire, Daryl 45
Mailman, Deborah 143
Mangeshkar, Lata 31
manufacturing in Australia 189
  Beyond Business in Australia: A 21st Century Manufacturing Culture in Australia 189–90
Maralinga nuclear testing 198
Maralinga Tjarutja people 198–9
Mardi Gras 34, 35

marginalised minority communities 5
Marie Stopes 125
marriage
  arranged 159
  criticism from Muslims for support of equality in 162
  forced 159
  same-sex marriage 85, 86, 105, 162
Menindee 85
  fish kill 2019 179–80
men's rights activists (MRAs) 133
mental health and climate anxiety 217
Menzies, Robert 198
migrant Muslim women 4
migrants to Australia
  colour, of 40
  culture preservation and 170
  current hostility towards 40–1
  engineers, difficulty in finding employment 16, 18
  participation in politics, motivations 96
  persons of colour 2
  pride, swallowing 27
  trying to fit in, pattern of 11
  white politicians 2
  workers, exploitation of 169
migration policies
  anti-immigration hysteria 12, 92, 235
  calls to change 'composition' of 40
  White Australia Policy 12
Morrison, Scott 11, 91
  climate action and 186
  Federal ICAC 51
  'quiet Australians' rhetoric 91
  social security increases and 20
  Women4Justice march comments 220

Morrison, Toni 224
Mosman Council 191
mother-in-law 37
Mullumbimby 85
multiculturalism 32, 168, 169, 170
  conditional Australianness 168–9
  culture preservation and 170
Murdoch media 74, 87, 151
Murray-Darling River system 180
  First Nations people's rights 180
Musk, Elon 209
Muslim people
  see also Islamophobia
  hostility towards 12, 40
  stereotypes of 156–7
  women see Muslim women
Muslim women 135–6, 154, 155, 157, 158, 161
  attacks against 154, 155, 158
  'the Great Replacement' conspiracy 200

Nakate, Vanessa 214
name
  identity, as part of 17
  mispronunciation and ridicule of 16–17
national parks and native title land 199
National Party 76, 146
  2019 federal election 94
  anti-environment 60
  political donations, acceptance 51
National Press Club 133
National Tertiary Education Union 125
native animals
  habitat destruction and fragmentation 60

INDEX

Native Vegetation Act 2003, repeal 59
natural disasters 186
neoliberalism 61, 183, 216, 235
NESPAK 22, 23
New South Wales Council for Civil Liberties 124
NSW Nurses and Midwives' Association 124
NSW Parliamentary Inquiry into Human Trafficking 159
New South Wales State Parliament 2013 swearing in 4, 43
  'bear pit' 44
  coalition government policies in 2013 45
  connections, privileged 53
  corporate donors and 53, 58
  extent of corruption 53
  grant funding rort 52
  Greens presence in 2013 45
  Legislative Council 45
  resignations under corruption cloud 50
  secret deals with crossbenchers 60–1, 68, 69
New South Wales Teachers Federation 125
Newman, Campbell 59
News Corp 153
  platform for racists 152
  progressive politicians engaging with 153
  racism, role in fuelling 152
Newsweek 186
Nile, Fred 109, 121

Obeid, Eddie 45, 50
O'Farrell, Barry 45, 50
Omar, Ilhan 142, 143
One Nation 69, 245
  hate, politics of 40

Pauline Hanson's One Nation (PHON) 67, 146
political donations, acceptance 51
Orange by-election 2016 75, 76
Oregon State University 22
'Orientalism' 156–7

Pacific Islanders and climate inequality 196
Pakistan
  Ahmadis, persecution of 24–6
  Christian population 8
  class divisions 8
  climate change impacts 196
  corruption, entrenched 21–2, 48
  creation of 25
  female prime minister, first 7
  feminism in 129–30
  gender disparities 7
  India-Pakistan wars 30–1
  military rule 48, 129
  politicians, view of 48
  politics, conversations about 88
  societal contradictions 7–8
  Tarbela Dam 212–13
  water rights 212–13
Panahi, Rita 133
parliamentary pledge of allegiance 5
parliaments, Australian
  federal *see* Australian Parliament
  first female Indigenous senator 140
  first female Muslim senator 140, 230
  first female prime minister 7, 140
  gender disproportion 112, 140
  lack of diversity 95, 140
  proportion born overseas 90, 95
patriarchy 10, 45, 88, 128

Patrick, Rex 64, 65, 69
Pauline Hanson's One Nation (PHON) 67, 146
Peris, Nova 141–2
permanent residency 22, 26–7
Peucker, Mario 145
phone calls, abusive 5, 144, 154, 171
photo-shopping 3
political career
  Australian Senate 91, 99, 166–7
  colleagues 223
  deciding to run for Senate 166
  door-knocking 228–9
  engineering knowledge and 63
  family and friends, impact 230–1
  first female Muslim MP 140, 230
  Heffron by-election 2012 230
  Heffron candidate 2011 227–8, 230
  inaugural NSW Parliament speech 55, 142–3
  inaugural Senate speech 248–50
  New South Wales Parliament 4, 43–5, 166, 230
  New South Wales Senate 96
political change 97
  community campaigns and 119
political decision-making
  community needs 53, 58
  expert evidence and 53, 58
  vested interests in 57, 60
political donations 50, 95
  decision-making and 53, 58
  fossil-fuel companies 51
  gambling industry 73
  resource industry, amount 50
political parties, major
  lobbyists, power 53
  political donations, acceptance 51
political scandals
  no real consequences 90
politicians
  career politicians 94
  cyclical incumbency 94
  lobbyists after Parliament 95
  Pakistan, view held of local 48, 49
  Pakistan, view held of Western 49
politics
  advice to people getting into 47
  corruption, omnipresence 50
polling, impact of flagging 91
'pork-barrelling' 51–2, 232
Port Macquarie 226
  2001 move to 38
  culture of 38–9
  house guests 39, 40
Port Macquarie-Hastings Council 38, 191–2
Possingham, Professor Hugh 59
poverty, feminisation 135
pregnancy discrimination in the workplace 80, 83–4
prejudice 5
preselections 232
prime ministers, overthrow of 91
prison, detaining people in 87
private school funding 87
privatisation of public assets 45
progressives
  abortion decriminalisation and 101–3, 113, 123
  'brogressives' 162
  complicity in racism 165–6
  Progressives On Everything But Israel (POEBI) 162
  religion, 'blind spots' 163, 164
Prophet Muhammad (PBUH) 24
'public consultation' tokenism 59
Public Health Association 124

INDEX

public housing funding 12
public education
  advocating for increased funding 2, 33
  funding 12
public investment in essential services 12
public sector cuts 12, 45

Queensland government
  land clearing laws, impact 59
Qur'an 5

racing industry, power of 76–7
racism 141–2, 235
  casual racism 40
  energy spent confronting 224
  everyday racism 40
  female politicians of colour, against 141–3
  political parties fanning 40–1
  race-baiting 151
  résumé racism 16
  right-wing media and 151–2
  speaking out against 2
  systemic against Aboriginal people 10
racist abuse, personal toll 3, 167–8, 171, 175, 246–7
  cost of speaking out 174
  'Love Letters to Mehreen' 172–3
racist comments 1
  Facebook page 3, 154, 171
  social media, on 2
  Twitter account 3, 154
Rafi, Mohammed 31
Ramsay, Dr Philippa 127
Ray, Sarah Jaquette 251
refugees, hostility towards 40, 41
religious equality 5
religious festivals 32, 122–3

renewable energy sector
  equality 209
  human rights and 210
representation 174
  Australians born overseas in Parliament 90
  equal, of women 134, 227
  proportional 94
résumé racism 16
right-wing media
  racism, role in mainstreaming 151–2
Rio +20 Summit 184
Rio Earth Summit 1992 182, 183, 184
Rio Tinto Juukan Gorge destruction 199
Roy, Arundhati 206
Royal Australian and New Zealand College of Obstetricians 124
Royal Commission into Aboriginal Deaths in Custody
  deaths in custody since 11
  recommendations, failure to fully implement 11
Royal Flying Doctors, Maralinga airstrip 37
RSPCA 74
Rudd, Kevin 91
Rushton, Gina 119

Said, Edward W. 156–7
St Vincent's Hospital Darlinghurst 35
same-sex marriage 85, 86, 105
sea level rise 196
Secord, Walt 123
secular system of governance 5
separation of state and religion 5
sexual consent education 129
sexuality equality 5
Shakti Community Council 148, 149

Sharkie, Rebekha 67, 68
Shooters and Fishers party 60, 76
Sky News 151, 153
slavery, reparations for 207
social justice, agitators for 47
social media, abuse on 2, 5, 143, 154, 155
  hate speech and 145
social welfare 18–19
  Centrelink robodebt 19
  COVID-19 measures 19
  payment levels 19
  stigmatisation of recipients 19, 20
  youth allowance 19
Southern, Lauren 151
Speakman, Mark 83, 84
Special Commission of Inquiry into Greyhound Racing 70, 71–2
Spence, Chris 109
'sports rorts' 51
STEM courses 62, 63
Sudanese community 41
sustainable development 182, 183
sustainable populationists 200, 201
Sydney Morning Herald 64
Sydney road projects
  destruction of habitat and ecological communities 204
  WestConnex motorway 62–3, 242–3

Tabbot Foundation 125
TABcorp 73
TAFE, abolition of fees 2, 161
Tarbela Dam, villages drowned 212–13
Tehan, Dan 64
terra nullius 10
Thai Airways 79
Thorpe, Lidia 150

Tlaib, Rashida 143
TransAfrica 207
transgender people
  disadvantage faced 105
  forced divorces 105
  trans women of colour 136
transport funding 12
Tripodi, Joe 50
trolls, impact of 4, 141
Trump, Donald 91, 142, 147
Trumpism 147
trust 239
tsunami 2004, female casualties 196
Turnbull, Malcolm 91
Twitter, abusive comments on 3, 86

Union Carbide, Bhopal gas leak 187–8
United Nations
  The Impact of COVID-19 on Women 134
universities
  advocating for abolition of fees 2, 62, 161
  casualisation of staff 67
  corporatisation 67
  COVID-19, impact on 66
  Liberal Party treatment of 66
  vice-chancellors 66–7
University of Engineering and Technology, Lahore 13
  living on campus 13
University of New South Wales (UNSW)
  Honey Pot childcare, campaign for 32, 190
  lecturing position UNSW 192
  Master of Engineering Science 10, 18, 26
  PhD Environmental Engineering 27, 188, 190

INDEX

School of Civil and
  Environmental Engineering
  10
University of Sydney Queer Action
  Collective 121
University of Sydney Women's
  Collective 121
UNSW *see* University of New
  South Wales

violence against women 10, 128,
  135
visa holders
  labour exploitation of 169, 170
  no right to vote 93
  protection and care of, by
    government 94, 170
voluntary euthanasia 85, 86
voters, traditional categories of
  235
voting
  citizens, restricted to 93
  compulsory 93
  proportional voting system 94

Walgett, water supply 180
WAPDA House 22
war and militarism 87
water pollution
  Flint, Michigan 198
water theft by irrigators 180
Wauchope 38
WestConnex motorway 62–3,
  242–3
Western supremacist narrative 53
WhatsApp 29, 96
White Australia Policy 12
white supremacy 40, 145
  see also far right-wing extremism

Christchurch mosque massacre
  149, 200
women
  Aboriginal, life expectancy 135
  COVID-19, impact on 133, 134
  credibility, attacks on 141
  decision-making, exclusion 197
  disasters, deaths in 196
  Parliament House, harassment in
    219, 221
  political representation 134
  poverty, number in 135, 196
  trans women of colour 136
  violence against 10, 134
  Women 4 Justice march 220
Women's Legal Services 124
Women's March 119
women's rights
  advocating for 2
  autonomy over body 103, 110
  denial of 44
worker's rights, restrictions 45
World Bank 213

xenophobia, flourishing of 40, 92

Yat Yuen greyhound track
  (Canidrome) 78
Yeampierre, Elizabeth 199
younger generation, activism of
  217–18

Zia-ul-Haq, General 129
Zoe's Law 83, 109
  campaign against bill 110–12
  personhood movement in the US
    109–10
Zoom 29

Dr Mehreen Faruqi is the Greens Senator for New South Wales. She is a civil and environmental engineer and lifelong activist for social and environmental justice. In 2013, she joined the New South Wales Parliament, becoming the first Muslim woman to sit in an Australian parliament. In 2018, she became Australia's first Muslim female senator. She is a passionate advocate against racism and misogyny.

Since emigrating from Pakistan in 1992, Mehreen has worked in leadership positions in local government, consulting firms and as an academic in Australia and internationally. This includes her roles as Manager of Environment and Services for Mosman Council, Manager of Natural Resources and Catchments for Port Macquarie–Hastings Council, Director of the Institute of Environmental Studies (UNSW) and as an Associate Professor in Business and Sustainability (AGSM, UNSW).

While in New South Wales Parliament, she introduced the first ever bill to decriminalise abortion. Mehreen has been a leading voice in opposition to the greyhound racing industry, privatisation of public transport, and removal of laws that protect native vegetation. Since joining the Federal Senate in August 2018, Mehreen has been an outspoken advocate for public education, anti-racism, public housing and animal welfare.